ALL ABOUT
Good Cooking

ALL ABOUT
Good Cooking

Myra Street and Jane Todd

Hamlyn
London · New York · Sydney · Toronto

Acknowledgements

The authors and publisher would like to thank
the following for their help in supplying props for
the colour photographs:

Casa Pupo
Emilia Ceramics
John Lewis Partnership
The Tupperware Company Limited
Royal Doulton
Josiah Wedgwood and Sons Limited

Photographs by John Lee
Illustrated by Marilyn Day and Tony Streek

Published by
The Hamlyn Publishing Group Limited
London · New York · Sydney · Toronto
Astronaut House, Feltham, Middlesex, England
© Copyright 1974 (text and line artwork)
The Hamlyn Publishing Group Limited
© Copyright 1974 (colour pictures) Tower Housewares
Limited, P.O. Box 16, Wolverhampton, WV5 8AQ.

ISBN 0 600 38700 3

Printed in England by Hazell, Watson and Viney, Aylesbury

Contents

Useful facts and figures

Metric measures

A convenient method of converting recipe quantities is to round off gramme and millilitre measurements to the nearest unit of 25. The chart below gives the exact conversion (to the nearest whole figure) of Imperial ounces and fluid ounces to grammes and millilitres, and the recommended equivalent based on the nearest unit of 25.

Ounces/fluid ounces	Approx. g. and ml. to nearest whole figure	Recommended conversion to nearest unit of 25
1	28	25
2	57	50
3	85	75
4	113	125
5 ($\frac{1}{4}$ pint)	142	150
6	170	175
7	198	200
8 ($\frac{1}{2}$ lb.)	226	225
9	255	250
10 ($\frac{1}{2}$ pint)	283	275
11	311	300
12	340	350
13	368	375
14	396	400
15 ($\frac{3}{4}$ pint)	428	425
16 (1 lb.)	456	450
17	484	475
18	512	500
19	541	550
20 (1 pint)	569	575

Note: When converting quantities over 1 lb. or 1 pint, add together the appropriate figures in the centre column (the direct conversion) before rounding off to the nearest unit of 25.

Throughout the book, we have converted each recipe individually, using the method explained but, where necessary, balancing the proportions of the more critical recipes, such as cakes. Decilitres (tenths of a litre) have been used for the liquid measures.

Note on metric units of measurement

1 litre (1000 millilitres, 10 decilitres) equals 1·76 pints, or almost exactly 1¾ pints. 1 kilogramme (1000 grammes) equals 2·2 pounds, or almost exactly 2 pounds 3 ounces.

Oven temperature guide

	Electricity		Gas Mark
	°F	°C	
Very cool	225	110	$\frac{1}{4}$
	250	130	$\frac{1}{2}$
Cool	275	140	1
	300	150	2
Moderate	325	170	3
	350	180	4
Moderately hot	375	190	5
	400	200	6
Hot	425	220	7
	450	230	8
Very hot	475	240	9

Notes for American users

Although each recipe has an American measures and ingredients column, the following list gives some American equivalents or substitutes for terms used in the book.

British	American
Deep cake tin	Spring form pan
Frying pan	Skillet
Greaseproof paper	Wax paper
Grill/grilled	Broil/broiled
Kitchen paper	Paper towels
Muslin	Cheesecloth
Patty tins	Muffin pans
Sandwich tin	Layer cake pan
Stoned	Pitted
Swiss roll tin	Jelly roll pan
Mixer/liquidiser	Mixer/blender

Note: The British pint is 20 fluid ounces whereas the American pint is 16 fluid ounces.
All cup and spoon measures in this book are level.

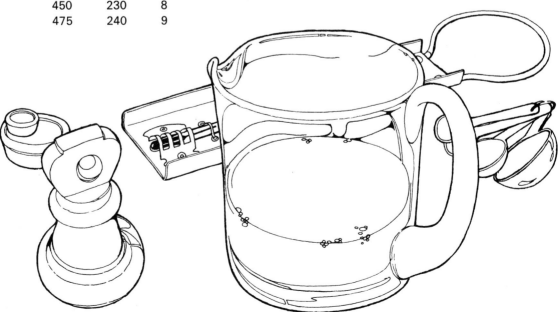

Introduction

There are many cook books to choose from and we have worked on a number of the ones which are to be found in the shops now. For an idea of what we thought was wanted we decided to look through our readers' letters—we often do this before embarking on a new project. It appeared that many people are keen to try new recipes but do not always have the knowledge to make basic recipes. When the basics of cooking have been mastered it is but a simple step to follow with exciting variations.

In the guides to the various cooking methods we have tried to provide you with colourful step by step photographs of the most difficult stages and then given recipes for expanding your repertoire. The recipes are given to enable you to cook with or without various kitchen gadgets and we have tried to add information for storage and freezing. We have been fortunate to have the use of the complete range of Tower cookware and Tower Power for our photographs which has made our task both more enjoyable and easier.

All About Good Cooking contains as much information as we could muster in the 160 pages and we hope that it will answer some of the needs you have expressed to us from time to time. There are many photographs of the more delicious recipes to show you, the reader, how the finished dishes should look.

Most people are interested in entertaining at home and after the guides have been followed we hope that entertaining will no longer present any problems. Cooking well requires a little love and it is so much easier to love doing something when you are more familiar with it. We hope that you are going to enjoy using this book as much as we have enjoyed working on it.

A guide to kitchen equipment

Today's woman is expected to be all things to her family, cook, hostess, nurse, laundress, seamstress, chauffeur and sometimes gardener, home handywoman and interior decorator. Homemaking is an important job for anyone and a little planning helps to ease the load.

If the plumber arrived to do some work in your house you would be horrified if he had a collection of broken tools and yet so many cooks inflict useless tools on themselves in the kitchen. For a reasonably small capital outlay it is possible to set yourself up with some good equipment.

A real look in the kitchen cupboards may be a shock to you . . . old pots with loose handles, perhaps some old rusty baking tins which stick and a collection of blunt knives.

Everyone with a kitchen, new or old, will find that one which is well equipped will save endless hours of unnecessary work and will really encourage creative cooking.

Let's start with the basic things which we all have to invest in at some time when we set up home.

The cooker

Thirty-eight per cent of housewives in this country have installed a new cooker over the last five years. Obviously you will buy this to suit the needs of your family, and there are so many to choose from that it must be an individual choice to suit the family budget. Working wives should remember that an automatic oven is worth its weight in gold when the train is late or you are kept at the office. Like a car, a cooker needs some loving care if it is to stay in good condition. Wipe it over with a damp cloth after use, and food which is spilt or splashed will not have a chance to burn onto the enamel. It is often worth lining the tray under the burners and the grill pan with foil as this saves food burning on and spoiling the appearance. Do read the manufacturer's instructions on cleaning and be very careful with abrasive pads. Once the cooker surface is scratched dirt collects more easily. Try to clean the oven after a cooking session (in particular roasting) otherwise food which has spilt and splashed will burn on firmly. Some new cookers have self-cleaning ovens, they work well and are to be recommended if the budget will stretch to it.

The refrigerator

Buy for the future—if there are only two of you now, remember there may be three or four in a couple of years. Very small refrigerators are ideal for bachelor pads and single dwellings but hopeless for families. Buy a sensible size for your family. It is difficult to plan meals ahead with no refrigerator space. The recommended capacity is 1 cubic foot per person, plus 1 cubic foot, but of course this varies as to how you use your refrigerator space and whether you use it in conjunction with a freezer. Food smells collect in the refrigerator and it should be defrosted according to the manufacturer's instructions, at least once every two weeks with a mild solution of bicarbonate of soda and warm water. This removes any strong food smells. Remember that food storage at low temperatures is effected by a circulation of cold air therefore the cabinet must be packed sensibly. If you jam everything onto the shelves blocking up the back, the air will not circulate and a low temperature throughout cannot be efficiently maintained and this goes back to the point previously mentioned which recommends buying a cabinet that is large enough for your needs. The domestic refrigerator is one of our most misused pieces of kitchen equipment. Strongly flavoured foods should be wrapped and it should be borne in mind that a low temperature only slows down the growth of bacteria. Food which is left uncovered for a long time before storing will not be 'cured' in the fridge. Bacteria will also start to multiply whenever food is removed. Remember to allow hot food to cool before putting into the refrigerator otherwise the temperature in the cabinet will rise and affect other things which are being stored (see notes on storage, page 14).

The freezer

This is not always a piece of kitchen equipment as many of our kitchens are too small to accommodate it. However more freezer manufacturers are developing freezer/fridges which can be kept in the kitchen. The freezer is more usually found in the spare room or the garage but of course the ideal place for convenience is in the kitchen. Choose a freezer which is large enough for your needs. Bulk buying saves money but small freezers cannot accommodate much and unless you wish to use your freezer as an extension of the refrigerator, for longer storage, do buy as much space as you can afford. Everyone we know who has a small freezer wishes they had more freezer space. Freezing is rather an addictive pastime and once you have taken the plunge you will wonder how you lived without one. The outside can be polished with a good quality furniture cream or car wax; this is especially important if the freezer is kept in the cellar, outhouse or garage, as dampness can cause rusting. The freezer should be defrosted once or twice a year depending on the amount of frost which appears. Beware of frost on the lid of a chest or the door of an upright as this effects the seal and therefore the inside temperature. There is a difference between a freezer which freezes down food and a conservator which stores commercially frozen food. Do make sure that you are buying a freezer and the new EEC marking is as follows ✱✱✱✱ which ensures that you are buying a freezer and not a conservator. For further information see notes on storage, page 14.

Pots and pans

There are so many marvellous saucepans to choose from today that surely our great grandmothers would be envious of these super easy-to-clean pans which we can buy. There are coloured sets which brighten any kitchen, or sparkling aluminium depending on your fancy. As aluminium is a good heat conductor, aluminium cookware heats up speedily, distributing heat over the base to ensure even cooking. The greatest invention to date is surely the non-stick saucepan—no more rubbing away the skin on the fingers with abrasive pads but a quick swish with a soapy cloth gives a clean pan! However whether you invest in decorated, coloured or gleaming aluminium pans, like most other kitchen appliances, they do need loving care if they are to remain in good condition.

Non-stick surfaces make work in the kitchen much easier. There are many types of non-stick surfaces but the most effective so far is known as polytetrafluoroethlyne otherwise known as ptfe. This very handy chemical with the long name is produced under the name Teflon and has proved to be excellent for coating the insides of cooking pans because food does not cling to it. Greasy frying pans and sticky casseroles dipped in hot soapy water come clean with a wipe. It seems like magic the first few times you use them but it's true and so it is worth while bearing the following points in mind for a long and happy life with your Teflon-coated, scratch-resistant, non-stick pans:
Before using your non-stick pan wash it in hot water made

bubbly with washing up liquid, rinse thoroughly and dry. Frying pans should be lightly greased with oil or cooking fat to pre-condition the non-stick coating. Heat the pan and wipe off surplus oil with soft kitchen paper. Use medium heat for cooking in non-stick pans, full heat should be avoided as this can cause the surface to stain and the food will then burn as in any saucepan.

Overheating an empty pan will affect its appearance and damage the coating.

Should small stains appear after long use; they do not affect the non-stick quality of the pan as long as they are not allowed to build up, and they can be effectively removed by boiling the following solution in the stained pan for 5–10 minutes *without* boiling over to avoid discolouring the outside of the saucepan.

1 cup water
½ cup liquid bleach
2 tablespoons bicarbonate of soda

After this treatment wash and lightly grease the pan, as previously described, to recondition it.

Some pans e.g. hard-base Teflon can be used with metal kitchen tools. This means that a scratch-resistant finish has been applied over a specially prepared metal base which protects the coating against scratching; these pans are therefore slightly more expensive but will last longer. If scratches do occur no real damage is done to the quality of the non-stick surface. These scratches do not widen with use, the coating does not peel and the food will not be affected in any way. However, do read the manufacturer's instructions to obtain full benefit from your non-stick pots, pans and casseroles.

To wash non-stick pans use hot soapy water and a soft nylon brush or use a sponge pad. Rinse with warm water and dry with a dry towel afterwards. It is important to dry the pans thoroughly as this prevents a layer of grease forming over the months which will eventually stain the non-stick surface. **Never use wire wool or scouring powder** or you will ruin the surface. The outside of the pan can be scoured if stained but you will find that the new coloured aluminium pans are very easy to clean on the outside as well.

Automatic dish washers do not affect the non-stick finish although unless rinsed thoroughly the dish washer detergents do tend to discolour the outsides and, in time, handles tend to become loose.

For everyday cooking you will need three saucepans (small, medium and large), a milk pan and a frying pan, preferably with a lid. Casseroles which can be used on top of the cooker as well as in the oven mean that food can be browned and cooked in the same pan, saving washing up. A new milk pan on the market which prevents milk from boiling over can also be used as a double sauce-pan. The double walls of the pan are filled with water and as this boils, the contents of the pan heat gently. An ideal pan for egg custards and egg-based sauces.

Baking tins

It is now possible to buy a comprehensive range of non-stick tins to meet most needs when baking. These tins require treating as the non-stick pans and they do not require lining. Treat as non-stick frying pans before using. Buy bakeware according to your baking needs and store carefully; so often we throw our tins into a cupboard on top of each other and this does tend to scratch the surface.

Light greasing of non-stick bakeware is essential as in ordinary tins when using mixtures containing eggs, sugar and fruit, but no fat. Cake tins may be floured and cakes should turn out without the aid of a knife. With non-stick coatings, other than Teflon, fruit fillings should not be allowed to come into contact with the surface because of the acid content of the fruit. Always line the pan first.

To complete your cook's tools of the trade, invest in a good quality kettle, can opener and some knives. It is impossible and even dangerous to try to prepare some foods with blunt knives—however do keep sharp knives out of the reach of children. A balloon whisk, palette knife, wooden spoons and a rolling pin complete the basic equipment and as an added bonus a set of measuring spoons is very handy.

Mixers and liquidisers

These could be called the second pair of hands. These particular pieces of kitchen equipment have grown enormously in popularity over the last few years and what a boon they can be to the overworked housewife. Some people may love stirring the batter for the Yorkshire pudding but most of us would rather spend the time relaxing with the family on Sunday. A quick whiz with either the mixer or liquidiser and the pudding batter makes itself. You will have to forgive us but we are both confirmed mixer and liquidiser converts and throughout the book we have tried to show you how to save time and effort by using this invaluable kitchen aid.

Your choice of machine will depend on the size of your family and the amount of specialised cooking you do. First find a home for your mixer and liquidiser on the kitchen wall or on a work top—a machine which is kept in a cupboard is no use to anyone so please keep this in mind. Once you have your mixer and liquidiser do make an effort to use it as you will be amazed at the way it can aid and abet you to produce more versatile meals.

Many people have small mixers and liquidisers and most of the recipes in this book have been made with a small cordless machine; this means that in some recipes the

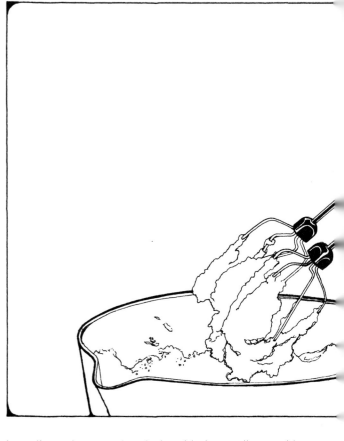

ingredients have to be dealt with in small quantities—particularly when using the liquidiser.

Mixers—hints for use

1 Read manufacturer's instructions if you want to obtain the best results from your machine. Use the recipe leaflet as a guide, for your own recipes, for speed, etc.

2 For cakes and puddings use your ingredients at room temperature.

3 When creaming fat and sugar, the bowl and beaters can be warmed by dipping in hot (not boiling) water.

4 Before whisking egg whites make sure bowl and beaters are completely clean and dry. Eggs should be at room temperature.

5 Do not bang beaters on the side of the bowl to remove mixture.

6 Beware of over mixing e.g. pastry dough and cream are prime examples for the inexperienced mixer cook.

7 Clean beaters and bowl in warm soapy water then rinse thoroughly. Do not immerse electrical parts in water and always refer to manufacturer's instructions if in doubt. One brand of small mixer is cordless and, as such, it is possible to take the mixer to the saucepan on the cooker, or any part of the kitchen without worrying about a trailing flex. This useful appliance works on a rechargeable power unit i.e. the unit is replaced on a base connected to the mains when not in use.

8 Mixers, even the smaller ones, can be bought with other attachments such as a liquidiser, coffee grinder, slicer, shredder, can opener, juice extractor and knife sharpener. Throughout the book you will see many recipes where we have used these appliances. They are most useful and can be added to your basic equipment gradually.

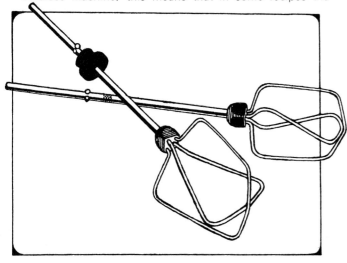

Some uses for the liquidiser

Making breadcrumbs When a recipe calls for fresh breadcrumbs, just put a few small pieces of crustless bread into the goblet and switch on for a few seconds.

Chopping nuts They can be chopped finely or coarsely, or ground to a powder, depending on the recipe.

Chopping herbs Washed and dried parsley and other fresh herbs can be chopped in next to no time.

Grating cheese Cubes of hard cheese can be grated finely.

Making soups The softened vegetables can be puréed, thus avoiding wasting any of the goodness.

Making babies food Small portions of cooked lean meat, vegetables and gravy liquid can be puréed.

Making fruit juices Put prepared fruit plus liquid and sugar in the goblet and blend.

Making mayonnaise Done in seconds in the liquidiser, see page 90.

Making milk shakes Blend milk, ice cream and flavouring.

Making biscuit crumbs Digestive, semi-sweet biscuits and gingernuts can be ground in a liquidiser, for flan cases, cheesecakes, toppings, etc.

Rescuing a lumpy sauce A lumpy sauce or custard can be blended until smooth.

Liquidisers

The adventurous cook will find this handy kitchen aid is superb value for money as it can save hours of valuable preparation time. Many dishes, such as cream soups, pâtés, stuffings and delicious desserts, can take a long time to prepare but are very easy and quick with the help of the liquidiser.

1 Read the manufacturer's instructions to give your machine a long, trouble-free life.

2 Do not allow the liquidiser to labour, or run the machine beyond the recommended time.

3 The goblet should not be filled beyond the recommended level as it will cease to liquidise the food properly. If the food is sticking in the liquidiser; add more liquid or remove some of the mixture.

4 If your goblet is made of plastic do not expose it to high temperatures—always allow boiling liquids to cool before ladling them into the goblet.

5 Do not clean the blades with your fingers, use a bottle brush. To clean the liquidiser rinse the food out with cold water then half fill the goblet with warm water and add a drop of washing up liquid, turn onto maximum speed for a few seconds, empty and rinse again with clean water.

6 Do remember that a liquidiser can be permanently damaged if it is not used according to the manufacturer's instructions. For example some machines (the larger ones) can deal with pieces of raw vegetables without the addition of liquid whereas with the smaller machines it is usually necessary to add liquid with certain ingredients.

7 With the type of liquidiser which is charged up on a mains-connected recharger always remove the power unit from the base before setting up the liquidiser for operation.

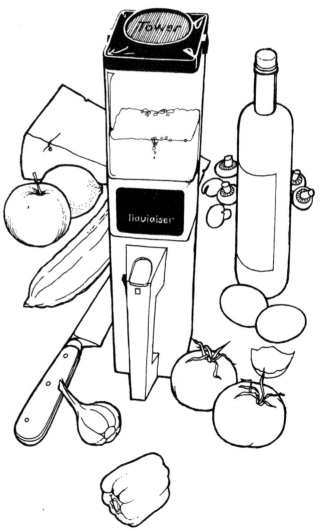

A guide to storage

Careful storage of food is essential to prevent any unnecessary wastage, and as food becomes increasingly expensive to budget for, knowing how to store food, combined with careful shopping can help to keep the cost of living down. When foods are in season they are at their cheapest, but it is no saving to buy a vast quantity of a fruit or vegetable just because it is offered at a bargain price, unless you can use it all fairly quickly, or the purchase is in good condition and it can be placed in a home freezer.

There are various ways of storing food, each depending on the type of food and how long it is intended for storage. Basically foodstuffs are kept either in a store cupboard, a refrigerator (and/or larder), a freezer or a vegetable rack.

The store cupboard

This is intended mainly for basic dry ingredients such as flour, cornflour, spices etc., for canned foods such as soups, vegetables, fruit, juices etc., for sauces and essences such as tomato, Worcestershire, pickles, chutneys, vinegar, tomato purée, meat pastes, cooking oils etc., for beverages such as instant coffee, coffee beans, cocoa powder, drinking chocolate, fruit squashes etc., for preserves such as jams, marmalades, honey etc.

If you don't own a home freezer or may sometimes want an instant meal, keep a selection of complete meals in cans or packets.

Bread needs to be stored in a cool, dry place. You can keep it in a bread bin which should have air holes to prevent the bread from going mouldy. Make sure that the bin is kept free from crumbs which could collect in the corners and become mouldy. It can be kept wrapped or unwrapped in the bin, according to how it is purchased.

If the shelves of your store cupboard are not made of a laminated plastic, which can be kept clean by wiping with a damp cloth, they should be lined with wax paper or shelf lining paper, or lined with an adhesive plastic covering such as Fablon.

What you store, and where it is stored in the cupboard is a matter of personal preference, but obviously the ingredients which you use most should be stored on the lower shelves and in the handiest position. If you are not able to reach some of your shelves without standing on a stool make sure that it is steady or, better still, invest in a step stool; do not keep heavy cans etc. on high shelves.

It is helpful, for identification purposes, to store certain dry ingredients in clear glass jars with airtight stoppers, or in labelled storage jars. There is a wide range of storage jars available; however as long as they have airtight lids and are made from glass, polythene or plastic and are available in varying sizes the choice of pattern and shape is an entirely personal one. Ingredients for storage jars include flour, sugar, pastas, rice, currants, sultanas, raisins and nuts. Always ensure that the jars are clean and dry before putting any ingredients in. Dry glass jars in a low oven.

The golden rule to all storage is to use the ingredients in rotation—always put new purchases behind the ones already on the shelf so that they will be used first. Often dented cans of tomatoes, beans etc. are offered at a reduced price, these are perfectly safe to buy, but cans which have blown, look as if they have been leaking or are rusty should not be purchased as the contents may be contaminated.

The refrigerator

All perishable foodstuffs should be stored in the refrigerator and where necessary wrapped or packed in a suitable covering or containers. It is important to wrap strong-smelling foods, such as fish, to prevent the cross-contamination of flavours. However, neither uncooked fish nor meat should be stored in an airtight container; the best way of covering it is to place the food on a plate and cover it loosely with a see-through wrap (this makes identification in the refrigerator easy). Frozen meat and poultry should always be placed on a plate or a shallow dish to catch the drips as it defrosts. (It is not a good idea to keep meat and poultry in the supermarket packaging for any length of time.) Cooked meat and poultry should be kept, covered, for a limited time only.

Cheese should be well protected to prevent it from drying in the refrigerator; wrap it in foil, wax or greaseproof paper and then store it in a plastic container in the coolest part of the refrigerator. (Remember to allow cheese to return to room temperature before serving it.)

Store eggs in the spaces provided—usually in the door of the refrigerator; however, it is useful to keep a few at room temperature for baking and making mayonnaise.

Fats (butter, margarine, cooking fat and lard) keep well stored in the refrigerator. Salted butter has a slightly longer storage life than unsalted.

You will find that salad vegetables such as lettuce and watercress will keep fresh and crisp longer if they are washed and very gently dried in a clean tea towel or with kitchen paper before being put in the refrigerator. Store the prepared vegetables in a polythene bag or a plastic container with an airtight lid in the section for the salads usually at the bottom (i.e. the coolest part of the refrigerator). If lettuce is placed too near the ice-making compartment of the refrigerator it may become partly frozen and will then have to be discarded as when defrosted it will go limp. Other salad vegetables such as tomatoes, cucumber and spring onions and green or red peppers can also be stored in the salad container of the refrigerator. Make sure that the salad container is kept dry.

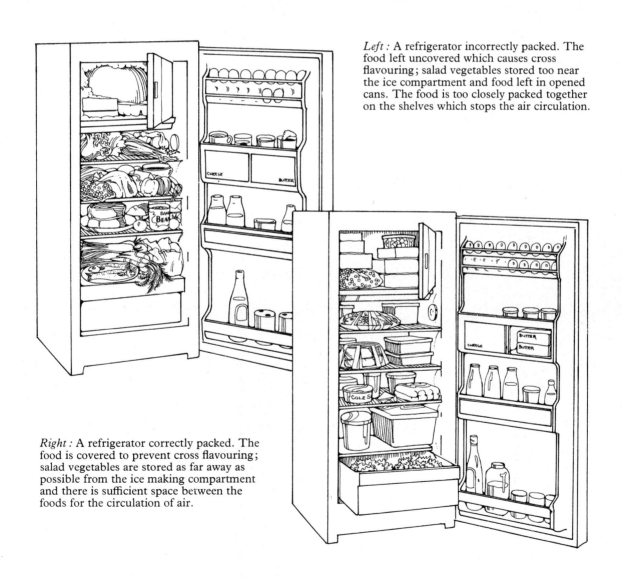

Left : A refrigerator incorrectly packed. The food left uncovered which causes cross flavouring; salad vegetables stored too near the ice compartment and food left in opened cans. The food is too closely packed together on the shelves which stops the air circulation.

Right : A refrigerator correctly packed. The food is covered to prevent cross flavouring; salad vegetables are stored as far away as possible from the ice making compartment and there is sufficient space between the foods for the circulation of air.

If you purchase ready-prepared vegetables in polythene bags they can be stored in the refrigerator, but should be used within the time recommended by the supplier.

You can store commercially-frozen produce in the freezer compartment of your refrigerator, but you must adhere to the manufacturer's recommendations for length of storage, according to the star markings on your refrigerator. The freezer compartment of the refrigerator cannot be used for freezing down food of any type, as it is not capable of achieving a low enough temperature.

The refrigerator must be defrosted (unless it has an automatic defrost) and cleaned regularly. If too much frost is allowed to build up in and around the ice-making compartment, it forces the motor of the refrigerator to work harder to maintain the temperature inside the cabinet. To defrost and clean your refrigerator turn off the switch and pull out the plug. Remove all the contents and allow the frost to melt (you can place a bowl of warm water in the refrigerator to hasten this process). Wipe the shelves and interior of the refrigerator over with a solution of warm water and bicarbonate of soda (this helps to absorb food smells)—never use a scouring powder as this will permanently scratch the interior surface. The outside of the refrigerator can be kept pristine and new-looking by wiping it over with a little white furniture cream.

The larder

If you are fortunate enough to have a larder attached to your kitchen make sure that you use it to its fullest advantage. If it has a marble shelf use this for storing foods which you want to be kept cool but not necessarily in the refrigerator. (The marble slab would also be ideal for pastry making.)

The larder—providing it is cool and dry—is an ideal area for storing jams, preserves, pickles, chutneys and all ingredients which would otherwise be kept in the store cupboard.

The freezer

The freezer can be a most useful item of kitchen equipment. The housewife with a family, the young career housewife and even a couple without children will find it invaluable. It can be used for storing commercially-frozen products, for freezing down your own dishes such as soups, pies, casseroles, puddings, cakes etc., and for storing fresh meat, poultry and game. However you utilise your freezer there are certain basic rules which must be followed; all food must be correctly packed to protect it from the cold, dry air inside the freezer; the food must be in good condition (you cannot freeze tough meat and expect it to come out tender!) and above all only suitable foods must be frozen. Freezing hints are given, where you see this symbol ❄, at the end of some recipes.

The vegetable rack

It is necessary to keep vegetables in a rack to allow the air to circulate around them freely. The vegetable rack can be free-standing, in which case it should be kept in a cool, dry place, or in the larder. Some kitchen units incorporate baskets for storing vegetables—make sure that you do not have these arranged in a cupboard next to the cooker which would then make the cupboard too warm to store vegetables adequately. Beware of storing vegetables in polythene bags for any length of time as they sometimes become soft and unpleasant—root vegetables, in particular, do not like being shut up in a polythene bag.

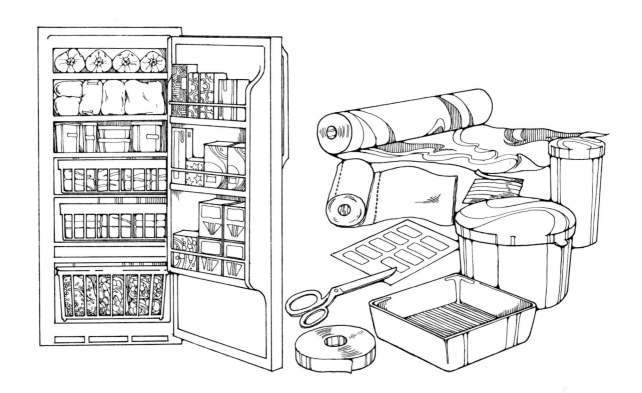

Minestrone, French onion soup and lettuce soup (see pages 22, 20)

A guide to soups

Soup making need not be a laborious process and with the aid of a liquidiser some really flavoursome soups can be made from the most inexpensive of ingredients: for example the outer leaves of a lettuce, an onion, stock, milk and seasoning will produce a most delicious lettuce soup which can be served either hot or cold. Soup, apart from being served as a meal starter at dinner, can be served with garlic bread, or with bread and cheese, and makes an ideal luncheon dish; a cold or hot soup can be taken on a picnic and is a nourishing and inexpensive way of feeding a growing family.

Soups can be thickened with flour or cornflour, beurre manié (equal quantities of fat and flour blended together and whisked in, a little at a time, at the end of the cooking), with a liaison of egg yolks and/or cream (which also add goodness) or a clear unthickened soup can be served. Soups blended in a liquidiser need not be thickened with flour or cornflour as the blended ingredients are usually thick enough. An egg yolk or cream can be added to a liquidised soup to enrich it.

The basis of soup is a good stock, but today very few people keep a stock pot going! (Although with the aid of a pressure cooker stock can be made very quickly and economically, see page 146.) However, a satisfactory stock can be made using the commercially-prepared stock cubes—beef for meat soups and the lighter chicken ones for vegetable soups. A little meat or vegetable extract can also be added to give more flavour. Remember to vary the flavour of your soups by adding different herbs—mace in a celery soup, sage in a broad bean soup and so on. A bouquet garni will do wonders for a mixed vegetable soup and the flavour of the homely lentil and pea soups is improved tremendously if the stock from boiling a bacon joint or a ham bone can be used (do not add any salt without first trying the soup—the stock may have been sufficiently salty).

When making a fish soup ask the fishmonger for the trimmings and use these to make a fish stock.

Most soups freeze well, so it is worth making at least double the amount. Allow the soup to cool before packing it in polythene containers or foil bags, leaving headspace. If a recipe contains an egg yolk or cream, omit them for freezing and add at the reheating stage.

It is essential to garnish all food—it not only makes the food look more appetising, but often, particularly with soups, the garnish makes the dish more substantial and without it the soup would be unfinished. No garnish must be overpowering either in colour, taste or texture—it must blend with and complement the dish. Many garnishes can be prepared in advance and it is no trouble at all to drop a few well dried parsley leaves into the liquidiser goblet and switch on for a few seconds. Chopped parsley can be stored in an airtight container in the refrigerator. At the end of the soup recipes you will find suggested garnishes. Before the soup recipes you will find basic instructions for making various types of soups. By following these instructions and looking at the recipes given, you will soon find that you can invent your own soup recipes using whatever ingredients you may have to hand and adding your flavourings and seasonings to suit your choice of menu and type of meal.

Making soup in the liquidiser

1 The most important point is to always follow the manufacturer's instructions for using your particular type of liquidiser. With most models—the smaller ones in particular—it is essential not to fill the goblet too full or to run the machine for longer than stated by the manufacturer.

2 Sauté the prepared vegetables in butter, fat or oil in a pan.

3 Add the liquid—this can be stock, water or milk, or a mixture of all three—together with the seasonings.

4 Bring the ingredients to the boil, cover the pan and simmer gently until the vegetables are softened.

5 Leave aside to cool slightly.

6 Ladle the cooled vegetables and liquid into the liquidiser goblet, a little at a time, and liquidise using a low speed.

7 Return the liquidised ingredients to a clean pan; reheat, stir in any additional ingredients (egg yolks, cream or milk) and check the seasoning. Be careful not to allow any soup to boil once cream or an egg yolk has been added, as it will curdle.

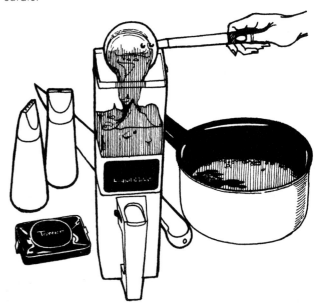

Making a purée soup (without a liquidiser)

1 Sauté the prepared vegetables in butter, fat or oil.
2 Add the stock and seasonings.
3 Cover and simmer until the vegetables are tender.
4 Cool slightly, then press the vegetables through a sieve, using a wooden spoon.
5 Reheat the resulting purée and add stock or milk. Thicken if necessary and add cream or egg yolks as required.
6 Check seasoning and serve.

Making a vegetable soup

1 Sauté the prepared vegetables in butter, fat or oil.
2 Add the stock and seasonings.
3 Cover and simmer until the vegetables are tender.
4 Check seasoning and serve.

Broad bean soup

Main utensils: saucepan, liquidiser
Preparation time: few minutes
Cooking time: 30 minutes
Serves: 4

Imperial/Metric	American
1 oz./25 g. butter	2 tablespoons butter
1 onion, chopped	1 onion, chopped
1 clove garlic, crushed	1 clove garlic, crushed
1 lb./½ kg. broad beans (shelled weight)	1 lb. fava or lima beans (shelled weight)
2–3 sprigs parsley	2–3 sprigs parsley
3 sage leaves, chopped	3 sage leaves, chopped
salt and pepper	salt and pepper
1 pint/6 dl. chicken stock	2½ cups chicken stock
½ pint/3 dl. milk	1¼ cups milk
¼ pint/1½ dl. single cream (optional)	⅔ cup coffee cream (optional)

Melt the butter in a saucepan and sauté the onion and garlic for 2–3 minutes, until softened. Add the beans, parsley, sage, seasoning, stock and milk. Bring to the boil, cover and simmer until the beans are tender and the outer skins have risen to the top. Discard the bean skins (they make the soup bitter) and allow the soup to cool slightly. Ladle into the liquidiser, a little at a time, and switch the machine to low speed until the ingredients are puréed.

Return to a clean saucepan, check the seasoning and reheat. Ladle into soup cups and if liked, swirl a little cream into each serving.
 ✳ Omit the cream for freezing and add it at the reheating stage. Garlic shortens the freezer storage life, so either store for 6 weeks only with the garlic, or omit the garlic and store for 4–6 months.

Leek soup

Main utensils: saucepan, liquidiser
Preparation time: 5 minutes
Cooking time: 30 minutes
Serves: 4–6

Imperial/Metric	American
1 oz./25 g. butter	2 tablespoons butter
4 large leeks, sliced	4 large leeks, sliced
4 large potatoes, chopped	4 large potatoes, chopped
2 pints/generous 1 litre stock	5 cups stock
salt and pepper	salt and pepper
2 egg yolks	2 egg yolks
2 tablespoons chopped parsley	3 tablespoons chopped parsley

Melt the butter in a saucepan and sauté the prepared leeks and potatoes for a few minutes. Add the stock and seasoning. Bring to the boil, cover and simmer for about 30 minutes, until the vegetables are tender. Cool slightly, then ladle into the liquidiser, a little at a time, and switch the machine on low speed until the vegetables are puréed. Return to a clean saucepan, check the seasoning, reheat and stir in the egg yolks and chopped parsley just before serving.
Note: Remember not to boil the soup after the egg yolks have been added, as it will curdle.
 ✳ This soup freezes well, but add the egg yolks at the reheating stage.

Chop the onion and potato finely before sautéing in the butter for the lettuce soup. The stock can be made from chicken stock cubes.

When the onion and potato have softened add the washed lettuce leaves, milk, stock and dill. Bring to the boil, cover and simmer for 10–15 minutes.

Allow the cooked vegetables and liquid to cool slightly, then ladle into the liquidiser, a little at a time. Switch on the liquidiser and let it run until the ingredients are reduced to a thin purée. Pour into a bowl, or clean saucepan for reheating.

Lettuce soup   (Illustrated above and on page 17)

Main utensils: saucepan, liquidiser
Preparation time: few minutes
Cooking time: 20 minutes
Serves: 6
	Imperial/Metric
	1 oz./25 g. butter
	1 onion, chopped
	1 potato, chopped
	1 lettuce or outside leaves
	   from 2 lettuces
	1½ pints/scant 1 litre milk
	½ pint/3 dl. chicken stock
	salt and pepper
	pinch dill
	¼ pint/1½ dl. cream
	Garnish:
	snipped chives
		American
		2 tablespoons butter
		1 onion, chopped
		1 potato, chopped
		1 lettuce or outside leaves
		   from 2 lettuces
		3¾ cups milk
		1¼ cups chicken stock
		salt and pepper
		pinch dill
		⅔ cup cream
		Garnish:
		snipped chives

Melt the butter in a saucepan and sauté the onion and potato until softened. Stir in the washed lettuce leaves and toss with the vegetables. Add the milk, stock, seasoning and dill. Bring to the boil, cover and simmer for 10–15 minutes. Cool slightly, then ladle into the liquidiser, a little at a time, and switch the machine on low speed until the ingredients are puréed. Return to a clean saucepan, check the seasoning, reheat and stir in the cream just before serving. Garnish with snipped chives.

Note: If liked, this soup can be served chilled.

☼ If freezing this soup, omit the cream and add it at the reheating stage.

Provençal soup

Main utensils: saucepan, liquidiser
Preparation time: 15 minutes
Cooking time: 45 minutes
Serves: 6

Imperial/Metric	**American**
1 lb./½ kg. tomatoes	1 lb. tomatoes
1 lb./½ kg. potatoes	1 lb. potatoes
3 pints/1½ litres stock	7 cups stock
salt and pepper	salt and pepper
1 clove garlic, crushed	1 clove garlic, crushed
few thyme leaves, chopped	few thyme leaves, chopped
1 large onion, chopped	1 large onion, chopped
1 oz./25 g. butter	2 tablespoons butter
Garnish:	*Garnish:*
chopped chervil	chopped chervil

Peel and slice the tomatoes and potatoes. Place in a saucepan with the stock, seasoning, garlic, thyme and onion. Bring to the boil, cover and simmer for 45 minutes. Cool slightly, then ladle into the liquidiser, a little at a time, and switch the machine on low speed until the vegetables are puréed. Return to a clean saucepan, check the seasoning, reheat and stir in the butter just before serving. Serve garnished with chopped chervil.

※ Omit the garlic if freezing this soup, or store for 6 weeks only with the garlic.

Lentil soup

Main utensils: saucepan, liquidiser
Preparation time: 5 minutes
Cooking time: about 1 hour
Serves: 4–6

Imperial/Metric	**American**
½ pint/3 dl. lentils	1¼ cups lentils
about 2 pints/generous 1 litre bacon stock (if available)	about 5 cups ham stock (if available)
1 large onion, chopped	1 large onion, chopped
2 carrots, chopped	2 carrots, chopped
1 small turnip, chopped	1 small turnip, chopped
1 stick celery, chopped	1 stalk celery, chopped
pepper	pepper
1 bay leaf	1 bay leaf
Garnish:	*Garnish:*
chopped parsley	chopped parsley

Wash the lentils, drain well and place in a saucepan with the bacon stock, prepared vegetables, pepper and bay leaf. Bring to the boil, cover and simmer for about 1 hour, until the lentils are thoroughly softened (add more stock during cooking if necessary). Cool slightly, then ladle into the liquidiser, a little at a time, and switch on low speed until the ingredients are puréed. Return to a clean saucepan, check the seasoning and reheat. Serve garnished with chopped parsley.

※ This soup freezes well.

Tomato and corn soup

Main utensils: 2 saucepans
Preparation time: few minutes
Cooking time: 5 minutes
Serves: 6–8

Imperial/Metric	**American**
1 medium can tomato juice	1 medium can tomato juice
1 bay leaf	1 bay leaf
pinch mace	pinch mace
4 peppercorns	4 peppercorns
2 oz./50 g. butter	¼ cup butter
2 oz./50 g. flour	½ cup all-purpose flour
1½ pints/scant 1 litre milk	3¾ cups milk
1 medium can sweetcorn	1 medium can kernel corn
salt and pepper	salt and pepper

Place the tomato juice in a saucepan with the bay leaf, mace and peppercorns. Place over a low heat and *very slowly* bring to the boil. Remove from the heat and leave to infuse. Meanwhile, melt the butter in a saucepan, stir in the flour and cook for 1–2 minutes. Off the heat, blend in the milk. Return to the heat and, stirring all the time, bring to the boil and cook, stirring, for 2–3 minutes. Add the drained corn and strained tomato juice. Check the seasoning, reheat and serve with croûtons.

※ This soup freezes well.

Minestrone soup (Illustrated on page 17)

Main utensil: saucepan
Preparation time: 15 minutes
Cooking time: 1½ hours
Serves: 6

Imperial/Metric	American
2 rashers streaky bacon	2 bacon slices
1 tablespoon oil	1 tablespoon oil
2 carrots, sliced	2 carrots, sliced
1 onion, chopped	1 onion, chopped
4 sticks celery, chopped	4 stalks celery, chopped
2 potatoes, chopped	2 potatoes, chopped
about 3 pints/1½ litres water	7½ cups water
1 clove garlic, crushed	1 clove garlic, crushed
1 bay leaf	1 bay leaf
2 sage leaves	2 sage leaves
salt and pepper	salt and pepper
2 tomatoes, skinned and chopped	2 tomatoes, skinned and chopped
8 oz./225 g. cabbage, shredded	3 cups shredded cabbage
4 oz./100 g. short macaroni	¼ lb. short macaroni
2 tablespoons chopped parsley	3 tablespoons chopped parsley
grated Parmesan cheese	grated Parmesan cheese

Rind and chop the bacon rashers. Place in a pan with the oil. Cook over a low heat until the fat from the bacon runs. Add the prepared carrots, onion, celery and potatoes. Sauté for about 5 minutes. Add the water, garlic, bay leaf, sage and seasoning. Bring to the boil, cover and simmer for 1 hour. Add the tomatoes, cabbage, macaroni and parsley and simmer, covered, for about a further 20 minutes (adding more stock if necessary), until the vegetables are tender and the macaroni softened. Remove the bay leaf and sage leaves and serve with grated Parmesan cheese.

Note: The ingredients in a minestrone soup can be varied according to what is available. There should always be a good selection of vegetables, and rice, pasta and soaked and cooked dried beans can be added according to choice. The flavour can be further varied by omitting the bay leaf and sage and adding a bouquet garni.

French onion soup (Illustrated on page 17)

Main utensils: saucepan, casserole
dish or individual ovenproof dishes
Preparation time: 5 minutes
Oven temperature: moderate
(350°F., 180°C., Gas Mark 4)
Cooking time: 50 minutes
Serves: 4

Imperial/Metric	American
8 oz./225 g. onions	½ lb. onions
2 oz./50 g. butter	¼ cup butter
2 teaspoons flour	2 teaspoons all-purpose flour
1½ pints/scant 1 litre stock	3¾ cups stock
salt and pepper	salt and pepper
1 bay leaf	1 bay leaf
1 small French loaf	1 small French loaf
4 oz./100 g. Gruyère cheese, grated	1 cup grated Gruyère cheese

Slice the onions thinly. Melt the butter in a saucepan and *very slowly* fry the onion slices until softened and lightly browned—this will take at least 15 minutes. Add the flour and stirring, add the stock. Add the seasoning and bay leaf. Bring to the boil, cover and simmer for 25–30 minutes. Place the slices of French bread in the bottom of a casserole dish, or individual ovenproof dishes. Discard the bay leaf and ladle over the soup. Sprinkle over the grated cheese and place the casserole (uncovered) in the centre of a preheated moderate oven for 15–20 minutes to brown. Serve from the casserole dish.

Note: Alternatively, the soup can be ladled into a tureen and toasted slices of French bread, sprinkled with the cheese, can be floated in the soup.

Bortsch

Main utensils: shredder attachment
or hand grater, saucepan
Preparation time: 5–10 minutes
Cooking time: about 30 minutes
Serves: 4–6

Imperial/Metric	American
1 lb./½ kg. raw beetroot	1 lb. raw beet
2 pints/generous 1 litre beef stock	5 cups beef stock
1 small onion, chopped	1 small onion, chopped
salt and pepper	salt and pepper
¼ pint/1½ dl. soured cream	⅔ cup sour cream

Grate the beetroot, using the shredder attachment to your mixer, if possible, or a hand grater. Place in a pan with the stock, onion and plenty of seasoning. Bring to the boil, cover and simmer until the vegetables are tender. Spoon into soup bowls and top each serving with a spoonful of soured cream.

Scotch broth

Main utensil: large saucepan
Preparation time: 10 minutes
Cooking time: 2 hours
Serves: 6

Imperial/Metric	**American**
1½–2 lb./about 1 kg. scrag or middle neck of mutton	1½–2 lb. mutton neck slices
4 pints/2¼ litres water	10 cups water
2 oz./50 g. pearl barley	¼ cup pearl barley
2 carrots, chopped	2 carrots, chopped
1 leek, sliced	1 leek, sliced
2 turnips, chopped	2 turnips, chopped
1 onion, chopped	1 onion, chopped
1 stick celery, chopped	1 stalk celery, chopped
bouquet garni	bouquet garni
salt and pepper	salt and pepper
2 tablespoons chopped parsley	3 tablespoons chopped parsley

Remove as much of the fat as possible and cut the mutton into small pieces. Put in a large saucepan with the water. Bring to the boil, remove the scum that rises, cover and simmer for 30 minutes. Add the pearl barley, prepared vegetables, bouquet garni and plenty of seasoning. Simmer, covered, for a further 1½ hours. Take out the bouquet garni and pieces of mutton and cut the nicest pieces of meat off the bones. Return the meat pieces to the broth, skim off any fat and stir in the chopped parsley.

Note: As this soup is so thick and full of vegetables it makes a meal in itself served with pieces of fresh bread to mop up the goodness.

Shrimp soup

Main utensils: 2 saucepans, liquidiser
Preparation time: 15 minutes
Cooking time: about 1 hour, including making the stock
Serves: 4–6

Imperial/Metric	**American**
Fish stock:	*Fish stock:*
fish trimmings	fish trimmings
1 bunch parsley	1 bunch parsley
1 bay leaf	1 bay leaf
1 onion, sliced	1 onion, sliced
salt and pepper	salt and pepper
2½ pints/1¼ litres water	6¼ cups water
¼ pint/1½ dl. white wine	⅔ cup white wine
1 lb./½ kg. potatoes	1 lb. potatoes
1 leek (white part only)	1 leek (white part only)
1 oz./25 g. butter	2 tablespoons butter
salt and pepper	salt and pepper
2 egg yolks	2 egg yolks
¼ pint/1½ dl. single cream	⅔ cup coffee cream
4 oz./100 g. fresh or frozen shrimps	about ¾ cup fresh or frozen shrimp
Garnish:	*Garnish:*
chopped parsley	chopped parsley

Prepare the fish stock: wash and drain the fish trimmings and place in a saucepan with the remaining ingredients. Bring to the boil and simmer until the liquid has reduced by about one-third. Strain.

Peel and slice the potatoes and slice the leek. Melt the butter in a saucepan and sauté the prepared vegetables for 2–3 minutes. Add the fish stock and seasoning. Bring to the boil, cover and simmer for about 20 minutes, until the vegetables are tender. Cool slightly then ladle into the liquidiser, a little at a time, and switch the machine on low speed until the vegetables are puréed. Return to a clean saucepan, check the seasoning, reheat and stir in the egg yolks, cream and shrimps. Allow to heat through (but do not boil) and serve garnished with plenty of chopped parsley.

Slimmers' soup

Main utensil: liquidiser
Preparation time: 5 minutes
Serves: 4

Imperial/Metric	**American**
1 bunch watercress	1 bunch watercress
4 oz./100 g. carrots, shredded or grated	1⅓ cups shredded or grated carrot
1 small can tomatoes	1 small can tomatoes
1 dessert apple, peeled, cored and chopped	1 dessert apple, peeled, cored and chopped
½ pint/3 dl. water	1¼ cups water
salt and pepper	salt and pepper
pinch sugar	pinch sugar
¼ pint/1½ dl. soured cream or natural yogurt (optional)	⅔ cup sour cream or unflavored yogurt (optional)
Garnish:	*Garnish:*
chopped parsley	chopped parsley

Wash the watercress and remove the stalks. Dry the leaves well. Mix all the ingredients together (except the soured cream) and liquidise, a little at a time. Chill well and if liked, before serving, stir in the soured cream or yogurt. Garnish with chopped parsley.

Gazpacho

Main utensil: liquidiser
Preparation time: 10 minutes
Serves: 6

Imperial/Metric	**American**
2 cloves garlic	2 cloves garlic
1 onion	1 onion
1 small cucumber	1 small cucumber
12 oz./350 g. ripe tomatoes	¾ lb. ripe tomatoes
1 green pepper	1 green sweet pepper
1 red pepper	1 red sweet pepper
1 thick slice white bread, crusts removed	1 thick slice white bread, crusts removed
1 tablespoon olive oil	1 tablespoon olive oil
1 tablespoon red wine vinegar	1 tablespoon red wine vinegar
iced water	iced water
ground black pepper	ground black pepper
Garnish:	*Garnish:*
chopped green or red pepper	chopped green or red sweet pepper
chopped cucumber	chopped cucumber

Peel the garlic, onion, cucumber and tomatoes. Chop them coarsely then feed into the liquidiser, a few at a time, and switch on the machine until the vegetables are finely chopped. Gradually add the chopped peppers while the machine is on medium speed. Add the remaining ingredients and as much iced water as necessary (or the liquidiser goblet will take) to make a fairly thin consistency. Pour into a bowl, check the seasoning and consistency and chill well. Serve with the chopped peppers and cucumber in small dishes.

Garnishes and accompaniments for soups

Croûtons Remove the crusts from fairly thick slices of day-old bread. Cut the slices into cubes and fry the cubes, over a gentle heat, in hot butter and oil until golden and crisp. Drain on absorbent paper and serve sprinkled over the soup, or in a separate bowl. Croûtons can also be cut from slices of lightly toasted bread.
Croûtes Cut ¼-inch (½-cm.) slices from a French loaf, place on a baking tray and bake in a cool oven (300°F., 150°C., Gas Mark 2) until golden brown. Serve with the soup, or place in the bottom of the tureen and ladle the hot soup over.
Garlic bread Cut a small French loaf, almost through, at 1-inch (2·5-cm.) intervals. Mix together 1 oz. (25 g.) butter and 1–2 crushed cloves of garlic (depending on taste) and spread between the slices. Wrap in foil and heat through in a moderate oven (350°F., 180°C., Gas Mark 4) for about 15–20 minutes. Serve hot with the soup.

Cheese straws, small savoury biscuits and crackers all make suitable store cupboard accompaniments for soup. Snipped chives, chopped mint, parsley, or a mixture of fresh chopped herbs can be sprinkled over a soup before serving. If fresh herbs are not available, use a small amount of the dried variety.
Grated cheese can be sprinkled over vegetable soups to make a more substantial dish.

Celery soup (see page 146)

A guide to starters and appetisers

When planning a menu, whether it is to serve to your family or for a special occasion, remember that the first course plays an important part as it is the opener to the kind of food that is to follow. How many times have you ordered a delicious starter in a restaurant only to find that instead of stimulating your appetite (as a starter should) it completely satisfied it and left you no room to enjoy your chosen main course dish? Delicious French onion soup with a round of French bread and Gruyère cheese floating in it could be followed by a light main course dish, but followed by goulash and rice would sink even the most ambitious gourmet!

It can often be a good idea to serve the first course with pre-lunch or dinner drinks, as this takes away some of the strain of being the cook/hostess. Dips and finger food—titbits on sticks, can be interesting and colourful. Pâtés and savoury mousses can be prepared well in advance and stored in the refrigerator or freezer. This means there need be no panic if your guests have been delayed.

A liquidiser is ideal for making pâtés quickly—without the help of a liquidiser making a pâté can be a time consuming operation.

We are fortunate in being able to buy avocado pears, grapefruit, various kinds of melons and a fine selection of smoked fish all of which make delicious, but simple starters which don't involve you in any cooking. However, do remember that the idea of an appetiser is to stimulate the appetite so do not fill your guests too full at the beginning of the meal or you will be disappointed at the response to your *pièce de résistance*.

Snacks to accompany drinks

As well as the more usual bowls of potato crisps, nuts etc., serve a selection of the following next time you offer drinks to your guests.

Devilled and salted almonds; stuffed and unstuffed olives; puff cracknels, each one stuffed with a prawn, or two shrimps moistened with mayonnaise; small savoury biscuits spread with pâté and garnished with half a stuffed olive, or spread with bloater cream and garnished with a curled anchovy fillet and either a slice of stuffed olive or a piece of canned pimento.

Olives

French, Spanish and black olives and olives stuffed with nuts or pimento all make good appetisers. Steep unstuffed olives for a few minutes in cold water, then drain well and serve in dainty dishes containing a little cold water. When serving them at a dinner party, put a spoonful of sherry or Madeira in the serving dishes instead of water. Black olives can be stoned and filled with fish paste or pâté (an easy way to fill them is to pipe the mixture in through a small piping tube). Serve on tiny round canapés of cold, buttered toast, or cooked pastry, thinly buttered, or small round savoury biscuits.

Windsor canapés

Main utensils: baking tray, saucepan (preferably non-stick)
Preparation time: 15 minutes, not including making the pastry
Oven temperature: hot (425°F., 220°C., Gas Mark 7)
Cooking time: about 10 minutes

Imperial/Metric
6 oz./150 g. flaky or rough puff pastry (see pages 106, 108)
6 oz./150 g. cooked smoked haddock
¼ pint/1½ dl. double cream
2 egg yolks
salt and pepper
paprika pepper

American
6 oz. flaky or rough puff pastry (see pages 106, 108)
6 oz. cooked smoked haddock
⅔ cup whipping cream
2 egg yolks
salt and pepper
paprika pepper

Roll out the pastry thinly and cut into rounds, about 3½ inches (9 cm.) in diameter. Place on a baking tray and bake near the top of a preheated hot oven for about 10 minutes, until risen and golden brown.

Meanwhile, flake the haddock finely. Place in a saucepan with the cream, egg yolks and seasonings to taste.

Stir over a low heat until thickened and heated through. (Do not allow the mixture to boil.) Pile the mixture onto the baked pastry rounds and serve at once.

Note: If wanted for a buffet party smaller pastry rounds can be made.

Anchovy and egg canapés

Main utensil: grill pan
Preparation time: 5 minutes
Cooking time: few minutes
Serves: 6

Imperial/Metric
4 anchovies
2 hard-boiled eggs, chopped
6 small squares toast
3 stuffed olives
little melted butter

American
4 anchovies
2 hard-cooked eggs, chopped
6 small squares toast
3 stuffed olives
little melted butter

Mix anchovies and eggs. Spread on the squares of toast. Press half a stuffed olive into centre of each. Brush with melted butter and place under a preheated grill for 3–4 minutes. Serve hot.

Salted almonds

Main utensil: frying pan or baking tray (preferably non-stick)
Preparation time: 5 minutes
Oven temperature: moderate (350°F., 180°C., Gas Mark 4)
Cooking time: 5 or 15 minutes according to method used

Imperial/Metric
8 oz./225 g. whole almonds
1 oz./25 g. butter or 2 tablespoons olive oil
salt and paprika pepper

American
1½ cups whole almonds
2–3 tablespoons butter or olive oil
salt and paprika pepper

Place almonds in a bowl and cover them with boiling water. Leave to stand for about 5 minutes. Then transfer to a bowl of cold water; the skins can then be removed easily by rubbing an almond between the right thumb and first finger. Dry with a paper towel. Heat the butter or oil in a frying pan, add the nuts and fry, turning frequently with a spoon until an even golden colour—about 5 minutes.

Alternatively, place the butter or olive oil on a flat baking tray, add the prepared nuts, and place them in a preheated moderate oven until nicely browned and most of the fat has been absorbed—this will take about 15 minutes. When nuts are ready remove with a spoon to a dish lined with brown paper, sprinkle heavily with salt, then with a dash of paprika pepper. Shake off any loose salt, and turn onto another piece of brown paper to dry. Store, when cold, in an airtight jar. Serve in crystal, silver or china dishes lined with a lace paper doily.

❊ To freeze, put in a heavy duty polythene bag without salt. For a long freezer life salt only on removing from the freezer.

Anchovy squares

Main utensil: liquidiser (optional)
Preparation time: 5 minutes

Imperial/Metric
butter
black olives
salt and pepper
small squares hot toast
anchovy fillets
mustard and cress

American
butter
ripe olives
salt and pepper
small squares hot toast
anchovy fillets
garden cress

To make olive butter, beat butter to a cream and stir in liquidised or chopped olives to taste; season lightly. Spread toast squares with this mixture and place a curled anchovy fillet in the centre of each. Serve on a dish lined with a paper doily and garnish with mustard and cress.

Cress or pimento butter can be made in the same way and used instead of olive butter. Allow twice as much butter as liquidised olives, 3 pimentos to 4 oz. (100 g.) butter, and 2 tablespoons chopped or liquidised mustard and cress or watercress to 2 oz. (50 g.) butter.

Favourite egg dip

Main utensil: liquidiser (optional)
Preparation time: few minutes, plus
   time to chill dip
Makes: 2 pints (generous 1 litre)

Imperial/Metric
12 hard-boiled eggs, liquidised or
   finely chopped
1 oz./25 g. soft butter or margarine
1 tablespoon lemon juice
2 teaspoons made mustard
2 teaspoons Worcestershire sauce
2 drops Tabasco sauce
1 teaspoon salt
¼ teaspoon white pepper
¼ pint/1½ dl. mayonnaise (see page
   90) or salad cream

American
12 hard-cooked eggs, liquidised or
   finely chopped
2 tablespoons soft butter or margarine
1 tablespoon lemon juice
2 teaspoons made mustard
2 teaspoons Worcestershire sauce
2 drops Tabasco sauce
1 teaspoon salt
¼ teaspoon white pepper
⅔ cup mayonnaise (see page 90) or
   cole slaw dressing

Mix all the ingredients together and beat until smooth—the mixture should be soft enough to dip potato chips etc. into it easily. Chill until ready to serve. About 20 minutes before serving, remove from the refrigerator and beat to a fluffy consistency. Serve piled in a bowl, with potato crisps, sticks of raw vegetables etc. for dipping.

Cheese and onion dip

Main utensil: liquidiser
Preparation time: 5 minutes, plus
   time to chill dip
Serves: 6–8

Imperial/Metric
½ packet French onion soup mix
4 tablespoons single cream
8 oz./225 g. cottage cheese
salt and pepper
Garnish:
chopped chives or parsley

American
½ package French onion soup mix
⅓ cup coffee cream
1 cup cottage cheese
salt and pepper
Garnish:
chopped chives or parsley

Mix the dried onion soup with the cream about 30 minutes before making up the dip. Liquidise the cottage cheese and then blend in the onion mixture with the seasoning. Pile

Variations

Celery cheese dip Use the celery soup instead of French onion soup.
Pineapple cheese dip (Illustrated on page 29) Use a 7-oz./200-g. can of pineapple pieces instead of the soup.

into a dish and leave to chill. Garnish with chopped chives or parsley and serve with potato crisps, raw carrot or celery sticks and cauliflower florets.

Blend most of the drained pineapple pieces in the liquidiser with the cottage cheese. Garnish with the reserved pineapple pieces.

Surprise hors d'oeuvre

Main utensil: bowl
Preparation time: 5 minutes
Serves: 8

Imperial/Metric
8 oz./225 g. liver sausage, unsliced
4 hard-boiled egg yolks
1 oz./25 g. softened butter
½ teaspoon made mustard
8 slices bread, toasted on one side
bunch watercress

American
½ lb. liver sausage, unsliced
4 hard-cooked egg yolks
2 tablespoons softened butter
½ teaspoon made mustard
8 slices bread, toasted on one side
bunch watercress

Scoop out the centre from the piece of liver sausage, (do not remove the casing) leaving a wall about ½ inch (1 cm.) thick. Fill the space with a mixture of sieved hard-boiled egg yolks, butter and mustard. Chill, then remove the casing from the liver sausage and cut the roll into thin slices. Place on the untoasted sides of the bread slices and serve on a bed of watercress.

Scallops au gratin

Main utensil: saucepan
  (preferably non-stick)
Preparation time: 15 minutes
Cooking time: 10 minutes
Serves: 4

Imperial/Metric	American
6 scallops	6 scallops
½ pint/3 dl. milk	1¼ cups milk
1 slice onion	1 slice onion
1 blade mace	1 blade mace
2 oz./50 g. butter or margarine	¼ cup butter or margarine
1 oz./25 g. flour	¼ cup all-purpose flour
2 oz./50 g. mushrooms	½ cup mushrooms
1 teaspoon chopped parsley	1 teaspoon chopped parsley
salt	salt
paprika pepper	paprika pepper
dried breadcrumbs	dry bread crumbs
1 tablespoon grated cheese	1 tablespoon grated cheese

Remove beards and black parts from the scallops, then place them in a saucepan. Cover with cold water and bring slowly to the boil. Drain and cut into four pieces. Grease four scallop shells. Heat the milk slowly in a saucepan with the onion and mace. Melt half the fat in a saucepan, stir in flour and, when frothy, strain in the hot milk. Stir until smooth and boiling. Peel and chop the mushrooms, then fry them in the remaining fat. Add scallops, mushrooms and parsley to the sauce. Bring to the boil, season to taste with salt and paprika pepper and cook for 2–3 minutes. Divide mixture between the shells. Sprinkle lightly with crumbs, then with cheese, and brown under the grill.

Grapefruit and avacado starter, three-minute liver pâté, smoked haddock cream and pineapple cheese dip (see pages 33, 32, 30, 28)

Salmon creams

Main utensils: nylon sieve or liquidiser, saucepan (preferably non-stick), individual moulds or a soufflé dish
Preparation time: 15 minutes
Serves: 4

Imperial/Metric	American
8 oz./225 g. canned or cooked fresh salmon	½ lb. canned or cooked fresh salmon
½ teaspoon juice from ½ an onion	½ teaspoon juice from ½ an onion
1 egg	1 egg
1 tablespoon butter	1 tablespoon butter
1 tablespoon flour	1 tablespoon all-purpose flour
¼ pint/1½ dl. milk	⅔ cup milk
½ teaspoon lemon juice	½ teaspoon lemon juice
salt and pepper	salt and pepper
1 teaspoon cream	1 teaspoon cream

Rub the fish through a fine sieve or purée in a liquidiser. (Allow to cool if using freshly cooked salmon.) Mix in the onion juice. Beat the egg white stiffly and fold into the salmon mixture, using a tablespoon. Melt the butter in a saucepan, then stir in the flour and when frothy, gradually stir in the milk. Stir until thickened, then remove the pan from the heat and stir in the egg yolk, lemon juice and seasoning to taste. Return the pan to a low heat and stir in the salmon purée and cream. Spoon into greased individual moulds or a soufflé dish and leave in a cool place to set. To serve, turn onto a bed of green salad—watercress or lettuce leaves—tossed in French dressing.

Potted shrimps

Main utensil: saucepan
Preparation time: few minutes
Cooking time: few minutes
Serves: 4

Imperial/Metric	American
½ pint/3 dl. picked shrimps	1¼ cups picked shrimp
2½ oz./65 g. butter	5 tablespoons butter
pinch ground mace	pinch ground mace
pinch grated nutmeg	pinch grated nutmeg
pinch cayenne pepper	pinch cayenne pepper

Put the shrimps into a saucepan with 1½ oz. (40 g.) of the butter. Season to taste with the ground mace, grated nutmeg and cayenne pepper. Place the saucepan over a low heat to melt the butter. Stir the mixture then turn it into small jars or pots, pressing the shrimps down firmly. Melt the rest of the butter and pour some over the top of each jar to seal. Serve chilled with slices of thin toast or with cream crackers.

Smoked haddock cream (Illustrated on page 29)

Main utensil: liquidiser
Preparation time: 10 minutes
Serves: 4–6

Imperial/Metric	American
8 oz./225 g. smoked haddock fillet	½ lb. smoked haddock fillet
¼ pint/1½ dl. double cream	⅔ cup whipping cream
juice of ½ lemon	juice of ½ lemon
salt	salt
freshly ground black pepper	freshly ground black pepper
pinch cayenne pepper	pinch cayenne pepper
Garnish:	*Garnish:*
lemon fans	lemon fans
chopped parsley	chopped parsley

Remove any skin and bones from the haddock and flake the raw smoked fish. Put half the fish in the liquidiser with half the cream, switch on until a creamy mixture is obtained. Empty into a bowl and liquidise the remaining half. Mix the creamed fish together in the bowl with lemon juice and seasoning to taste. Pile into a dish and garnish with lemon fans and parsley. Serve with crispbread or hot buttered toast.

Variations
Arbroath smoked cream Use delicious Arbroath smokies in place of the smoked haddock to make this cream.

Smoked salmon cream Make the mixture with smoked salmon and use to spread on canapés. Garnish with caviare.

Shrimp toasts

Main utensil: double saucepan
Preparation time: 10 minutes
Cooking time: 20 minutes
Serves: 4

Imperial/Metric
¼ pint/1½ dl. milk
¼ pint/1½ dl. single cream
generous 1 lb./½ kg. picked shrimps
2 tablespoons sherry
salt
pinch cayenne pepper
pinch grated nutmeg
1 oz./25 g. butter
1 tablespoon flour
hot buttered toast

American
⅔ cup milk
⅔ cup coffee cream
1 lb. picked shrimp
3 tablespoons sherry
salt
pinch cayenne pepper
pinch grated nutmeg
2 tablespoons butter
1 tablespoon all-purpose flour
hot buttered toast

Pour milk and cream into the top of a double saucepan. Add shrimps and sherry, and cook over the boiling water for 15 minutes. Season to taste with salt, cayenne pepper and grated nutmeg. Knead the butter and flour together, then mix into the creamed shrimps, a little at a time. Cook for 3 minutes, stirring all the time. Serve on squares of buttered toast.

Creamed oysters

Main utensils: saucepan
(preferably non-stick), sieve
Preparation time: 10 minutes
Cooking time: about 15 minutes
Serves: 4

Imperial/Metric
1 pint/generous ½ litre oysters
½ pint/3 dl. milk
3 tablespoons butter
5 tablespoons flour
salt and pepper
celery salt
4 vol-au-vent cases or 8 small
bouchées (see page 116)

American
2½ cups oysters
1¼ cups milk
4 tablespoons butter
6 tablespoons all-purpose flour
salt and pepper
celery salt
4 vol-au-vent cases or 8 small
bouchées (see page 116)

Clean the oysters, then cook in boiling water for about 2 minutes, until plump. Drain and measure off ¼ pint (1½ dl.) of the liquid and mix it with the milk. Melt the butter in a saucepan, stir in the flour and when frothy, stir in the liquid by degrees. Season to taste with salt, pepper and celery salt; stir until well blended, then add the oysters. Heat the mixture until piping hot, then turn into the hot pastry cases and serve at once.
Note: The creamed oysters can be served on rounds of buttered toast, if preferred.

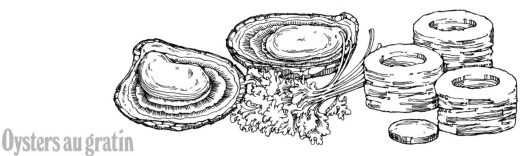

Oysters au gratin

Main utensils: 2 saucepans
(preferably non-stick), ovenproof
dish
Preparation time: 5 minutes
Oven temperature: moderate
(350°F., 180°C., Gas Mark 4)
Cooking time: about 20 minutes
Serves: 4

Imperial/Metric
12 oysters
2 oz./50 g. butter
1 teaspoon chopped parsley
about ¼ pint/1½ dl. white wine
1 oz./25 g. flour
3 tablespoons fresh breadcrumbs
1 tablespoon melted butter

American
12 oysters
4 tablespoons butter
1 teaspoon chopped parsley
about ⅔ cup white wine
¼ cup all-purpose flour
4 tablespoons fresh bread crumbs
1 tablespoon melted butter

Shell the oysters and put into a saucepan of boiling water and cook for 1–2 seconds. Drain and reserve liquor. Beard, place in a pan containing their own liquor. Add half the butter, the parsley and wine. Bring just to boiling point, but do not boil. Remove the oysters to a shallow ovenproof dish. Melt the remainder of the butter in another pan. Stir in the flour and when frothy, ½ pint (3 dl.) mixed hot wine and reserved liquor. Bring to the boil and spread over the oysters. Mix the breadcrumbs with melted butter and sprinkle on top of the sauce. Bake in the preheated oven until brown, about 20 minutes.

Veal and rice custards

Main utensils: saucepan (preferably non-stick) double saucepan, individual moulds, baking tin (preferably non-stick)	Imperial/Metric	American
Preparation time: 15 minutes	6 oz./150 g. long-grain rice	scant 1 cup long-grain rice
Oven temperature: moderate (350°F., 180°C., Gas Mark 4)	4 oz./100 g. cooked veal, diced	½ cup diced cooked veal
Cooking time: 20 minutes	1 teaspoon grated onion	1 teaspoon grated onion
Serves: 4	salt	salt
	paprika pepper	paprika pepper
	celery salt	celery salt
	½ pint/3 dl. milk	1¼ cups milk
	2 eggs	2 eggs

Cook the rice in boiling, salted water until tender, then drain well. Turn into a basin and mix in the veal, onion, salt, paprika pepper and celery salt to taste. Beat in the milk and beaten eggs. Turn into the top of a double saucepan with boiling water below (or place in a bowl over a pan of boiling water) and cook, stirring, until the mixture is warm but not hot. Divide the mixture between eight greased individual moulds. Place in a baking tin containing hot water and cook in a preheated moderate oven until set. Serve hot or cold.

Eggs in artichokes

Main utensils: saucepan (preferably non-stick), individual ovenproof dishes	Imperial/Metric	American
Preparation time: 20 minutes	4 globe artichokes	4 globe artichokes
Oven temperature: hot (425°F., 220°C., Gas Mark 7)	2 oz./50 g. butter	¼ cup butter
Cooking time: few minutes	salt and pepper	salt and pepper
Serves: 4	4 eggs	4 eggs
	grated Parmesan cheese	grated Parmesan cheese

Boil the artichokes, then remove leaves and chokes. With a stainless knife, scrape the edible part of the leaves into a basin, mix to a paste with half the butter, and season with salt and pepper. Arrange an artichoke bottom in each of four ovenproof dishes. Poach the eggs and, when cooked, place one on top of each artichoke bottom. Spoon the artichoke paste over the eggs. Sprinkle with the cheese, dot with the remaining butter and place in a hot oven for 2–3 minutes.

Note: Poached eggs can also be served as a starter on a bed of spinach or green peas in individual soufflé dishes.

Three-minute liver pâté (Illustrated on page 29 and opposite)

Main utensils: 1-lb. (½-kg.) loaf tin (preferably non-stick), liquidiser, roasting tin (preferably non-stick)	Imperial/Metric	American
Preparation time: 5 minutes	12 thin slices streaky bacon	12 bacon slices
Oven temperature: moderate (325°F., 170°C., Gas Mark 3)	3 bay leaves	3 bay leaves
Cooking time: about 1 hour	6 oz./175 g. chicken liver	6 oz. chicken liver
Serves: 6	4 oz./100 g. pig's liver	¼ lb. pork liver
	1 clove garlic	1 clove garlic
	1 egg	1 egg
	3 tablespoons cream	scant ¼ cup cream
	salt	salt
	freshly ground black pepper	freshly ground black pepper
	few drops brandy (optional)	few drops brandy (optional)

Smooth out the streaky bacon rashers with a knife to make them as thin as possible. (If you can get your bacon cut, ask for it to be cut on No. 2.) Place the bay leaves in the bottom of the loaf tin and then line it with the bacon rashers. Put the liver, garlic and egg into the goblet and blend until smooth. Blend in the cream, seasoning and brandy, if used. Pour the liver mixture into the bacon-lined tin and fold the ends of the rashers over the liver mixture. Cover securely with foil and place the loaf tin in a roasting tin half filled with water. Cook in the centre of the preheated over for about 1 hour. When cooked allow to cool, chill then turn out and serve cut in slices. Serve with toast and butter.

Stretch thinly cut bacon rashers with a knife and use to line a small loaf tin. The rashers should be long enough to fold over the liver mixture.

Blend together the liver, garlic and egg in the liquidiser. Blend in the cream, seasoning and brandy. Spoon the mixture into the bacon-lined tin and fold the ends of the rashers over the liver mixture.

Cover the top with tinfoil and secure it under the edges of the loaf tin. Place the tin in a roasting tin half filled with water and cook in the centre of a preheated moderate oven for about 1 hour.

Avocado and grapefruit starter

(Illustrated on page 29)

Halve, stone and peel an avocado pear. Cut the flesh into thin slices and sprinkle with lemon juice. Arrange on a serving dish with fresh grapefruit segments.

Crème de menthe melon cocktail

Main utensil: potato ball cutter	**Imperial/Metric**	**American**
Preparation time: 10 minutes, plus 30 minutes' standing time	1 large honeydew melon or 2 ogen melons	1 large honeydew melon or 2 ogen melons
Serves: 4	1 bunch fresh mint	1 bunch fresh mint
	2–3 tablespoons castor sugar	about $\frac{1}{4}$ cup granulated sugar
	$\frac{1}{2}$ pint/3 dl. boiling water	$1\frac{1}{4}$ cups boiling water
	4 teaspoons crème de menthe	4 teaspoons crème de menthe

Scoop out the melon balls with a potato ball cutter, allowing about eight per person and place in a basin. Wash and drain the mint. Sprinkle with sugar, cover with boiling water and leave to stand for 30 minutes. Strain the liquid over the melon balls. Chill and divide between four glasses. Pour a teaspoon of crème de menthe into each glass and garnish with a sprig of fresh mint, a tiny cube of mint jelly, or a piece of crème de menthe.

A guide to fish

Often, fish seems to be left off many housewives' shopping lists—it should not be so neglected as fish can provide a nourishing and appetising meal at a very competitive price. There is a great variety of fish available, either fresh or frozen, so there need be no excuse for not including it in your menus. It is ideal to serve to a growing family as it is a good source of protein, and the oily fish are rich sources of Vitamins A and D. As fish is a low-calorie source of protein it can be included in your menus if you are on a calorie-controlled diet.

The types of fish readily available can be divided into the following categories:

White fish which includes plaice, sole, haddock, cod and turbot.
Freshwater fish which includes trout, salmon and carp.
Oily fish which includes herrings, sprats and mackerel.
Shellfish which includes prawns, scampi, lobster, scallops and mussels.

Buying and preparation

Whatever type of fish you are purchasing it is particularly important that it is fresh (there is nothing more off-putting than being presented with a herring that should have been removed from the counter days ago!). The signs of freshness to look for when buying white fish are that the flesh should be firm and elastic and the eyes bright and clear. Oily fish should have bright eyes and gills and plenty of scales. If you press your finger into a herring or mackerel and the imprint stays in the flesh do not buy—it is a sure sign that the fish has had a long journey from the sea. It is important to be particularly careful about the freshness of shellfish. Apart from having an unpleasant flavour, stale shellfish can be dangerous to eat. When buying mussels make sure that the shells are tightly closed. Fresh prawns should not look dry and be a pleasant pink colour. And last but not least all fish should smell pleasant.

If you are in doubt about the freshness of the fish which your fishmonger has on his slab then it is better to play safe and buy frozen fish. This will have been deep frozen within hours of being caught and although you may possibly sacrifice a little bit of flavour and moistness, it is certainly a much better buy than fish which is not as fresh as it ought to be. Of course, if you are fortunate enough to live at the coast you should be able to get the freshest of fish.

Ask your fishmonger for a few fish trimmings to make a fish stock with. Simmer them in water, plus a little dry white wine if possible, with an onion, a carrot, a bouquet garni, some peppercorns, a blade of mace and seasoning for about 30 minutes. Strain before using.

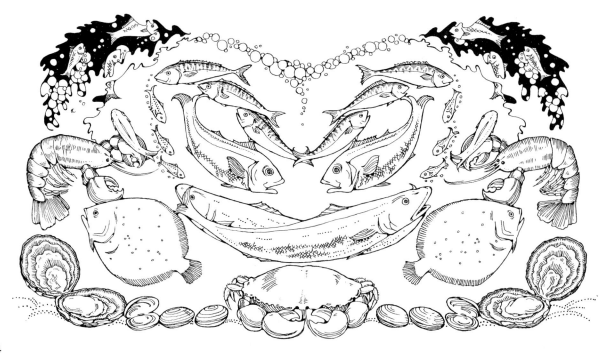

Preparation

Mostly, the fish that you buy will be prepared or the fishmonger will do it for you when you have chosen your purchase. However, it is useful to know how fish should be prepared in order that you can deal with any you may be offered straight from the sea or river!

Whole white fish should be cleaned, washed and dried. Cutlets and fillets should be washed and dried. It looks more attractive if the centre bone is removed from cutlets. It is easier to remove after the fish has been cooked, but if you want to stuff the centre then it should be removed before cooking.

Small whole fish need to be scaled and the head and entrails removed.

Shellfish—fresh prawns and shrimps need to be picked, although a few whole prawns or shrimps make an attractive garnish. To prepare mussels and crab see the recipes on page 43.

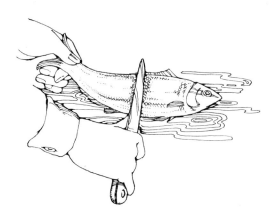

Scaling

Place the fish on a board with the tail towards you. Hold the fish firmly by the tail and, with a small knife, scrape from the tail towards the head—against the grain of the scales. Rinse thoroughly under the cold tap to wash all the loose scales away.

Cleaning

Remove the head, unless the recipe calls for the head to be left on. Pull off the gills and make a slit down the underside and remove the intestines. Wash the inside of the fish under cold running water until no traces of blood remain. Dry with absorbent paper.

To skin fillets

Place the fillets on a board with the flesh side up and the tail end towards you. Rub the fingers of your left hand in salt (to give a good grip) and take hold of the tail. Take a sharp knife, with a firm blade, and work the knife along the fillet between the skin and the flesh.

To prepare herrings

Take the whole herring and slit it open on the underside. Discard the intestines (the roe can be served separately) and turn the herring over so that the flesh side is on the board. Beat along the backbone with a rolling pin to loosen it. Carefully remove the backbone together with the smaller side bones.

To store fish

If fish cannot be cooked on the day it is purchased it needs to be stored carefully. Wash and dry the fish and place it on a plate. Cover it lightly (to prevent cross-flavours) and store in the refrigerator.

Garnishes for fish dishes

Lemon (cut in various ways) is the most usual garnish for fish dishes, but many others can be used to give colour and to enhance the appearance of the dish. Here are a few ideas:

Lemon butterflies Cut a thin slice of lemon in half and then almost in half again. Pull the quarter sections apart to look like a butterfly.

Lemon twists Cut a thin slice of lemon almost in half and twist it into an S shape.

All the lemon garnishes can be dusted with paprika pepper or finely chopped parsley. Before cutting slices from the lemon, the skin can be scored to give each slice a fancy edge.

A slice of stuffed olive or a curled strip of canned anchovy can be placed in the centre of a lemon slice.

Chopped parsley or chives.

Sprigs of fresh herbs—parsley, dill, rosemary.

Chopped raw onion or radish.

Sprigs of watercress.

Tomato or cucumber slices or twists (make as for lemon twists).

Pimentos cut in strips, or chopped.

Capers and gherkins Gherkins can be cut in a fan shape—slice a small gherkin almost through, from top to bottom, and spread the slices out to look like a fan.

To prepare fish fillets for deep frying they must be coated in beaten egg and fresh breadcrumbs. Breadcrumbs can be made very easily in a liquidiser. Remove the crusts from slices of bread and put pieces of bread, a few at a time, into the liquidiser goblet. Switch on for a few seconds until the bread is reduced to fine crumbs.

Lower the fish into the heated fat or oil and fry for 2–3 minutes, until the fish is cooked and the coating golden brown and crisp. Lift from the oil and put onto absorbent paper to drain.

Methods of cooking

Deep frying Used for portions and fillets of white fish, scampi and very small fish—whitebait. Any food that is to be deep fried needs to be protected with some form of coating so that the hot fat or oil can cook the fish through to the centre without overcooking the outside. Fish fillets for deep frying can be coated in a batter or beaten egg and breadcrumbs. It helps to flour the fillets lightly first to absorb any excess moisture and enable the chosen coating to adhere better. If using an egg and breadcrumbs don't use the violently-coloured packaged crumbs, make bread-crumbs from slices of day-old bread—these can be made in a trice in a liquidiser, or alternatively rub the bread through a sieve. You can make fresh breadcrumbs in advance and store them in an airtight container in the refrigerator. For deep frying you need a fairly large saucepan and a basket to contain the food. Use a good quality white fat (not lard or dripping as it can impart a certain flavour to the food) or oil and fill the pan two-thirds full. Heat the fat until a cube of day-old bread turns golden brown in 1 minute. (If you have a fat thermometer, 360°F., 180°C., is the recommended frying temperature.) Gently lower in the basket containing the prepared food. Beware of putting too much food in the basket at one time, as this will cause the coating to become soggy by lowering the heat of the fat too much. When the food is cooked and the coating crisp and an even golden brown, lift out the basket and drain the food on absorbent paper, then transfer it to a serving dish (if possible lined with

a dish paper to absorb any further excess fat). Allow the fat or oil to cool before straining it for re-use. Providing it is stored in a cool place and strained after each frying, the fat or oil can be used again and again (topping up with new fat or oil as necessary) without absorbing any flavour from the food previously fried. When deep frying whitebait they just need to be dipped in seasoned flour before frying.

Shallow frying This is a method suitable for frying thinner fillets of fish which have been coated in egg and bread-crumbs. (Batter is not a suitable coating for food that is to be shallow fried.) For shallow frying you can use a white fat, oil, butter, margarine, or a mixture of oil and butter (the oil prevents the butter from over-browning). Heat the fat in a frying pan (a non-stick pan is ideal for frying coated fish fillets as it ensures that the coating has no possibility of sticking to the pan) and fry the fillets for 2–3 minutes on each side, depending on the thickness. Drain the fish on absorbent paper before serving.

To ensure crisp chips they need to be blanched, before the final cooking. Heat the fat or oil and gently lower in a basket of well dried chipped potatoes. Fry for 3–4 minutes, until they are softened, but not crisp or coloured. Tip out and drain on absorbent paper. Just before serving, reheat the oil and fry the chips for 1–2 minutes, until crisp and golden brown. Drain and serve.

Deep fried haddock, garnished with a wedge of lemon served with crisp and golden chipped potatoes.

Poaching Suitable for cooking whole fish and fillets. The cooking liquid can be milk, stock, water, wine or a court bouillon (used for poaching a whole trout or salmon) made by simmering water, wine, a few carrots and onions, peppercorns, a bay leaf and a blade of mace for 30–40 minutes; the court bouillon is strained before use.

Add salt and pepper to the poaching liquid and a little vinegar or squeeze of lemon juice—this helps to keep the flesh of white fish firm and white. When poaching a salmon in a court bouillon omit the lemon juice and vinegar and gently lower the fish into the hot court bouillon to preserve the colour. Whichever poaching liquid is used it must never be allowed to boil rapidly—it should just simmer gently during the whole of the cooking time. Allow 10 minutes cooking time per lb. ($\frac{1}{2}$ kg.) for salmon and poach fillets for

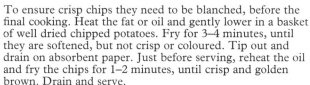

5–10 minutes, depending on their size and thickness. If serving a whole salmon cold, allow it to cool in the court bouillon to give a good flavour and moist texture.

Steaming Suitable for cutlets and fillets of white fish. Place the prepared fish on an ovenproof dish, sprinkle with salt and pepper and dot with butter. Cover with a lid or foil and place over a saucepan of boiling water. Steam for 10–20 minutes according to the thickness of the fish. (Be careful not to allow the water in the saucepan to boil away.)

Grilling Suitable for fillets of plaice or sole; herring, bloaters, kippers and small mackerel, or cutlets and steaks. Place the prepared fish on the greased rack of the grill pan, sprinkle with salt and pepper and brush with oil, melted butter or a marinade. Cook under the preheated grill for about 5 minutes for fillets and cutlets, and 10–15 minutes for herrings and mackerel. Halfway through the cooking time turn the fish over and again brush with oil. When grilling whole fish make diagonal slits across the skin and, if necessary, lower the heat halfway through the cooking time.

Baking This method of cooking is suitable for whole fish, cutlets and steaks. Place the prepared fish in a non-stick baking tin or an ovenproof dish and dot with butter. Sprinkle with salt and pepper, plus any other suitable seasonings, cover with butter papers, foil or a lid and cook in a moderate oven (350°F., 180°C., Gas Mark 4), until the flesh is firm and white throughout. If the flesh is still pink or a clear liquid runs out when a knife is inserted, cook for a further 10–15 minutes.

Fish with creole sauce

Main utensils: 2 saucepans
   (preferably non-stick)
Preparation time: 10 minutes
Cooking time: 20 minutes
Serves: 4

Imperial/Metric
1 lb./½ kg. cod or haddock fillets
Creole sauce:
2 tablespoons oil
1 small onion, chopped
1 clove garlic, crushed
1 stick celery, chopped
1 green pepper
1 medium can tomatoes
1 tablespoon tomato purée
pinch sugar
salt and pepper
pinch basil
few drops Tabasco sauce
pinch chilli powder

American
1 lb. cod or haddock fillets
Creole sauce:
3 tablespoons oil
1 small onion, chopped
1 clove garlic, crushed
1 stalk celery, chopped
1 green sweet pepper
1 medium can tomatoes
1 tablespoon tomato paste
pinch sugar
salt and pepper
pinch basil
few drops Tabasco sauce
pinch chili powder

Place the fish fillets in a shallow pan with just sufficient water to cover and poach over a moderate heat for 15 minutes. Drain and keep hot. Heat the oil in a saucepan and fry the prepared onion until softened but not browned. Add the prepared garlic, celery, seeded and chopped pepper and sauté for a further 3–4 minutes, until the vegetables are softened. Stir in the remaining ingredients, bring to the boil, cover and simmer for 15 minutes. Arrange the fish fillets on a serving dish and spoon over the creole sauce.

Cider-baked haddock

Main utensils: ovenproof dish,
   frying pan (preferably non-stick)
Preparation time: 10 minutes
Oven temperature: moderate
   (350°F., 180°C., Gas Mark 4)
Cooking time: about 30 minutes
Serves: 4

Imperial/Metric
1½ lb./¾ kg. fresh haddock fillets
salt and pepper
squeeze lemon juice
pinch mixed dried herbs
1 oz./25 g. butter
1 onion, peeled and finely chopped
4 oz./100 g. button mushrooms
¼ pint/1½ dl. dry cider
Garnish:
1 can anchovy fillets
parsley sprigs

American
1½ lb. fresh haddock fillets
salt and pepper
squeeze lemon juice
pinch mixed dried herbs
2 tablespoons butter
1 onion, peeled and finely chopped
1 cup button mushrooms
⅔ cup cider
Garnish:
1 can anchovy fillets
parsley sprigs

Remove the skin from the haddock and cut the fillets into four portions. Place in an ovenproof dish, sprinkle over the seasoning, lemon juice and mixed herbs. Heat the butter in a frying pan and sauté the onion and mushrooms for 2–3 minutes, until the onion becomes transparent. Add to the ovenproof dish. Pour in the cider. Cover with a lid, foil or butter papers and bake in the centre of the preheated oven for about 30 minutes, until the fish flakes easily with a fork. Garnish the fish with strips of drained anchovy fillets and parsley sprigs and serve from the ovenproof dish.

Marinated plaice

Main utensil: baking tray
   (preferably non-stick)
Preparation time: just over 1 hour,
   including marinating time
Cooking time: about 5 minutes
Serves: 4

Imperial/Metric
¾ pint/4½ dl. olive oil
salt and pepper
1 tablespoon wine vinegar
4 plaice fillets, skinned
few thyme leaves
1 bay leaf
grated rind and juice of 1 orange
Garnish:
orange slices

American
scant 2 cups olive oil
salt and pepper
1 tablespoon wine vinegar
4 plaice or flounder fillets, skinned
few thyme leaves
1 bay leaf
grated rind and juice of 1 orange
Garnish:
orange slices

Mix together the olive oil, seasoning and wine vinegar. Place the fish fillets in a shallow (not metal) dish and pour over the olive oil mixture. Add the thyme and bay leaf. Leave in a cool place for at least 1 hour to marinate; turn the fish once during marinating. Remove the plaice from the marinade and arrange on a baking tray. Brush with some of the marinade and cook under a preheated grill for about 3 minutes on each side. When cooking the second side, brush over more of the marinade. Transfer the plaice to a serving dish and sprinkle over the grated orange rind and juice. Serve garnished with orange slices. A green salad goes well with this dish.

Mushroom-stuffed plaice fillets

Main utensils: frying pan, saucepan (preferably non-stick), ovenproof dish
Preparation time: 10 minutes
Oven temperature: moderate (350°F., 180°C., Gas Mark 4)
Cooking time: 20 minutes
Serves: 4

Imperial/Metric	American
4 oz./100 g. butter	½ cup butter
8 oz./225 g. button mushrooms, sliced	2 cups sliced button mushrooms
8 plaice fillets	8 plaice or sole fillets
salt and pepper	salt and pepper
4 tablespoons dry white wine	⅓ cup dry white wine
1 pint/generous ½ litre fish stock (see page 34)	2½ cups fish stock (see page 34)
2 oz./50 g. flour	½ cup all-purpose flour
2 tablespoons cream	3 tablespoons cream
Garnish:	*Garnish:*
watercress sprigs	watercress sprigs

Melt half the butter in a frying pan and sauté the sliced mushrooms for 3–4 minutes. Drain on absorbent paper, cool slightly and place a portion in the centre of each fillet. Sprinkle with salt and pepper and roll up each fillet, starting from the tail end. Arrange in an ovenproof dish and pour in the wine and some of the stock to come halfway up the sides of the fillets. Cover with butter papers, foil or a lid. Cook in the centre of a preheated oven for about 15 minutes, until the fish is tender. Remove the fish to a serving dish and keep warm. Add the cooking liquor to the fish stock. Melt the remaining butter in a saucepan and stir in the flour. Cook, stirring over a low heat for 1–2 minutes; do not allow the mixture to brown. Off the heat, gradually blend in 1 pint (generous ½ litre) fish stock. Return to the heat, bring to the boil and cook, stirring, until thickened. Check the seasoning and stir in the cream and pour the sauce over the fish fillets. Garnish with sprigs of watercress and serve at once.

Cod à la provençale (Illustrated on page 41)

Main utensil: saucepan (preferably non-stick)
Preparation time: 5 minutes
Cooking time: 15 minutes
Serves: 4

Imperial/Metric	American
1 lb./½ kg. cod	1 lb. cod
seasoned flour	seasoned flour
oil and butter for frying	oil and butter for frying
1 onion, chopped	1 onion, chopped
1 clove garlic, crushed	1 clove garlic, crushed
12 oz./350 g. tomatoes	¾ lb. tomatoes
salt and black pepper	salt and black pepper
1 tablespoon chopped parsley	1 tablespoon chopped parsley
few sage leaves, chopped	few sage leaves, chopped
few thyme leaves, chopped	few thyme leaves, chopped
4 oz./100 g. black olives, stoned	scant 1 cup pitted ripe olives

Cut the cod into fairly large pieces and coat in the seasoned flour. Heat the oil and butter in a saucepan and fry the cod pieces until lightly browned on all sides. Remove to a plate. Add the onion and garlic to the pan and fry until softened but not browned. Add the skinned and sliced tomatoes, seasoning and herbs. Cover and simmer for about 5 minutes. Stir in the pieces of cod and the black olives. Stir over the heat until the cod and olives are hot, then spoon into a serving dish.

Seafood kebabs

Main utensils: 4 kebab skewers
Preparation time: 5 minutes
Cooking time: 10 minutes
Serves: 4

Imperial/Metric	American
2 lb./1 kg. cod or haddock	2 lb. cod or haddock
4 tomatoes	4 tomatoes
1 green pepper	1 green sweet pepper
few black olives, stoned	few ripe olives, pitted
salt and pepper	salt and pepper
2 tablespoons lemon juice	3 tablespoons lemon juice
2 oz./50 g. butter, melted	¼ cup butter, melted

Cut the fish into fairly large pieces. Halve the tomatoes, seed the pepper and cut the flesh into fairly large pieces. Alternate pieces of fish, tomato halves, pieces of pepper and whole black olives onto four skewers. Season well with salt and pepper; mix the lemon juice and butter and brush liberally over the kebabs. Cook under a moderate grill, turning the skewers, until all the ingredients are cooked through. Brush with the melted butter mixture from time to time during the cooking. Serve on a bed of long-grain rice and accompany with a tossed green salad.

Oven-braised fish

Main utensils: frying pan
(preferably non-stick), ovenproof
dish
Preparation time: 10 minutes
Cooking time: about 45 minutes
Oven temperature: moderately hot
(375°F., 190°C., Gas Mark 5)
Serves: 4–5

Imperial/Metric	**American**
3 tablespoons oil	scant $\frac{1}{4}$ cup oil
3 leeks, sliced	3 leeks, sliced
3 sticks celery, chopped	3 stalks celery, chopped
4 oz./100 g. button mushrooms	1 cup button mushrooms
2 carrots, sliced	2 carrots, sliced
salt and black pepper	salt and black pepper
1 2$\frac{1}{2}$-lb./about 1$\frac{1}{4}$-kg. cod or haddock, prepared	1 2$\frac{1}{2}$-lb. cod or haddock, prepared
2 oz./50 g. butter	$\frac{1}{4}$ cup butter
lemon juice	lemon juice
pinch tarragon	pinch tarragon
$\frac{1}{4}$ pint/1$\frac{1}{2}$ dl. dry white wine	$\frac{2}{3}$ cup dry white wine
$\frac{1}{4}$ pint/1$\frac{1}{2}$ dl. water	$\frac{2}{3}$ cup water

Heat the oil in a frying pan and sauté the prepared vegetables until slightly softened, but not browned. Transfer them to an ovenproof dish. Season the fish inside and out and spread half the butter inside and dot the remainder on the top. Place on the vegetables, sprinkle with lemon juice and tarragon and pour in the wine and water. Cover closely with butter paper, foil or a lid and cook in the preheated oven for about 45 minutes, until the fish is cooked and the vegetables tender. Garnish with chopped parsley and serve from the ovenproof dish.

Kedgeree (Illustrated opposite)

Main utensil: saucepan
(preferably non-stick)
Preparation time: 5 minutes
Cooking time: 15 minutes
Serves: 3–4

Imperial/Metric	**American**
6 oz./175 g. long-grain rice	about 1 cup long-grain rice
3 oz./75 g. butter	6 tablespoons butter
1 small onion, finely chopped	1 small onion, finely chopped
6 oz./175 g. cooked smoked haddock	6 oz. cooked smoked haddock
2 hard-boiled eggs	2 hard-cooked eggs
salt and pepper	salt and pepper
1 tablespoon cream	1 tablespoon cream
Garnish:	*Garnish:*
chopped parsley	chopped parsley
sieved hard-boiled egg yolk	sieved hard-cooked egg yolk

Cook the rice in boiling, salted water until just tender. Drain thoroughly and rinse cold water through the grains to separate them. Meanwhile, melt the butter in a saucepan and sauté the onion until softened but not browned. Add the flaked fish and chopped hard-boiled eggs. (Sieve one of the egg yolks and use to garnish.) Mix well and heat through, stirring. Add plenty of seasoning and the rice and mix gently, until thoroughly hot. Finally, stir in the cream and turn into a hot serving dish; sprinkle with chopped parsley and sieved egg yolk and serve at once.
Note: If you want to make this dish for more than three or four people, remember to have equal amounts of rice and smoked haddock and a generous amount of butter to keep the kedgeree moist.

Normandy trout

Main utensils: ovenproof dish,
small saucepan (preferably
non-stick)
Preparation time: 5 minutes
Oven temperature: moderate
(350°F., 180°C., Gas Mark 4)
Cooking time: about 15 minutes
Serves: 4

Imperial/Metric	**American**
2 oz./50 g. butter	$\frac{1}{4}$ cup butter
4 trout	4 trout
1 tablespoon water	1 tablespoon water
squeeze lemon juice	squeeze lemon juice
salt and pepper	salt and pepper
2 tablespoons chopped parsley	3 tablespoons chopped parsley
1 tablespoon snipped chives	1 tablespoon snipped chives
$\frac{1}{4}$ pint/1$\frac{1}{2}$ dl. single cream	$\frac{2}{3}$ cup coffee cream
1 oz./25 g. fresh white breadcrumbs	$\frac{1}{2}$ cup fresh soft bread crumbs

Put three-quarters of the butter in an ovenproof dish and place in the oven to melt. Remove and place in the trout. Sprinkle over the water, lemon juice, seasoning, parsley and chives. Cover and cook in the centre of the oven for about 10–15 minutes. Meanwhile, place the cream in a small saucepan and, stirring, bring to the boil and simmer for 1–2 minutes. Remove the trout from the oven and pour over the cream. Sprinkle with breadcrumbs and dot with the remaining butter. Place under a heated grill for 1–2 minutes to brown the top. Serve at once, garnished with lemon fans.

Russian salmon pie, cod à la provençale, kedgeree and Danish herring salad (see below, pages 39, 40, 46)

Russian salmon pie (Illustrated above)

Main utensils: saucepan, baking
   tray (preferably non-stick)
Preparation time: 20 minutes
Cooking time: 30—40 minutes
Oven temperature: hot (425°F.,
   220°C., Gas Mark 7)
Serves: 4

Imperial/Metric
3 oz./75 g. butter
1 small onion, finely chopped
4 oz./100 g. button mushrooms,
   sliced
2 oz./50 g. flour
½ pint/3 dl. milk
salt and pepper
12 oz./350 g. canned or fresh,
   cooked salmon
1 hard-boiled egg, chopped
8 oz./200 g. flaky or puff pastry
   (see pages 106, 108)
beaten egg to glaze

American
6 tablespoons butter
1 small onion, finely chopped
1 cup sliced button mushrooms

½ cup all-purpose flour
1¼ cups milk
salt and pepper
¾ lb. canned or fresh,
   cooked salmon
1 hard-cooked egg, chopped
½ lb. flaky or puff pastry
   (see pages 106, 108)
beaten egg to glaze

Heat the butter in a saucepan and fry the prepared onion until softened but not browned. Add the mushrooms and fry for a further 2—3 minutes. Stir in the flour and cook over a low heat for 1—2 minutes. Gradually add the milk, bring to the boil, stirring, and cook for 2—3 minutes, until thickened. Season and stir in the flaked fish (drain the canned salmon and remove the bones) and chopped egg. Leave aside to cool. Roll the pastry out thinly to a square, trim the edges and spoon the filling into the centre of the square. Brush the edges with water and bring the two opposite points to

the centre of the filling. Overlap them slightly and secure. Bring up the other two points and press lightly together. Press all four seams together. Carefully lift the pie onto a baking tray. Decorate the top with leaves made from the pastry trimmings. Brush with beaten egg and cook near the top of a preheated oven for 30—40 minutes, until the pastry is crisp and golden brown.
Note: This fish pie can be served hot or cold and also makes a good meal starter.

Mustard herrings

Main utensils: frying pan (preferably non-stick), ovenproof dish
Preparation time: 15 minutes
Oven temperature: moderate (350°F., 180°C., Gas Mark 4)
Cooking time: 25 minutes
Serves: 4

Imperial/Metric
4 herrings
2 oz./50 g. butter
1 onion, sliced
salt and black pepper
½ oz./15 g. flour
2 teaspoons Dijon mustard
pinch castor sugar
½ pint/3 dl. water
¼ pint/1½ dl. single cream
Garnish:
lemon wedges

American
4 herring
¼ cup butter
1 onion, sliced
salt and black pepper
2 tablespoons all-purpose flour
2 teaspoons Dijon mustard
pinch granulated sugar
1¼ cups water
⅔ cup coffee cream
Garnish:
lemon wedges

Split and bone the herrings (see page 35). Melt half the butter in a frying pan and sauté the onion for a few minutes, until soft but not browned. Transfer to a fairly shallow ovenproof dish. Place the herrings on top of the onions, flesh side down. Sprinkle with salt and generously with black pepper, cover and cook in the centre of the preheated oven for about 20 minutes. Meanwhile, melt the remaining butter in a saucepan, remove from the heat and stir in the flour, mustard and sugar. Return to the heat and cook, stirring for 1–2 minutes. Gradually add the water, stirring; bring to the boil and cook for 1–2 minutes, stirring. Stir in the cream and heat, but do not boil. Remove the herrings from the oven and arrange, with the onions, on a serving dish. Pour over the sauce and serve at once, garnished with lemon wedges.

Mackerel with gooseberry sauce

Main utensils: grill pan, saucepan (preferably non-stick), liquidiser
Preparation time: 5 minutes
Cooking time: 10–15 minutes
Serves: 4

Imperial/Metric
4 fresh mackerel
melted butter or olive oil
salt and black pepper
Gooseberry sauce:
8 oz./225 g. gooseberries or 1 8-oz./225-g. can gooseberries
4 tablespoons water
pinch nutmeg
1 tablespoon castor sugar
1 oz./25 g. butter

American
4 fresh mackerel
melted butter or olive oil
salt and black pepper
Gooseberry sauce:
½ lb. gooseberries or 1 ½-lb. can gooseberries
⅓ cup water
pinch nutmeg
1 tablespoon granulated sugar
2 tablespoons butter

Place the prepared mackerel on the greased grid of the grill pan. Make 3 or 4 diagonal slits across the top, brush with melted butter or oil and sprinkle with salt and plenty of black pepper. Cook under the preheated grill, for 10–15 minutes, turning the fish over halfway through the cooking time and brushing with more butter or oil.

To make the gooseberry sauce, place the topped and tailed gooseberries in a saucepan with the water. Bring to the boil, cover and simmer until softened. (Omit this stage with canned gooseberries.) Cool slightly, then blend, a few at a time, in a liquidiser with some of the cooking liquid until puréed. (Or press through a sieve.) Reheat the purée and stir in the nutmeg, sugar and butter. Spoon into a sauce boat and serve with the mackerel.

Moules marinière

Main utensil: saucepan
(preferably non-stick)
Preparation time: 15 minutes
Cooking time: 20 minutes
Serves: 4

Imperial/Metric
4 pints/2¼ litres mussels
1 oz./25 g. butter
1 onion, chopped
2 sticks celery, chopped
½ bottle dry white wine
few sprigs parsley
few sprigs thyme
1 bay leaf
black pepper
Garnish:
chopped parsley

American
5 pints mussels
2 tablespoons butter
1 onion, chopped
2 stalks celery, chopped
½ bottle dry white wine
few sprigs parsley
few sprigs thyme
1 bay leaf
black pepper
Garnish:
chopped parsley

Prepare the mussels by scrubbing them well under cold running water. Make sure that all the mud, seaweed etc. is washed away. Remove the beards with a small sharp knife and discard any mussels which are open and will not close when sharply tapped, or any that are cracked. Melt the butter in a saucepan and sauté the onion and celery until softened, but not browned. Add the wine, herbs and a generous amount of black pepper. Cover and simmer for 10 minutes. Add the mussels, cover and cook over a low heat, shaking the pan from time to time, until the shells open; take out the top shells and place the mussels, in their half shell, in soup plates or bowls and keep warm. Strain the cooking liquor and boil it, uncovered, until reduced by about half. Pour over the mussels, sprinkle with plenty of chopped parsley and serve with crusty French bread.

Crab au gratin

Main utensil: baking tray
(preferably non-stick)
Preparation time: 15 minutes
Oven temperature: moderately hot
(400°F., 200°C., Gas Mark 6)
Cooking time: 25 minutes
Serves: 4 (as a starter)

Imperial/Metric
1 medium crab, cooked
1 oz./25 g. fresh white breadcrumbs
4 oz./100 g. cheese, grated
salt and pepper
pinch dry mustard
pinch paprika pepper
few drops Tabasco sauce
2 tablespoons single cream
Garnish:
watercress sprigs

American
1 medium crab, cooked
½ cup fresh soft bread crumbs
1 cup grated cheese
salt and pepper
pinch dry mustard
pinch paprika pepper
few drops Tabasco sauce
3 tablespoons coffee cream
Garnish:
watercress sprigs

Lay the crab on its back and prise up the apron and lift off. Remove and discard the stomach bag, near the head, and the gills or dead man's fingers. Scrape all the meat from the shell into a basin. Gently tap the inside edge of the shell to break it along the line of the natural marking, then wash and scrub the shell and oil it lightly. Remove the flesh from the claws (keep the tiny claws for garnish) and mix it with the other meat. Mix the crab meat, breadcrumbs, grated cheese, seasonings, Tabasco sauce and cream to give a fairly soft consistency. Replace this mixture in the shell, place on a baking tray and cook in a moderately hot oven for 20–25 minutes, until lightly browned and heated through. Serve garnished with watercress and the reserved claws.

Scrape the meat from the crab shell into a basin.

Remove the meat from the claws and add it to the basin.

Replace the crab meat mixture in the shell. Cook in a moderately hot oven for 20–25 minutes and serve garnished with watercress and the reserved claws.

Grilled salmon steaks with hollandaise sauce

Main utensils: small saucepan
  (preferably non-stick),
  double saucepan
Preparation time: 5 minutes
Cooking time: 15 minutes
Serves: 4

Imperial/Metric
4 salmon steaks
3 oz./75 g. butter, melted
salt and pepper
lemon juice
Hollandaise sauce:
2 tablespoons wine vinegar
4 peppercorns
4 tablespoons water
3 egg yolks
6 oz./175 g. softened butter
salt and pepper
lemon juice
Garnish:
lemon

American
4 salmon steaks
6 tablespoons butter, melted
salt and pepper
lemon juice
Hollandaise sauce:
3 tablespoons wine vinegar
4 peppercorns
$\frac{1}{3}$ cup water
3 egg yolks
$\frac{3}{4}$ cup softened butter
salt and pepper
lemon juice
Garnish:
lemon

Brush the salmon steaks on both sides with melted butter; sprinkle with seasoning and lemon juice. Cook the steaks, under a moderate grill, for about 5 minutes on each side, until the flesh flakes easily with a fork. (Brush over with more butter during grilling.) Remove the dark skin and keep the salmon warm while making the hollandaise sauce.

Boil the vinegar, peppercorns and water in a small saucepan until reduced by one-third. Strain into a double saucepan (or use a basin placed over a pan of hot water) and add the egg yolks. Whisk over a *very low heat* until the sauce begins to thicken. Divide the butter into portions and whisk

it into the sauce, a portion at a time. Season and add a few drops of lemon juice; garnish the salmon with lemon and serve the hollandaise sauce separately.

Note: Maître d'hôtel butter can be served with the salmon in place of hollandaise sauce. Soften 4 oz. (100 g.) butter in a bowl and mix in 1 tablespoon finely chopped parsley, a little seasoning and a squeeze of lemon juice. Form into a roll, wrap in wax paper or foil and leave in the refrigerator to harden. Divide into 4 pats and serve one on each piece of salmon. Rolls of maître d'hôtel can be made in advance, wrapped in freezer film and stored in the freezer.

Boil the vinegar, peppercorns and water in a saucepan. When reduced by one-third strain into a double saucepan (the one illustrated is a pan with a water jacket around the outside; the water is poured in through a hole in the handle).

Add the egg yolks and whisk over a very low heat until the sauce begins to thicken. To ensure that there is no chance of the egg yolks overheating have the pan to one side of the heat. The cordless mixer shown here is ideal for making hollandaise sauce as it can be used over the cooker without the danger of a trailing flex.

When the sauce has thickened, whisk in the pieces of softened butter, a few at a time. Add the lemon juice and the sauce is ready to serve.

Hollandaise sauce can be served with fish, in particular salmon; it is also delicious served with vegetables.

Prawns with savoury rice

Main utensil: saucepan
  (preferably non-stick)
Preparation time: 5 minutes
Cooking time: about 20 minutes
Serves: 4

Imperial/Metric
1 oz./25 g. butter
1 onion, finely chopped
1 clove garlic, crushed
8 oz./225 g. long-grain rice
salt and pepper
squeeze lemon juice
1 pint/generous ½ litre fish stock
  or water
8 oz./225 g. frozen prawns
1 oz./25 g. grated Parmesan cheese
Garnish:
few whole prawns
chopped parsley

American
2 tablespoons butter
1 onion, finely chopped
1 clove garlic, crushed
generous 1 cup long-grain rice
salt and pepper
squeeze lemon juice
2½ cups fish stock or water

1⅓ cups frozen prawns or shrimp
¼ cup grated Parmesan cheese
Garnish:
few whole prawns or shrimp
chopped parsley

Heat the butter in a saucepan and fry the onion and garlic until softened, but not browned. Stir in the rice, seasoning and lemon juice. Cook over a low heat for 2–3 minutes, stirring. Add the liquid, bring to the boil, cover and simmer until most of the liquid has been absorbed. Stir in the defrosted prawns and continue to cook until all the liquid has been absorbed. Check the seasoning and stir in the Parmesan cheese. Turn into a dish and serve garnished with whole prawns and chopped parsley.

Danish herring salad (Illustrated on page 41)

Main utensil: liquidiser
Preparation time: 5 minutes, plus
  overnight marinating
Serves: 4

Imperial/Metric
4 rollmops
1 onion, sliced
2 bay leaves
Marinade:
2 tablespoons vinegar
2 tablespoons French mustard
6 tablespoons oil
2 tablespoons tomato purée
black pepper
few drops Worcestershire sauce
Garnish:
parsley

American
4 rollmops
1 onion, sliced
2 bay leaves
Marinade:
3 tablespoons vinegar
3 tablespoons French mustard
½ cup oil
3 tablespoons tomato paste
black pepper
few drops Worcestershire sauce
Garnish:
parsley

Drain the rollmops and cut into thick slices. Arrange in a dish with the slices of onion and bay leaves. Mix the ingredients together for the marinade, using a liquidiser if possible. Pour over the rollmops, cover and leave in a cool place overnight. Serve garnished with parsley.
Note: If you do not want to marinate this dish overnight, pour the marinade into a serving dish and arrange the rollmops in the marinade.

Taramasalata

Main utensil: liquidiser
Preparation time: few minutes
Serves: 4

Imperial/Metric
1 slice white bread
8 oz./225 g. smoked cod's roe
1 small potato, boiled
1 clove garlic
juice of 1 lemon
2–3 sprigs parsley
1 tablespoon olive oil
salt and pepper
Garnish:
lemon wedges
black olives

American
1 slice white bread
½ lb. smoked cod's roe
1 small potato, boiled
1 clove garlic
juice of 1 lemon
2-3 sprigs parsley
1 tablespoon olive oil
salt and pepper
Garnish:
lemon wedges
ripe olives

Remove the crusts from the bread and make breadcrumbs, using the liquidiser. Add the cod's roe, potato, garlic, lemon juice and parsley and blend until smooth (add the ingredients a little at a time if your liquidiser is a small one). Add the oil, gradually, with the liquidiser on a low speed. Blend until smooth and season to taste. Turn into a dish, smooth the top and chill. Serve, garnished with lemon wedges and black olives, as a first course. Accompany with melba toast or fingers of hot toast.

A guide to meat, poultry and game

This guide deals with the most expensive item on our shopping list. It is essential to cook meat properly and it is sometimes neglected by even the most enthusiastic cooks as it is often put into the oven without due care and attention. In these days of rising prices it is worth while getting to know about meat, as the traditional Sunday sirloin is almost a luxury beyond most of us. We must become more familiar with the less expensive cuts and the more interesting ways of cooking them; our European counterparts have been coping with this problem for many years and are experts at producing delicious meals from offal and the cheaper cuts of beef and lamb.

The days of the small butcher seem to be numbered because the supermarkets and chain stores now have meat cut and wrapped ready to be picked up. In self-service stores it is difficult for the young housewife to become familiar with the various cuts of meat which are suitable for different methods of cooking. This is why a good butcher is still a housewife's best friend, so if you are still able to find one try to go in one day when the shop is quiet and ask some of the questions about meat that so many people want to know but feel shy in front of other customers! Once you are familiar with the different cuts shopping in a supermarket will not be such a problem and you will avoid falling into the trap of always buying the most familiar looking joint or chop in the shop.

There is one tip which we would like to pass on to you and in these days of chilled and frozen meat it is worth its weight in gold—that is the use of a meat thermometer. This little gadget costs about £1 and saves any guess work when it comes to cooking beef, lamb, pork and poultry. The following tables will of course guide you but if you want to know exactly when the beef is medium cooked, the pork thoroughly cooked and the turkey is done your thermometer will tell you. All meat and poultry shrinks and dries if overcooked and this is something we can do without when paying the present prices! It is also possible to cook beef, lamb, pork and veal straight from the frozen state, and again the thermometer will tell you when the meat is cooked right through. DO NOT cook frozen poultry or game without fully defrosting it as this can be dangerous.

The following simple diagrams will help you to become familiar with the different cuts of beef, pork, lamb and veal and the cooking methods will be a guide for the less experienced cook. It is worth while remembering that some cookery terms do not always mean what they say— boiled meat is not really boiled, it should just simmer. There was a cookery teacher who used to recite to the class the magic words 'A stew boiled is a stew spoiled!' There is often a tendency to cook casseroles and stews too quickly thus rendering the meat tough and stringy.

Meat

Beef
It is most confusing for a new housewife to choose meat as the old tests can only be applied when the beef is fresh and not chilled or frozen. For fresh meat the flesh should be a good dark red colour with a slight marbling of fat through the lean; the fat should be pale yellow without mottling and the suet hard and dry. Rolled joints should be examined at both ends as one end can often be much fattier than the one displayed.

Lamb
This is best when the fat is pearly white and the flesh is pink. Much of our lamb is frozen and with careful cooking an excellent result can be obtained. Do examine frozen chops carefully as they can be fatty with very little flesh if one is not buying from a reliable source.

Mutton
The flesh of mutton is a darker red than that of lamb, it should be firm, close-textured and not grained with fat like beef. The fat should be hard and waxy and mutton, like beef, should be well hung.

Pork
Choose pork which has a pinky white colour, is smoothly grained and firm to the touch. The skin should not be too thick and the fat should be pearly white with no spots.

Veal
This is an expensive meat now for the better cuts. Good veal should be firm, pale in colour and finely grained and the fat should be white.

Offal
This consists of liver, kidneys, brains, sweetbreads, tongue and head. The best known of these is the liver and kidneys, but it is well worthwhile experimenting with all types of offal as they add so much variety to the menu.

47

Cooking methods

Roasting

This can be done at a fairly high heat throughout the period of cooking. This method is one of the most popular in this country; roasting is a slightly misleading term here—really it is baking the meat in an enclosed space as opposed to true roasting on a spit in front of an open fire. Only prime cuts of meat should be used for roasting. (If in doubt as to the quality of a joint of meat it is better to pot-roast it.) Unless cooking in foil or roastabags, the meat or poultry should be basted with fat or dripping during cooking. Meat can also be roasted slowly in the oven at a low temperature throughout; with this method the joint is put into a cold oven. This is a useful method when cooking meat in a pre-set automatic oven; it is also suitable for joints which are not absolutely prime quality. All roasts can be cooked directly from the freezer, but the cooking time must be extended to allow the meat to cook right through.

Spit roasting In this method the meat or poultry is secured on a spit which rotates under a source of direct heat. Only prime cuts should be used and the food should be basted with fat and meat juices, or possibly a marinade, during cooking.

Many years ago sides of beef, pork and lamb were roasted this way in front of an open fire. It was the job of the spit boy to sit by the side of the fire, and with a long-handled ladle, spoon the fat over the rotating sides of meat.

Pot-roasting Sometimes it is more convenient to cook small joints or birds in a heavy pot on top of the cooker. For this method it is necessary to melt a little fat or dripping in the pan and allow it to become very hot then seal the meat on all sides in the hot fat. When pot-roasting remove the lid of the saucepan at least 20 minutes before the end of the cooking time to allow the meat to brown.

Grilling

Cooking on a grill pan under direct heat. This is one of the quickest methods of cooking meat, but is only suitable for small good quality pieces of meat—chops, steaks, chicken portions, kidneys, etc. The meat should be brushed with oil or melted butter and sealed on both sides under a high heat; then lower the heat to allow the food to cook through.

Frying

Cooking in a shallow pan in a small quantity of fat or oil. Kidneys, liver, chops, sausages and steak can be cooked by this method.

Meat being prepared for a casserole is often cooked this way (sautéing) to seal the meat on all sides and to brown it—this gives the dish a good flavour.

Deep frying (as described on page 36) is only suitable for cooking made-up meat dishes such as rissoles, meat cakes etc. or for thin slices of tender meat protected by a coating of egg and breadcrumbs, or slices of canned beef or luncheon meat coated in a batter.

Steaming

This is done most successfully under pressure (see pages 141 to 146); small fillets of fish can be steamed over a pan of water (see page 37).

Braising

This method of cooking meat has always been popular in France and is suitable for thicker slices of meat or small joints. It is a combination of roasting and stewing which is economical and gives a delicious flavour to the finished dish. The meat is sealed in a little hot fat as for pot-roasting and is most successful if done in a deep pan or a flame-proof casserole. Usually the meat is braised on a layer of prepared seasoned vegetables—onions, carrots, turnip and celery and some herbs or a bouquet garni are added. The meat should be cooked on top of the cooker for 10–15 minutes, shaking the pan from time to time to prevent the meat from sticking. Before covering the pan with a lid, add just enough liquid, which can be stock, water, sauce or wine, to cover the vegetables. The dish is then cooked very slowly in the oven or on top of the cooker until the meat is tender. Baste from time to time with the juice and add more liquid if the quantity reduces too much.

Very lean joints of meat are often larded before being braised. Thin strips of fat are threaded through the joint of meat, using a special larding needle, to give moisture to the meat during the cooking.

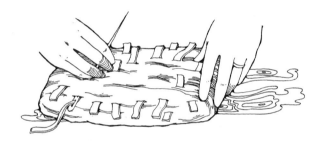

Stewing

This is a long, slow method of cooking in a small amount of liquid over a low temperature, in a covered saucepan. It is a popular and economical way of dealing with the cheaper cuts of meat. A better flavour results if the prepared meat is first browned by sautéing (see above). A selection of root vegetables are usually added to a stew. If using vegetables which take a shorter time to cook than the meat add them about halfway through the cooking period. Stews can also be cooked in a casserole in a slow oven. Whether a stew is cooked on top of the cooker or in the oven the method of preparation is the same—it is usually a little easier to ensure an even low heat during the entire cooking time when cooking in the oven and a little less attention is required to see that the liquid does not boil away.

Boiling

This is a method which can produce excellent results but the meat or poultry can become tough and tasteless (if not cooked carefully) instead of tender and juicy. This method is suitable for joints of mutton, silverside, ham or bacon. It is more successful to plunge the meat into boiling water, making sure it is covered and bring it back to the boil for 5 minutes so that the meat is sealed on the outside. Turn down the heat and allow to simmer for the required cooking time while will be 20–30 minutes to the lb. ($\frac{1}{2}$ kg.) depending on the type of meat or poultry that is being cooked. However, boiled meat is never actually *boiled* after the first 5 minutes cooking time; do keep this in mind for good results. The water should only bubble very gently on the surface during cooking. Boiled meat should not be under-cooked.

Roast pheasant garnished with sausages and sprigs of watercress and served with game chips and a watercress and walnut salad

Cuts of meat

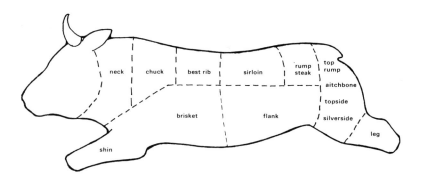

Beef

Roasting Sirloin, ribs, fillet (the undercut of the sirloin), aitchbone, topside (pot-roasting), top rump

Grilling, frying or barbecuing Rump steak, fillet, sirloin

Stewing or braising Chuck, brisket, flank, oxtail

Pickling or boiling Brisket, shin or leg, silverside, flank

Stock making Neck, shin or leg, flank, marrow bone

Lamb

Roasting Leg, loin, saddle, best end of neck, shoulder, breast (stuffed and rolled)

Grilling, frying or barbecuing Loin chops, chump chops, cutlets

Stewing, braising or boiling Neck, breast, leg, shoulder

Stock making Scrag end of neck, feet

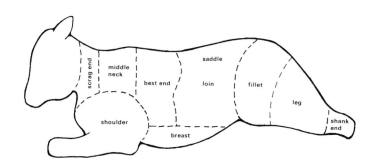

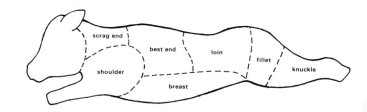

Pork

Roasting Loin, leg, bladebone, spareribs, fillet

Frying, grilling or barbecuing Chops, fillet

Boiling or stewing Head, hand, belly, spareribs, trotters

Veal

Roasting Shoulder, breast, best end of neck, loin, fillet

Frying, grilling or barbecuing Loin chops, fillet, best end of neck chops, escalopes (thin leg slices)

Boiling Head, breast

Stock making Knuckle, feet

Meat and poultry roasting chart

To roast	Temperature	Time	Accompaniments
	Put all meat into a hot oven for 10–15 minutes—450°F., 230°C., Gas Mark 8.		
Beef	Reduce to 350°F., 180°C., Gas Mark 4 (thermometer reading 140°F., 60°C., rare, 160°F., 71°C. medium).	15 minutes per lb. ($\frac{1}{2}$ kg.) and 15 minutes over	Yorkshire pudding (see page 55) Horseradish sauce (see page 56) Thin gravy
Lamb	Reduce to 325°F., 170°C., Gas Mark 3 (thermometer reading 170°F., 76°C.).	25 minutes per lb. ($\frac{1}{2}$ kg.) and 25 minutes over	Mint sauce Medium, thick gravy
Pork	Reduce to 350°F., 180°C., Gas Mark 4 (thermometer reading 185°F., 85°C.).	30 minutes per lb. ($\frac{1}{2}$ kg.) and 30 minutes over	Sage and onion stuffing Apple sauce Thickened gravy
Veal	Reduce to 325°F., 170°C., Gas Mark 3 (thermometer reading 175°F., 79°C.).	30 minutes per lb. ($\frac{1}{2}$ kg.) and 30 minutes over	Bacon rolls Thickened gravy
Turkey	425°F., 220°C., Gas Mark 7 for 15 minutes, reducing to 350°F., 180°C., Gas Mark 4	20 minutes per lb. ($\frac{1}{2}$ kg.) and 20 minutes over	Stuff the neck with yule stuffing (see page 55) or American stuffing (see page 54). Stuff the tail with 1–2 lb. ($\frac{1}{2}$ kg.) sausagemeat stuffing. Cover the breast with fat bacon. Baste.
Goose	425°F., 220°C., Gas Mark 7 for 15 minutes, reducing to 350°F., 180°C., Gas Mark 4	15 minutes per lb. ($\frac{1}{2}$ kg.) and 15 minutes over	Stuff with sage and onion, or American stuffing (see page 54). Baste.
Duck	400°F., 200°C., Gas Mark 6	20 minutes per lb. ($\frac{1}{2}$ kg.)	Younger birds do not require stuffing but older, larger ducks are usually stuffed with sage and onion at the tail end. Baste.
Chicken	400°F., 200°C., Gas Mark 6	20 minutes per lb. ($\frac{1}{2}$ kg.) and 20 minutes over	Stuff between the skin and flesh at the wishbone end until the bird is plump. Baste.
Pheasant	400°F., 200°C., Gas Mark 6 for 15 minutes, reducing to 350°F., 180°C., Gas Mark 4	40–50 minutes for small young birds, 1–1$\frac{1}{2}$ hours for larger older birds	Put a knob of butter inside the bird. Baste.

Barbecuing

The increasing popularity of barbecues shows that many people are finding out the pleasures of open air cooking and the marvellous flavours of charcoal-cooked chops and steaks. Even the humble sausage takes on a new glamour when cooked on the barbecue. Although there are expensive barbecues with spits and various luxury fittings there is nothing to stop anyone building a barbecue with a few bricks and some netting in the back yard, garden or patio. The one in the picture opposite was built by the photographer in his garden and it proved to be most efficient. A shelf from the oven was used as the top grid for cooking. It is an excellent idea to marinate meat before barbecuing and the marinade can then be used to brush over the steaks etc. during cooking.

Spicy barbecue sauces can be bought or made very easily, especially if you have a liquidiser. Use them to paint the food while cooking. Potatoes and corn in its husk can be barbecued most successfully with the meat.

Having a barbecued meal is an ideal way of raising wild enthusiasm for cooking from the man or men in your household, even if they won't touch a saucepan in the kitchen!

Barbecue cooking times

Build the fire up and only start cooking when the coals start to glow. A good barbecue fire usually takes in the region of 1 hour to be in perfect condition for cooking. Buy charcoal brickettes and beware of using any fuel which will taint the food.

Sausages	20–25 minutes
Frankfurter sausages	20–25 minutes
Hamburgers	5–8 minutes depending on size
Steaks 1–1½ inches (2·5–3·5 cm.) thick	5–15 minutes depending whether required well cooked or rare, or rare to medium, or medium to well done
Lamb chops	8–10 minutes depending on thickness
Kebabs	10–15 minutes depending on meats used
Chicken pieces	20–25 minutes
Ham steaks 1 inch (2·5 cm.) thick	15–20 minutes
Pork chops 1 inch (2·5 cm.) thick	15–18 minutes
Foil-wrapped potatoes (large)	1–1½ hours
(medium)	1 hour

Garlic bread (see page 24) is marvellous to serve with barbecued food and can be heated, wrapped in foil, on the barbecue. If liked, mix chopped parsley and chives into the garlic butter.

❋ The flavoured butter can be frozen and used with chops and steaks when cooking them on the barbecue or under the grill.

Left : A large capacity, cast iron barbecue with a double grill. The battery-operated rotary spit is an optional extra.

Below left : A do-it-yourself barbecue made from ordinary bricks and an oven shelf. Use charcoal, which can be bought from most ironmongers, for the fire.

Below : A dual purpose cast iron barbecue which can be used indoors in a chimney, or outdoors. It is ideal for cooking kebabs.

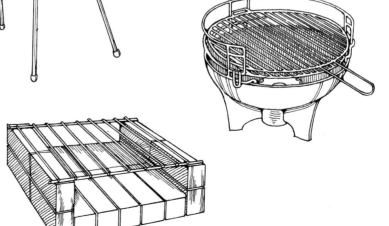

Steak, kebabs and foil-wrapped potatoes cooked over a barbecue

Popular accompaniments for roasts

Sage and onion stuffing

Main utensils: liquidiser or sieve,
  ovenproof dish
Preparation time: 10 minutes
Oven temperature: moderate
  (350°F., 180°C., Gas Mark 4)
Cooking time: 25 minutes

Imperial/Metric	American
6 slices white bread	6 slices white bread
4 onions	4 onions
1 egg	1 egg
1 teaspoon sage	1 teaspoon sage
$\frac{1}{4}$ teaspoon thyme	$\frac{1}{4}$ teaspoon thyme
few sprigs parsley	few sprigs parsley
salt and pepper	salt and pepper

Remove the crusts from the bread. Quarter the slices and make into breadcrumbs in the liquidiser (or rub through a sieve). Meanwhile partly boil the roughly chopped onions for a few minutes. Put the breadcrumbs in a bowl, then put the onions into the liquidiser (or chop finely) with the other ingredients and blend together. Mix together with the breadcrumbs; smooth into a greased ovenproof dish and bake until the stuffing is firm and golden brown. Put the stuffing in the oven about 25 minutes before the pork is due to be taken out.

Oatmeal stuffing

Main utensil: bowl
Preparation time: few minutes

Imperial/Metric	American
6 oz./175 g. oatmeal	1 cup oatmeal
3 tablespoons chopped suet	4 tablespoons chopped suet
2 onions, chopped	2 onions, chopped
pinch mixed herbs	pinch mixed herbs
salt and pepper	salt and pepper
milk or beaten egg to bind	milk or beaten egg to bind

Mix the oatmeal, suet, onions and herbs together; add salt and pepper to taste. Bind with a little milk or egg. Use to stuff a chicken for boiling, or rabbit for roasting.

American stuffing for roast goose or turkey (Illustrated on page 57)

Main utensils: saucepan
  (preferably non-stick), liquidiser
Preparation time: about 15 minutes
Cooking time: about 10 minutes

Imperial/Metric	American
1$\frac{1}{2}$ oz./40 g. butter or margarine	3 tablespoons butter or margarine
1 shallot, finely chopped or liquidised	1 shallot, finely chopped or liquidised
6 oz./175 g. mushrooms, chopped	generous 1 cup chopped mushrooms
8 oz./225 g. pork sausagemeat	1 cup pork sausagemeat
1 tablespoon chopped parsley	1 tablespoon chopped parsley
4 tablespoons unsweetened chestnut purée	5 tablespoons unsweetened chestnut purée
salt and pepper	salt and pepper
24 whole chestnuts, cooked and skinned	24 whole chestnuts, cooked and skinned
2 oz./50 g. fresh breadcrumbs	1 cup soft bread crumbs

Melt the fat in a saucepan, add the shallot and mushrooms and fry gently for 5 minutes, then add the sausagemeat and fry for 2 minutes. Stir in the parsley, chestnut purée, salt and pepper. Tip into a bowl with the whole chestnuts and breadcrumbs and mix well. Allow to cool before using. If liked the whole chestnuts can be blended in the liquidiser to make a smooth stuffing.

Yule stuffing for roast turkey

Main utensil: liquidiser
Preparation time: 15 minutes

Imperial/Metric	American
9 oz./250 g. fresh breadcrumbs	4½ cups soft bread crumbs
¾ pint/4½ dl. hot milk	scant 2 cups hot milk
3 oz./75 g. butter or margarine	6 tablespoons butter or margarine
4 oz./100 g. sausagemeat	½ cup sausagemeat
turkey liver	turkey liver
4 oz./100 g. lean bacon or ham, chopped	½ cup chopped lean bacon or ham
3 teaspoons chopped or liquidised onion	3 teaspoons chopped or liquidised onion
2 teaspoons chopped parsley	2 teaspoons chopped parsley
3 egg yolks	3 egg yolks
grated rind of 1 lemon	grated rind of 1 lemon
salt and pepper	salt and pepper
pinch paprika pepper	pinch paprika pepper
celery salt (optional)	celery salt (optional)

Make the crumbs in the liquidiser and turn into a basin; heat the milk almost to boiling point and pour over the crumbs and allow to stand for 10 minutes. Stir in the butter, sausagemeat, minced liver, bacon or ham, onion, parsley, beaten egg yolks, lemon rind, and seasonings to taste. Mix well and use to stuff the turkey.

Yorkshire pudding

Main utensils: wooden spoon or hand mixer or liquidiser
Preparation time: 10 minutes by hand. 4 minutes in the liquidiser
Oven temperature: hot (450°F., 230°C., Gas Mark 8)
Cooking time: 15–30 minutes depending on size
Serves: 4

Imperial/Metric	American
4 oz./100 g. plain flour	1 cup all-purpose flour
pinch salt	pinch salt
1 egg	1 egg
½ pint/3 dl. milk	1¼ cups milk

Sieve the flour and salt into the mixer bowl, make a well in the centre, and break the egg into it. Add a little milk and beat with the mixer until a smooth batter is obtained. Gradually stir in the remaining milk with a spoon. To make the batter in the liquidiser place the salt, egg and milk in the goblet and switch on at minimum speed for 30 seconds. Remove the lid and pour in the sieved flour. Replace the lid and blend for a further 30 seconds. If possible, allow to stand in a cool place for at least 15 minutes before using. Pour the meat fat into a Yorkshire pudding tin or put 3 tablespoons into a shallow ovenproof dish. Allow the fat to heat until very hot and then pour in the batter and bake in a hot oven for 15 minutes for individual puddings and 30 minutes for a large one.

Beef gravy

Pour off the fat from the roasting tin very slowly so that all the sediment and meat juices remain. Season the sediment which remains in the tin and mix well over the heat until it is dark brown. Add about ½ pint (3 dl.) stock (make up with a beef cube) and bring to the boil in the tin, stir well, and boil until a good flavour is obtained. Pour into a gravy boat and skim any fat off before serving.

Lamb gravy

Keep about 1 tablespoon fat in the tin with sediment and mix this with 1 tablespoon flour. Blend well and then continue as for beef gravy.

Pork gravy

Pork must be well cooked, therefore, it is important to know the exact weight of the joint to ensure that it is cooked throughout. It may be cooked straight from the freezer but allow 1 hour per lb. (½ kg.) cooking time. Serve with thickened gravy as for lamb.

Horseradish sauce 1

Main utensil: double saucepan
Preparation time: few minutes
Cooking time: about 20 minutes
Makes: ½ pint (3 dl.)

Imperial/Metric	American
1 horseradish, grated	1 horseradish, grated
½ pint/3 dl. milk	1¼ cups milk
3 tablespoons fresh breadcrumbs	4 tablespoons fresh bread crumbs
½ teaspoon salt	½ teaspoon salt
pepper	pepper
1 oz./25 g. butter or margarine	2 tablespoons butter or margarine

Place the horseradish, milk and breadcrumbs in the top of a double saucepan (or a bowl placed over a pan of hot water) and cook for 20 minutes. Season with salt and pepper to taste, and add the butter in small pieces. Stir until blended. Serve with hot roast beef, boiled beef, salt beef, ham or tongue.

Horseradish sauce 2

Main utensil: saucepan (preferably non-stick)
Preparation time: few minutes
Cooking time: few minutes
Makes: ½ pint (3 dl.)

Imperial/Metric	American
1 oz./25 g. butter	2 tablespoons butter
2 tablespoons flour	3 tablespoons all-purpose flour
½ pint/3 dl. stock	1¼ cups stock
1 horseradish, grated	1 horseradish, grated
½ teaspoon castor sugar	½ teaspoon granulated sugar
1 tablespoon vinegar	1 tablespoon vinegar
salt	salt

Melt the butter in a saucepan. Stir in the flour and cook until brown, stirring. Add the stock and bring to the boil, stirring constantly. Cook for 3 minutes, then add the horseradish, sugar and vinegar and salt to taste. Serve at once.

Cranberry sauce (Illustrated opposite)

Main utensils: saucepan (preferably non-stick), sieve or liquidiser
Preparation time: few minutes
Cooking time: 5–10 minutes
Serves: 4–6

Imperial/Metric	American
8 oz./225 g. cranberries	½ lb. cranberries
6 tablespoons water	½ cup water
2 oz./50 g. sugar	¼ cup sugar
1 oz./25 g. butter	2 tablespoons butter
2 tablespoons port (optional)	3 tablespoons port (optional)

Put the cranberries in a saucepan with the water and simmer over a moderate heat until tender. Remove from the heat and allow to cool slightly then blend in a liquidiser or rub through a sieve. Add the sugar, butter and port to taste, if used.

If you prefer a cranberry sauce with whole cranberries make a syrup with the sugar and water. Add the cranberries and simmer until tender. Stir in the butter and port, if used.

Note: Use an extra 2 tablespoons water if omitting the port.

Roast stuffed turkey, bacon rolls and chipolata sausages garnished with watercress and served with cranberry sauce, Brussels sprouts and roast potatoes

Prepare the stuffings for the turkey. To make a smoother American stuffing blend the chestnuts in the liquidiser.

Stuff the neck end with the yule stuffing and use the American stuffing for the other end.

Before roasting the turkey cover the top with rashers of streaky bacon. Pour a little stock around the turkey and place a coarsely chopped onion in the pan.

Tomato sauce

Main utensils: saucepan (preferably non-stick), liquidiser
Preparation time: 5 minutes
Cooking time: about 1½ hours
Makes: about ¾ pint (scant ½ litre)

Imperial/Metric	American
1 Spanish onion	1 Spanish onion
1 clove garlic	1 clove garlic
1 carrot	1 carrot
1 oz./25 g. butter	2 tablespoons butter
2 tablespoons olive oil	3 tablespoons olive oil
1 5-oz./150-g. can tomato purée	½ cup tomato paste
1 15-oz./425-g. can peeled tomatoes	1 15-oz. can peeled tomatoes
2 bay leaves	2 bay leaves
2 tablespoons chopped parsley	3 tablespoons chopped parsley
¼ tablespoon oregano	¼ tablespoon oregano
salt and pepper	salt and pepper
1 small strip lemon peel	1 small strip lemon rind
¼ pint/1½ dl. chicken stock	⅔ cup chicken stock
1 teaspoon sugar	1 teaspoon sugar
1 teaspoon Worcestershire sauce	1 teaspoon Worcestershire sauce

Prepare the vegetables by peeling and chopping finely. Sauté onion, garlic and carrot in the butter and olive oil until soft but not coloured. Stir in the tomato purée and continue to cook for a few minutes. Pour in the peeled tomatoes, herbs, seasoning, lemon rind, stock, and sugar then simmer gently in a covered pan for 1½ hours, stirring occasionally. Cool slightly then blend in the liquidiser or rub through a sieve. Return to the rinsed out saucepan, add Worcestershire sauce, reheat and use as required.

Variation

Milanese sauce Make the tomato sauce as above. Slice 6 oz. (175 g.) mushrooms and shred 6 oz. (175 g.) lean ham. Heat 1 oz. (25 g.) butter in a pan and sauté the mushrooms for 3–4 minutes. Add the sauce, then simmer, uncovered for 5 minutes. Stir in the prepared ham. Serve with spaghetti or tagliatelli and grated Parmesan cheese.

Spicy barbecue sauce

Main utensil: saucepan
Preparation time: 3 minutes
Cooking time: about 20 minutes

Imperial/Metric	American
2 tablespoons oil	3 tablespoons oil
1 medium onion, chopped	1 medium onion, chopped
¼ pint/1½ dl. vinegar	⅔ cup vinegar
¼ pint/1½ dl. water	⅔ cup water
1 beef stock cube	1 beef bouillon cube
1–2 tablespoons Worcestershire sauce	1–2 tablespoons Worcestershire sauce
1 teaspoon salt	1 teaspoon salt
¼ teaspoon pepper	¼ teaspoon pepper
½ teaspoon Tabasco sauce	½ teaspoon Tabasco sauce

Heat the oil in the pan and add the onions; cook slowly until the onion is just beginning to brown. Add all the other ingredients and stir well, bring slowly to the boil and simmer for about 15 minutes.

Dumplings

These go well with beef stews and casseroles. They can either be cooked separately in boiling water or stock for about 20 minutes, or placed on top of the stew 20 minutes before the end of the cooking time. If cooking them this way it may be necessary to add a little more liquid to the stew.

To make dumplings, blend 4 oz. (100 g.) self-raising flour, 2 oz. (50 g.) shredded suet, seasonings and herbs (if liked) with water to give a sticky dough. Form into small balls and cook.

❅ Cooked dumplings freeze well. They can be frozen in the stew (and reheated together) or packed separately and reheated in hot liquid.

Grilled steak with béarnaise sauce

Main utensils: frying pan, small
   saucepan (preferably non-stick),
   double saucepan, grill pan
Preparation time: 15 minutes
Cooking time: 20 minutes
Serves: 4

Imperial/Metric
2 oz./50 g. butter
freshly milled pepper
4 fillet or rump steaks
4 medium mushrooms
Béarnaise sauce:
1 teaspoon dried tarragon or
   2 teaspoons chopped fresh
   tarragon
2 teaspoons chopped shallots or
   spring onions
salt and pepper
3 tablespoons wine
   vinegar
3 egg yolks
2 teaspoons water
4 oz./100 g. butter

American
¼ cup butter
freshly milled pepper
4 beef tenderloin steaks
4 medium mushrooms
Béarnaise sauce:
1 teaspoon dried tarragon or
   2 teaspoons chopped fresh
   tarragon
2 teaspoons chopped shallots or
   scallions
salt and pepper
scant ¼ cup wine
   vinegar
3 egg yolks
2 teaspoons water
½ cup butter

Divide half the butter between the steaks and sprinkle the tops with freshly milled pepper. Sauté the mushrooms in the remaining butter in a frying pan. Grill the steaks on either side, until cooked to your liking. Garnish with the mushrooms and serve with the béarnaise sauce.

Put the tarragon, chopped shallots or spring onions, seasoning and wine vinegar in a pan. Boil over a moderate heat until reduced to about 1 tablespoon. Put the egg yolks, water and strained reduced liquid into a double saucepan. (Do not allow the water under the sauce to boil or it will cause the sauce to curdle.) Add the butter in small pieces, a few at a time, stirring briskly all the time with a wooden spoon or a small balloon whisk. Remove from the heat as soon as the sauce begins to thicken. Turn into a sauce boat and sprinkle the top with chopped tarragon or parsley.

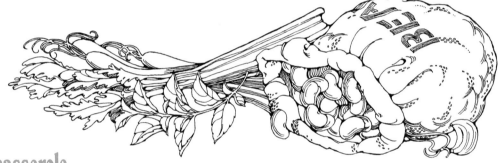

Italian casserole

Main utensils: frying pan,
   casserole (preferably non-stick)
Preparation time: 10 minutes
Oven temperature: moderate
   (325°F., 170°C., Gas Mark 3)
Cooking time: 2½ hours
Serves: 6

Imperial/Metric
1½ oz./40 g. butter
2 large onions
1 clove garlic
2-lb./1-kg. slice lean beef
2 carrots
1 stick celery
salt and pepper
¼ teaspoon basil
¼ pint/1½ dl. white wine
1 tablespoon tomato purée
¼ pint/1½ dl. water
2 oz./50 g. haricot beans (fresh if
   possible)

American
3 tablespoons butter
2 large onions
1 clove garlic
2-lb. slice lean beef
2 carrots
1 stalk celery
salt and pepper
¼ teaspoon basil
⅔ cup white wine
1 tablespoon tomato paste
⅔ cup water
¼ cup navy beans

Melt the butter in a frying pan and fry the sliced onions and crushed garlic gently without allowing them to brown. Transfer to a casserole and quickly brown the slice of meat on both sides. Place in the casserole with the onions. Cut the carrots into sticks, chop the celery and place in the casserole around the meat. Season with salt and pepper and sprinkle with basil. Pour in the white wine and blend the tomato purée with the water and pour over the vegetables. Cover and cook in the centre of the preheated oven for 1 hour. Check that the liquid has not evaporated and add the haricot beans (with more liquid if necessary). Continue cooking for a further 1½ hours.

❋ This dish freezes well, but add a little extra wine or stock when reheating.

Beef à la mode

Main utensil: flameproof casserole
  (preferably non-stick)
Preparation time: 15 minutes
Oven temperature: moderate
  (325°F., 170°C., Gas Mark 3)
Cooking time: about 1½ hours
Serves: 4–6

Imperial/Metric
1 calf's foot
6 streaky bacon rashers
3 lb./1½ kg. rolled beef topside
4 tablespoons Madeira
4 tablespoons white wine
bouquet garni
salt and pepper
24 small onions
3 carrots
1 tablespoon flour

American
1 calf foot
6 bacon slices
3 lb. rolled beef round
⅓ cup Madeira
⅓ cup white wine
bouquet garni
salt and pepper
24 small onions
3 carrots
1 tablespoon all-purpose flour

Ask the butcher to cut up the calf's foot. Blanch the pieces in boiling water, then drain. Wrap the bacon around the topside and secure with fine string. Brown on all sides in a large flameproof casserole. Pour in the Madeira, heat it slightly then ignite it. When the flames have died down add the wine, calf's foot pieces, bouquet garni and seasoning. Cover and bring to simmering point on top of the cooker. Prepare the onions and carrots and cut the carrots into fairly small pieces. Add to the beef, then cover and transfer to a moderate oven and continue cooking until the meat is tender; turn the meat once during cooking. To serve, remove the string and bacon from the meat and slice it. Serve with the vegetables and a gravy made from the strained cooking liquid thickened with the flour.

Goulash (Illustrated opposite)

Main utensils: frying pan, casserole
  (preferably non-stick)
Preparation time: 15 minutes
Oven temperature: moderate
  (350°F., 180°C., Gas Mark 4)
Cooking time: 1½ hours
Serves: 4

Imperial/Metric
1 lb./450 g. stewing steak
2 tablespoons seasoned flour
2 onions
1 green pepper
3 tablespoons oil
2 teaspoons paprika pepper
½ pint/3 dl. stock
2 large tomatoes
bouquet garni
2 tablespoons tomato purée
salt and pepper
grated nutmeg
2 tablespoons soured cream

American
1 lb. beef stew meat
3 tablespoons seasoned flour
2 onions
1 green sweet pepper
scant ¼ cup oil
2 teaspoons paprika pepper
1¼ cups stock
2 large tomatoes
bouquet garni
3 tablespoons tomato paste
salt and pepper
grated nutmeg
3 tablespoons sour cream

Cut the beef into small cubes and coat in seasoned flour. Peel the onions and cut into small pieces; seed the pepper and cut into small pieces. Sauté the onion and pepper lightly in the oil. Remove to the casserole and fry the floured meat until browned on all sides, sprinkle with the paprika pepper. Stir round with a wooden spoon and turn into the casserole dish. Sprinkle lightly with any remaining flour add the stock, peeled and sliced tomatoes, the bouquet garni, tomato purée, seasoning and nutmeg. Cover and cook in the oven for 1½ hours. Spoon over the soured cream before serving and if liked sprinkle a little paprika pepper on the cream.

Stew with dumplings, spring lamb casserole and goulash (see pages 48, 58, 67, 60)

Boiled beef

Main utensil: large saucepan (preferably non-stick)
Preparation time: 10 minutes
Cooking time: 3 hours
Serves: 4–6

Imperial/Metric	American
3 lb./1¼ kg. rolled brisket	3 lb. rolled fresh brisket
2 teaspoons salt	2 teaspoons salt
4 carrots	4 carrots
4 small onions	4 small onions
4 small turnips	4 small turnips
1 head celery	1 head celery
3 leeks	3 leeks
3 cloves	3 cloves
8 peppercorns	8 peppercorns
1 bay leaf	1 bay leaf
salt	salt

Place the meat in a large saucepan of boiling water and bring back to the boil. Add the salt, skim carefully, cover and allow the meat to simmer for 1½ hours, removing the scum from time to time. Prepare the vegetables and cut into fairly large pieces; add to the meat. Tie the herbs in a small piece of muslin and add to the pan; continue simmering until the meat is tender. To serve hot, remove the meat carefully to a serving dish and arrange the vegetables around it. Serve a little liquid separately in a sauce boat. To serve boiled brisket cold, remove from the saucepan, place in a dish and press with a heavy weight. If liked a little liquid can be reduced to make a glaze for the meat. Use the remaining liquid for making soup.

Steak and kidney pie

Main utensil: 1½-pint (about 1-litre) pie dish
Preparation time: 15 minutes
Oven temperature: hot (425°F., 220°C., Gas Mark 7) then moderate (350°F., 180°C., Gas Mark 4)
Cooking time: 2 hours
Serves: 4

Imperial/Metric	American
1 lb./½ kg. shoulder steak	1 lb. beef shoulder steak
2 lamb's kidneys	2 lamb kidneys
1 tablespoon flour	1 tablespoon all-purpose flour
salt and pepper	salt and pepper
1 onion, finely chopped	1 onion, finely chopped
stock or water	stock or water
8 oz./225 g. flaky pastry (see page 106)	½ lb. flaky pastry (see page 106)
beaten egg to glaze	beaten egg to glaze

Cut the steak into small cubes. Split, skin, core and slice the kidneys. Mix flour with salt and pepper to taste. Dip meat in seasoned flour; place in a pie dish with the onion, allowing filling to come a little higher than the top of the dish. Fill up with the stock or water. Roll out the pastry and use to cover the pie (see page 111). Brush with beaten egg, make a hole in the centre and bake in a preheated hot oven for 30 minutes, then lower the heat to moderate and bake for a further 1½ hours. Cover the pastry with foil after 1 hour. When cooked, add more hot stock, if liked.

To make a pie with a really rich brown gravy, fry the floured and seasoned meat lightly in a little oil with the chopped onion until the meat is brown. Add a dash of Worcestershire sauce and ½ pint (3 dl.) stock and allow to cook slowly in the oven or on top of the cooker for about 1 hour. Pack the cooked meat into the pie dish and pour on the juice. Allow to cool, insert a pie funnel and cover the pie dish with the pastry. Bake in a hot oven for 35–40 minutes.

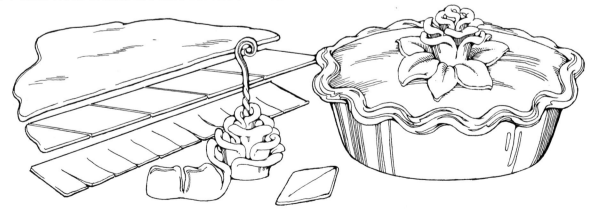

Any pastry trimmings or small pieces of leftover pastry can be rolled out and cut into leaves or a rose to decorate the top of a pie. Use a skewer to roll the pastry rose around so that it can be lifted onto the pie without spoiling the shape.

Spaghetti with bolognese sauce

Main utensils: saucepan (preferably non-stick), liquidiser or sieve
Preparation time: 10 minutes
Cooking time: about 1¼ hours
Serves: 6–8

Imperial/Metric	American
3 rashers bacon, chopped	3 bacon slices, chopped
2 oz./50 g. butter	¼ cup butter
2 small onions, finely chopped	2 small onions, finely chopped
2 small carrots, finely chopped	2 small carrots, finely chopped
2 sticks celery, finely chopped	2 stalks celery, finely chopped
8 oz./225 g. lean beef, minced	½ lb. lean beef, ground
4 oz./100 g. veal, minced	¼ lb. veal, ground
4 oz./100 g. pork, minced	¼ lb. pork, ground
½ pint/3 dl. chicken stock	1¼ cups chicken stock
¼ pint/1½ dl. dry white wine	⅔ cup dry white wine
1 10-oz./275-g. can tomatoes	1 10-oz. can tomatoes
1 teaspoon salt	1 teaspoon salt
freshly ground black pepper	freshly ground black pepper
1 clove	1 clove
freshly grated nutmeg	freshly grated nutmeg
8 oz./225 g. mushrooms, sliced	2 cups sliced mushrooms
3 chicken livers, chopped	3 chicken livers, chopped
4 tablespoons double cream	⅓ cup whipping cream
1-1¼ lb./about ½ kg. spaghetti	1-1¼ lb. spaghetti
1 oz./25 g. butter	2 tablespoons butter
grated nutmeg	grated nutmeg

Cook the bacon in the butter in a pan for about 2 minutes. Add the onions, carrots and celery, and allow to cook gently with bacon for about 5 minutes. Stir in the beef, veal and pork and cook for about 10 minutes. Stir in the stock and wine. Increase the heat slightly and cook until the sauce thickens, stirring constantly. Liquidise the tomatoes, or rub them through a sieve and add to the pan. Add seasonings, cover and simmer gently for 1 hour. Add the mushrooms and chicken livers and simmer for a further 5 minutes. Stir in the cream just before serving.

Cook the spaghetti as directed on the packet. The thickness may vary from brand to brand, but it will usually take about 10–12 minutes to be cooked *al dente*. This means that it is still chewy, definitely not soft or mushy. Drain the cooked spaghetti into a colander. Melt the butter in the saucepan, return the spaghetti to the pan and shake well. Sprinkle with grated nutmeg and serve with the sauce.
❋ This sauce can be frozen without the cream. At the reheating stage add the cream and to give more flavour 1 crushed clove of garlic and a pinch of oregano.

Hunters' stew

Main utensils: frying pan, casserole (preferably non-stick)
Preparation time: 10 minutes
Oven temperature: moderately hot (375°F., 190°C., Gas Mark 5)
Cooking time: 20–25 minutes
Serves: 4

Imperial/Metric	American
8 oz./225 g. onions, chopped	½ lb. onions, chopped
2 oz./50 g. butter	¼ cup butter
8 oz./225 g. cooked beef or pork, finely chopped	1 cup finely chopped cooked beef or pork
½ pint/3 dl. stock	1¼ cups stock
salt and pepper	salt and pepper
freshly grated nutmeg	freshly grated nutmeg
1 tablespoon chutney	1 tablespoon chutney
8 oz./225 g. apples, peeled and chopped	2 cups diced apple
1 lb./450 g. mashed potato	2 cups mashed potato
1 tablespoon breadcrumbs	1 tablespoon bread crumbs

Fry the onions in half the butter until pale golden. Add the meat, stock, seasoning and chutney and blend together. Spread some of the remaining butter on the bottom of a casserole and put in the meat mixture; top the meat with the apples and finally pipe or fork mashed potatoes on the top. Dot with the remaining butter and sprinkle with bread-crumbs. Bake in a moderately hot oven for 20–25 minutes.

Carbonade à la flamande

Main utensils: frying pan,
 flameproof casserole (preferably
 non-stick)
Preparation time: 15 minutes
Oven temperature: moderate
 (325°F., 170°C., Gas Mark 3)
Cooking time: 2 hours
Serves: 4–6

Imperial/Metric
1½ lb./¾ kg. stewing beef
4 large onions
2 oz./50 g. butter or oil
2 oz./50 g. lean bacon, chopped
1 tablespoon flour
salt and pepper
½ pint/3 dl. brown ale
¼ pint/1½ dl. stock
1 teaspoon French mustard
2 teaspoons sugar
bouquet garni
Garnish:
6 slices French bread
French mustard

American
1½ lb. beef stew meat
4 large onions
¼ cup butter or oil
2 bacon slices, chopped
1 tablespoon all-purpose flour
salt and pepper
1¼ cups dark beer
⅔ cup stock
1 teaspoon French mustard
2 teaspoons sugar
bouquet garni
Garnish:
6 slices French bread
French mustard

Cut the meat into strips about 1½ inches (3·5 cm.) long, or cubes. Peel and thinly slice the onions. Heat the butter or oil in a frying pan and sauté the onions and bacon. Transfer to the casserole. Coat the meat in the flour seasoned with salt and pepper and sauté for several minutes, until browned on all sides. Place in the casserole with the onions and add the remaining ingredients. Bring to the boil, cover and cook in the centre of the preheated oven for 1¾ hours. Spread the slices of French bread with the mustard and arrange, mustard-side down, on top of the meat. Return to the oven, uncovered, for another 15 minutes.

❋ This dish freezes. Put the bread on at the reheating stage.

Trim the beef and cut into cubes or thin strips. Coat the prepared meat in seasoned flour.

Heat the butter or oil in a frying pan and sauté the prepared onions and bacon for a few minutes. Transfer to a casserole dish. Sauté the meat until nicely browned. Place in the casserole with the remaining ingredients.

Fifteen minutes before the end of the cooking time, cut the French loaf into slices and spread each slice with mustard. Arrange the slices of bread, mustard-side down, on top of the meat. Return the casserole, uncovered, to the oven for the last 15 minutes cooking time.

Pork chops with apples

Main utensil: casserole (preferably
 non-stick)
Preparation time: 10 minutes
Oven temperature: moderate
 (350°F., 180°C., Gas Mark 4)
Cooking time: 40 minutes
Serves: 4

Imperial/Metric
4 pork chops
3 cooking apples
4 teaspoons brown sugar
2 teaspoons cinnamon
2 oz./50 g. butter
6 tablespoons dry sherry

American
4 pork chops
3 baking apples
4 teaspoons brown sugar
2 teaspoons cinnamon
¼ cup butter
½ cup dry sherry

Grill the pork chops for about 5 minutes on each side until golden brown, then place in the casserole and put into the oven for 10 minutes. Peel, core and cut the cooking apples into eight pieces, then slice thinly. Take the chops out of the oven and surround with slices of apple. Sprinkle the apple with brown sugar and cinnamon, dot with butter and pour the sherry over the chops. Return to the oven and cook for a further 15–20 minutes. Serve with broccoli.

Devonshire pie

Main utensil: 1½-pint (1-litre) pie dish
Preparation time: 25 minutes
Oven temperature: hot (450°F., 290°C., Gas Mark 8) then moderate (350°F., 180°C., Gas Mark 4)
Cooking time: 1 hour 15 minutes
Serves: 6

Imperial/Metric	American
6 pork chops	6 pork chops
2 lb./1 kg. tart apples	2 lb. baking apples
2 teaspoons sugar	2 teaspoons sugar
½–1 teaspoon allspice	½–1 teaspoon allspice
2 onions, sliced	2 onions, sliced
salt and pepper	salt and pepper
¼ pint/1½ dl. gravy	⅔ cup gravy
8 oz./225 g. flaky or puff pastry (see pages 106, 108)	½ lb. flaky or puff pastry (see pages 106, 108)
beaten egg to glaze	beaten egg to glaze

Trim chops and cut them short; grill lightly on each side and retain the juices to make gravy. Peel, core and slice the apples. Put a layer of apples in the bottom of a pie dish. Sprinkle with sugar and ground allspice to taste, then add a layer of sliced onions. Season with salt and pepper, then cover with a layer of prepared chops. Repeat layers until ingredients are used up. Insert a pie funnel and pour in the gravy. Allow to cool. Roll out the pastry and use to cover the pie (see page 111). Decorate with the pastry trimmings and make a hole in the top. Glaze with beaten egg and bake near the top of a preheated hot oven for about 15 minutes, until the pastry is risen and set, then reduce the heat to moderate and bake for a further 1 hour. Cover the pastry with foil or greaseproof, if necessary to prevent it from becoming too brown.

American chop suey

Main utensils: saucepan, frying pan (preferably non-stick)
Preparation time: 10 minutes
Cooking time: 20 minutes
Serves: 4–6

Imperial/Metric	American
6 oz./175 g. long-grain rice	about 1 cup long-grain rice
6 pork chops or 1 lb./½ kg. pork fillet	6 pork chops or 1 lb. pork tenderloin
1 oz./25 g. butter	2 tablespoons butter
1 large onion, sliced	1 large onion, sliced
1 stick celery, chopped	1 stalk celery, chopped
1 egg, beaten	1 egg, beaten
2 tablespoons soy sauce	3 tablespoons soy sauce

Cook the rice, Chinese fashion—wash rice and place in a large saucepan. Cover with cold, salted water and bring to the boil, then lower the heat and simmer for 15 minutes. Do not stir; when ready, the rice should have absorbed all the water. Meanwhile, remove meat from bones (if using chops) and cut in cubes. Heat butter and when hot, fry the meat with sliced onion and celery for 5 minutes. Stir in beaten egg. Stir for a few moments, then add the soy sauce. Season to taste and spoon into a hot dish. Serve the rice separately.

Gammon steaks with cherry sauce

Main utensils: casserole, saucepan (preferably non-stick)
Preparation time: 15 minutes
Oven temperature: moderate (350°F., 180°C., Gas Mark 4)
Cooking time: 40 minutes
Serves: 4

Imperial/Metric	American
4 thick gammon steaks	4 thick ham steaks
4 tablespoons water	⅓ cup water
1 teaspoon ground ginger	1 teaspoon ground ginger
2 tablespoons sugar	3 tablespoons sugar
1 20-oz./550-g. can sour stoned cherries	1 20-oz. can sour pitted cherries
1 tablespoon flour	1 tablespoon all-purpose flour

Trim any excess fat from the gammon, snip the edges and place in a casserole and cook in the oven for 10 minutes. Put the water, ginger and sugar in a pan and cook over a high heat for 5 minutes. Drain the stoned cherries and add to the saucepan, lower the heat and simmer for 5 minutes. Mix the flour with 2 tablespoons cold water and add a little of the hot cherry mixture to the flour blend well then return the thickening to the saucepan; cook and stir until thickened. Pour the cherry sauce over the ham and return to the oven for a further 30 minutes. Serve with green beans.

Danish kebabs

Main utensil: large saucepan
   (preferably non-stick)
Preparation time: 10 minutes
Cooking time: 25 minutes
Serves: 4

Imperial/Metric
1¾-lb./¾-kg. piece lean bacon
   (slipper or forehock)
4 oz./100 g. butter
1 onion, chopped
8 oz./225 g. long-grain rice
1¼ pints chicken stock
1 tablespoon chopped parsley
salt and pepper
3 large bananas
8 small tomatoes

American
1¾-lb. piece lean ham or bacon

½ cup butter
1 onion, chopped
generous 1 cup long-grain rice
generous 3 cups chicken stock
1 tablespoon chopped parsley
salt and pepper
3 large bananas
8 small tomatoes

Remove rind and fat from the bacon and cut the meat into ¾-inch (1½-cm.) cubes; drain. Simmer the bacon cubes in plenty of water for 25 minutes. Melt half the butter in a pan, add the onion and cook to soften. Stir in the rice and add the stock. Bring to the boil, stir and cover. Simmer for 12–15 minutes, until rice is tender, adding more stock if necessary. Add parsley and seasonings. Keep the rice hot.

Cut bananas into 4 or 5 pieces. Thread bacon, banana and tomatoes alternately onto skewers. Melt remaining butter, brush over kebabs. Grill kebabs about 8 minutes, turning frequently and brushing with more butter from time to time. Serve with the rice to which any remaining butter may be added.

Gammon with cream sauce

Main utensil: frying pan (preferably
   non-stick)
Preparation time: 10 minutes
Cooking time: about 10 minutes
Serves: 4

Imperial/Metric
4 gammon steaks
4 oz./100 g. tomatoes
2 oz./50 g. butter
1 onion, chopped
2 oz./50 g. mushrooms, chopped
1 green pepper, seeded and sliced

½ pint/3 dl. double cream
salt and pepper

American
4 ham steaks
¼ lb. tomatoes
¼ cup butter
1 onion, chopped
½ cup chopped mushrooms
1 green sweet pepper, seeded and
   sliced
1¼ cups whipping cream
salt and pepper

Remove rind from the steaks, snip fat at ½-inch (1-cm.) intervals. Skin tomatoes and chop flesh. Melt the butter and brush some over the steaks, then cook them under a hot grill until fat is brown, about 4 minutes each side. Keep steaks hot. Use remaining butter to cook the onion,

mushrooms and peppers for about 5 minutes. Add the chopped tomato and stir in the cream. Let the mixture cook over a moderate heat for about 4 minutes, until slightly reduced and creamy. Season to taste. Pour the sauce over the hot steaks and serve at once.

Barbecued spareribs

Main utensils: roasting tin
   (preferably non-stick), liquidiser
Preparation time: few minutes
Oven temperature: hot (450°F.,
   230°C., Gas Mark 8) reducing to
   moderate (350°F., 180°C.,
   Gas Mark 4)
Cooking time: 1½ hours
Serves: 4

Imperial/Metric
2–3 lb. pork spareribs
Liquidised barbecue sauce:
1 large onion
½ green pepper
1 chilli pepper
1 teaspoon mustard
2 tablespoons vinegar
salt
few drops Tabasco sauce
1 tablespoon Worcestershire sauce
4 tablespoons oil
4 tablespoons red wine (optional)

American
2–3 lb. pork spareribs
Liquidised barbecue sauce:
1 large onion
½ green sweet pepper
1 chili pepper
1 teaspoon mustard
3 tablespoons vinegar
salt
few drops Tabasco sauce
1 tablespoon Worcestershire sauce
⅓ cup oil
4 tablespoons red wine (optional)

Put the spareribs in a roasting tin and cook in the pre-heated oven for about 30 minutes then remove from the oven and brush with the barbecue sauce. Reduce the oven temperature to moderate and cook for a further hour, basting the spareribs frequently with the barbecue sauce. It is also advisable to turn the ribs from time to time.

Serve the remainder of the sauce, heated with the spareribs. Serve a large mixed salad and hand round plenty of paper napkins.
   To make the barbecue sauce, chop the vegetables coarsely and put all the ingredients in the liquidiser until the vegetables are finely chopped.

Irish stew

Main utensil: saucepan (preferably non-stick)
Preparation time: 15 minutes
Cooking time: about 1¾ hours
Serves: 4–5

Imperial/Metric	American
2 lb./1 kg. middle neck of lamb	2 lb. lamb neck slices
water	water
3 lb./1½ kg. potatoes	3 lb. potatoes
1 lb./450 g. onions	1 lb. onions
salt and pepper	salt and pepper
2 teaspoons Worcestershire sauce	2 teaspoons Worcestershire sauce
1 packet frozen mixed vegetables (optional)	1 package frozen mixed vegetables (optional)
chopped parsley (optional)	chopped parsley (optional)

Remove skin, and any excess fat from the meat; cut the meat into neat pieces and place in a saucepan. Cover with water and bring to the boil; remove the scum which rises to the top. Peel and cut all but three of the potatoes and the onions into slices; cut the reserved potatoes into quarters. When the scum has stopped appearing on the meat add the prepared potatoes and onions. Cover and simmer for 1 hour. Check the liquid in the pan then add the quartered potatoes and seasonings; continue to cook for 30-45 minutes. A packet of frozen mixed vegetables and some chopped parsley can be added about 20 minutes before the end of the cooking time to give this delicious dish a little more eye appeal.

☼ This dish freezes well in foil trays.

Lamb chops with ham

Main utensil: frying pan (preferably non-stick)
Preparation time: 15 minutes
Cooking time: 15 minutes
Serves: 6

Imperial/Metric	American
1 tablespoon olive oil	1 tablespoon olive oil
½ teaspoon salt	½ teaspoon salt
3 teaspoons white pepper	3 teaspoons white pepper
2 oz./50 g. butter	¼ cup butter
6 large mushrooms, peeled	6 large mushrooms, peeled
garlic salt (optional)	garlic salt (optional)
6 thin slices ham	6 thin slices ham
6 lamb chops	6 lamb loin chops
1 teaspoon chopped parsley	1 teaspoon chopped parsley
juice of ½ lemon	juice of ½ lemon
Garnish:	*Garnish:*
cooked peas	cooked peas

Mix the oil with the salt and pepper. Trim the chops and place in a shallow glass dish; pour over the oil mixture. Melt half the butter in a frying pan. Add the mushrooms and season with salt, pepper and garlic salt, if liked. Fry for 5 minutes each side. Meanwhile, grill the ham slices and arrange on a hot dish. Grill chops and place one on each slice of ham. Top with a mushroom. Add the rest of the butter to the frying pan and when hot, stir in parsley and lemon juice. Pour over the chops. Garnish with peas and serve with new potatoes.

Spring lamb casserole (Illustrated on page 61)

Main utensil: casserole dish
Preparation time: few minutes
Oven temperature: moderate (325°F., 170°C., Gas Mark 3)
Cooking time: about 1½ hours
Serves: 6

Imperial/Metric	American
6 lamb chops	6 lamb chops
4 onions, sliced	4 onions, sliced
2 small carrots	2 small carrots
1 pint/generous ½ litre stock	2½ cups stock
salt and pepper	salt and pepper
8 oz./225 g. fresh or frozen peas	½ lb. fresh or frozen peas
8 oz./225 g. small new potatoes	½ lb. small new potatoes

Trim the chops and arrange in a casserole with the sliced onions, peeled carrots, stock and seasoning. Cover and cook in the centre of the preheated oven for about 45 minutes. Add the peas and potatoes and cook for a further 30–40 minutes, until the meat is tender and the vegetables cooked. Check the seasoning and serve from the casserole dish.

If more convenient this dish can be cooked in a saucepan on top of the cooker in which case increase the amount of stock slightly.

Stuffed chops

Main utensils: liquidiser, frying
   pan, ovenproof dish with rack
   (preferably non-stick)
Preparation time: 15 minutes
Oven temperature: moderately hot
   (375°F., 190°C., Gas Mark 5)
Cooking time: 45 minutes
Serves: 6

Imperial/Metric	American
6 chump chops or veal chops	6 rib chops or veal chops
flour	flour
salt	salt
celery salt	celery salt
pepper	pepper
paprika pepper	paprika pepper
chopped fresh herbs	chopped fresh herbs
garlic salt (optional)	garlic salt (optional)
1 oz./25 g. butter or margarine	2 tablespoons butter or margarine
1 small onion, finely chopped or liquidised	1 small onion, finely chopped or liquidised
2 teaspoons chopped parsley	2 teaspoons chopped parsley
1 stick celery, finely chopped or liquidised	1 stalk celery, finely chopped or liquidised
2 oz./50 g. fresh breadcrumbs	1 cup fresh bread crumbs
3 cooking apples	3 baking apples
Garnish:	*Garnish:*
parsley	parsley

Cut a slit through the fat of the edge of each chop to give you a pocket for stuffing. Rub chops and inside the pocket lightly with flour seasoned with salt, celery salt, pepper and paprika pepper and chopped herbs to taste. Add a dash of garlic salt, if liked. Melt the fat in a frying pan. Add the onion, parsley and celery. Cook for 2–3 minutes, then add the breadcrumbs and season to taste. Remove to a plate. Place the chops in a frying pan, fat edge down, until the fat has run sufficiently to brown the chops. Fill each pocket with stuffing and secure the edges together with wooden cocktail sticks. Place on a rack in an ovenproof dish. Cut the apples in half and remove cores but not peel. Place half an apple on each chop. Cover closely and bake in a preheated moderately hot oven for about 45 minutes. Remove cocktail sticks and arrange chops, on a serving dish. Serve garnished with parsley.

Moussaka

Main utensils: frying pan,
   saucepan (preferably non-stick),
   casserole
Preparation time: 20 minutes
Oven temperature: moderate
   (325°F., 170°C., Gas Mark 3)
Cooking time: about 1½ hours
Serves: 4–6

Imperial/Metric	American
2 aubergines	2 eggplants
2 tablespoons oil	3 tablespoons oil
1 large onion, chopped	1 large onion, chopped
12 oz./350 g. potatoes, thinly sliced	12 oz. potatoes, thinly sliced
1 lb./450 g. cooked lamb, minced	2 cups ground cooked lamb
1 lb./450 g. tomatoes, skinned and chopped	1 lb. tomatoes, skinned and chopped
salt	salt
freshly ground black pepper	freshly ground black pepper
1 teaspoon rosemary	1 teaspoon rosemary
Cheese sauce:	*Cheese sauce:*
1 oz./25 g. butter	2 tablespoons butter
1 oz./25 g. flour	¼ cup all-purpose flour
½ pint/3 dl. milk	1¼ cups milk
2 oz./50 g. cheese, grated	½ cup grated cheese
½ teaspoon ground nutmeg	½ teaspoon ground nutmeg
1 egg	1 egg
1 carton natural yogurt	1 carton unflavored yogurt

Peel the aubergines and slice thinly. Sprinkle with salt and leave for 20 minutes. Rinse off the salt. Heat the oil in a frying pan and sauté the onions for a few minutes, until softened but not browned; remove to a plate. Sauté the rinsed aubergine slices and the potatoes in the oil remaining in the pan for about 10 minutes. Mix the minced lamb with the tomatoes and onions and season with salt, pepper and rosemary.

Melt the butter in a pan and stir in the flour. Cook over the heat for 1–2 minutes, stirring. Gradually blend in the milk, then stirring, bring to the boil and cook until thickened. Remove from the heat and stir in two-thirds of the grated cheese, the seasoning, nutmeg and beaten egg.

To assemble the moussaka, place a potato and aubergine layer in the bottom of a fairly deep ovenproof dish, then add a layer of sauce. Now add a layer of meat, then more sauce; continue to fill the dish this way, ending with potatoes and sauce. Cover and cook in the centre of the oven for about 1½ hours. Towards the end of the cooking time spread the yogurt over the top and sprinkle with the remaining cheese. Return, uncovered, to the oven.

Raised game pie (see page 72)

Lamb terrapin

Main utensil: saucepan (preferably non-stick)
Preparation time: 15 minutes
Cooking time: 10 minutes
Serves: 4

Imperial/Metric	**American**
2 oz./50 g. butter	¼ cup butter
1 teaspoon dry mustard	1 teaspoon dry mustard
1 tablespoon flour	1 tablespoon all-purpose flour
½ teaspoon salt	½ teaspoon salt
paprika pepper	paprika pepper
1 tablespoon Worcestershire sauce	1 tablespoon Worcestershire sauce
½ pint/3 dl. stock	1¼ cups stock
1 lb./½ kg. diced cooked lean lamb	2 cups diced cooked lean lamb
2 hard-boiled eggs	2 hard-cooked eggs
4 slices buttered toast	4 slices buttered toast
Garnish:	*Garnish:*
2 tomatoes, halved	2 tomatoes, halved
4 tablespoons cooked long-grain rice	5 tablespoons cooked long-grain rice

Melt the butter in a saucepan and stir in the mustard, flour and seasonings to taste. Mix well and stir in the Worcestershire sauce and stock. Bring to the boil and cook for 5 minutes. Stir in the prepared lamb and the sieved egg yolks and chopped egg whites. Heat thoroughly and serve on buttered toast. Garnish each serving with a grilled tomato half and surround with a ring of boiled rice.

Braised sheep's tongues

Main utensil: saucepan (preferably non-stick)
Preparation time: 15 minutes, not including soaking time
Cooking time: about 2½ hours
Serves: 4

Imperial/Metric	**American**
4 sheep's tongues	4 lamb tongues
1 stick celery	1 stalk celery
1 carrot	1 carrot
1 onion	1 onion
½ turnip	½ turnip
1 oz./25 g. butter	2 tablespoons butter
½ bay leaf	½ bay leaf
1 sprig thyme	1 sprig thyme
1 sprig parsley	1 sprig parsley
6 peppercorns	6 peppercorns
½ pint/3 dl. stock	1¼ cups stock
1 rasher bacon	1 bacon slice

Soak the tongues in salted water for 2 hours. Drain and place in a saucepan. Cover with cold water, then bring to the boil. Drain and dry. Cut celery, carrot, onion and turnip into slices and place in the bottom of a pan. Add butter, herbs and peppercorns. Arrange tongues on top, then pour in stock. Remove the rind from bacon rasher and chop finely, then sprinkle on top of tongues. Cover with a greased paper, then with a lid. Simmer very gently until tongues are tender, about 2½ hours. Remove tongues from pan. Skin and cut in half and serve on a bed of mashed potatoes or buttered spinach.

Devilled sheep's kidneys

Main utensils: frying pan (preferably non-stick)
Preparation time: few minutes
Cooking time: about 5 minutes
Serves: 2

Imperial/Metric	**American**
2 sheep's kidneys	2 lamb kidneys
2 oz./50 g. butter or margarine, melted	¼ cup butter or margarine, melted
¼ teaspoon curry powder	¼ teaspoon curry powder
1 teaspoon French mustard	1 teaspoon French mustard
1 teaspoon Worcestershire sauce	1 teaspoon Worcestershire sauce
salt and cayenne pepper	salt and cayenne pepper

Skin the kidneys. Split but do not halve, and remove the cores. Dip in melted butter or margarine. Mix the curry powder, mustard, Worcestershire sauce and salt and cayenne pepper to taste with enough melted butter to make a paste. Spread the paste all over the kidneys. Heat the remaining butter in a frying pan and fry the kidneys for 2–3 minutes, on the cut side, then turn and fry on the other side for 2–3 minutes.

Lambs' kidneys in piquant yogurt sauce

Main utensil: saucepan (preferably non-stick)
Preparation time: 5 minutes
Cooking time: about 20 minutes
Serves: 4

Imperial/Metric	**American**
8 lambs' kidneys	8 lamb kidneys
¼ pint/1½ dl. beef stock	⅔ cup beef stock
4 oz./100 g. mushrooms, sliced	1 cup sliced mushrooms
1 tablespoon tomato purée	1 tablespoon tomato paste
2 teaspoons prepared English mustard	2 teaspoons prepared English mustard
1 carton natural yogurt	1 carton unflavored yogurt
salt and pepper to taste	salt and pepper to taste
1 tablespoon chopped parsley	1 tablespoon chopped parsley

Skin the kidneys, cut them in half and remove the cores. Place in the pan with the stock, mushrooms and tomato purée. Cook, covered, for 20 minutes, or until tender. Stir in the mustard and yogurt. Reheat (but do not boil) and season to taste. Sprinkle with parsley before serving.

Sweetbreads à la poulette

Main utensils: saucepan, frying pan with lid (preferably non-stick)
Preparation time: 30 minutes, plus blanching time for sweetbreads
Cooking time: 10–15 minutes
Serves: 4–5

Imperial/Metric	**American**
1 pair sweetbreads	1 pair sweetbreads
1 oz./25 g. butter	2 tablespoons butter
1 onion, chopped	1 onion, chopped
4 oz./100 g. mushrooms, chopped	1 cup chopped mushrooms
1 teaspoon chopped parsley	1 teaspoon chopped parsley
salt and pepper	salt and pepper
1 tablespoon flour	1 tablespoon all-purpose flour
about ½ pint/3 dl. stock or water	1 cup stock or water

To prepare sweetbreads, wash them and soak in cold water for 1 hour, then wash again. Place in a saucepan, cover with cold water and bring to the boil, then cool slightly and remove the skin. Bring to the boil again and simmer for 30 minutes. Melt the butter in a saucepan. Add the onion, mushrooms, parsley and seasoning to taste. Place the drained sweetbreads on top. Sprinkle in the flour and add the stock or water. Stirring, bring to the boil; lower the heat, cover and cook slowly until the mushrooms and onion are tender. Serve with tomato sauce (see page 58) and garnish with baked pastry shapes.

Haggis

Main utensil: saucepan (preferably non-stick)
Preparation time: 25 minutes
Cooking time: 4–5 hours
Serves: 4–6

Imperial/Metric	**American**
stomach bag of sheep	stomach bag of sheep
sheep's heart, lights and liver	sheep's heart, lights and liver
8 oz./225 g. mutton suet	½ lb. mutton suet
3 onions	3 onions
1 lb./450 g. oatmeal	2½ cups oatmeal
salt and pepper	salt and pepper

Wash the bag clean with cold water, then turn it inside out. Scald and scrape it with a knife, then steep in salted water until required. Parboil heart, lights and liver, then mince finely together with the suet. Parboil and chop the onions. Toast the oatmeal to expand during cooking and add a little of the water in which the onions were boiled. Stuff the bag with the prepared heart etc., onions and oatmeal. Sew up the bag then prick all over with a long needle to prevent it bursting. Place on a plate in a saucepan with enough boiling water to cover. Cover and boil for 4–5 hours, keeping the haggis covered with boiling water all the time. After cooking, the haggis can be hung in a dry place until required. To serve, boil the haggis again, but only long enough to make it piping hot. Serve with well seasoned mashed potatoes enriched with milk and butter, and a glass of Scotch whisky.
Note: Some cooks omit the onions and only use the water in which onions have been boiled for flavouring.

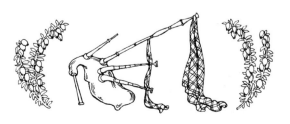

Raised pies

Veal and ham pie

Main utensils: pie mould (optional), baking tray (preferably non-stick)
Preparation time: 30 minutes, not including making the pastry
Oven temperature: hot (425°F., 220°C., Gas Mark 7) then moderate (350°F., 180°C., Gas Mark 4)
Cooking time: 1 hour 50 minutes
Serves: 6

Imperial/Metric	American
1 lb./450 g. hot water crust pastry (see page 109)	1 lb. hot water crust pastry (see page 109)
12 oz./350 g. pie veal	¾ lb. boneless pie veal
4 oz./100 g. raw ham	¼ lb. uncooked ham
juice and grated rind of 1 lemon	juice and grated rind of 1 lemon
1 tablespoon chopped parsley	1 tablespoon chopped parsley
salt and pepper	salt and pepper
stock or water	stock or water
2 hard-boiled eggs	2 hard-cooked eggs
beaten egg to glaze	beaten egg to glaze
Jelly:	*Jelly:*
1 tablespoon gelatine	1 tablespoon gelatin
½ pint/3 dl. chicken stock	1¼ cups chicken stock

Make the pastry case in the raised pie mould as shown in step by step pictures. (If you have no pie mould see line drawings opposite on how to make a mould by hand.) Trim the veal, and cut into small pieces; chop the ham into small pieces. Put the meat in a bowl and mix with the juice and rind of the lemon, the chopped parsley, seasoning and add a little stock or water. Place half this mixture in the pastry mould then place the hard-boiled eggs in the centre with a little space between and cover with the remaining meat. Cover with the pastry lid and decorate with pastry trimmings as shown in the pictures. Glaze the top of the pie with a little beaten egg and bake in the centre of the preheated oven for 20 minutes then reduce heat to moderate and continue cooking for 1½ hours, when the meat should be tender when tested with a skewer. Remove the pie from the oven and make up the jelly by dissolving the gelatine with the stock. Pour into the pie through the centre hole. Allow the pie to cool before serving.

Variations

Pork pie Substitute 1½ lb. (¾ kg.) lean pork for the veal. Omit the lemon and ham and add a little chopped sage with the parsley, if liked.
Game pie (Illustrated on page 69) Substitute 1 lb. (½ kg.) cooked game (pheasant, grouse, snipe, partridge, wild duck, woodcock, hare or rabbit) for the meat. Retain the ham for extra flavour; cook for about 1¼ hours.
Poultry pie Use chicken or turkey in place of the veal.
❄ Raised pies freeze successfully for short periods, but are really better eaten fresh.

Prepare the filling for the pie by chopping the cooked game into small pieces. Use some ham as well for extra flavour.

To make the hot water crust pastry, sieve the flour and salt into a bowl. Place the lard and water in a saucepan and bring gradually to the boil, then pour into the flour mixture. Beat the mixture with a wooden spoon until it clings together.

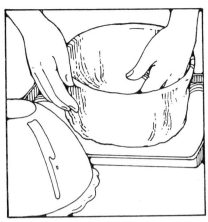

Mould the hot water crust pastry, on a baking tray, into the shape of a hollowed out shell.

Cut a double thickness of greaseproof paper, the height of the sides, and secure it around the outside of the pie. Fill the pie with the chosen filling.

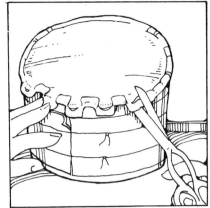

Brush the edges with water. Roll out the reserved pastry for the lid and fit into position, pressing the two edges together. Cut the rim at $\frac{1}{2}$-inch (1-cm.) intervals and fold down the alternate pieces to give a finished edge.

To shape a raised pie by hand

1 Cut off a quarter of the pastry and cover it over to use for the lid. (Raised pie pastry must be kept warm so that it can be moulded easily.)

2 Mould the remaining pastry, on a baking tray, into the shape of a hollowed out shell. Although soft at first, when cold the pastry will firm to hold the shape.

3 Cut a double thickness of greaseproof paper the height of the sides and secure around the outside to help hold the shape. Fill the pie as directed in the recipe.

4 Damp the uneven edges to form a rim and roll out the pastry which has been set aside for a lid, place on top of the pie and press two edges together to form a rim.

5 Cut the rim at $\frac{1}{2}$-inch (1-cm.) intervals and fold down alternate pieces to make an edge. Make a hole in the centre. Pastry trimmings can be used to make a rose (using a skewer, see drawings) or leaves to decorate the top of the pie.

Alternatively, you can use a loose-bottomed 7-inch (19-cm.) cake tin.

Cut off some of the pastry for a lid and keep it warm under an upturned basin. Place the pastry in the pie mould and, with your hands, work it up the sides of the mould until it lines the mould evenly. Bring the pastry up a little higher than the mould so that the extra can be turned over the filling.

Fill the lined mould with the prepared filling, roll out the reserved pastry for a lid. Dampen the turned-in pastry and put the lid in position. Make a hole in the centre and pinch the edges. Make leaves from the pastry trimmings and put in position. Glaze with beaten egg before baking.

Spanish meat loaf

Main utensils: mincer, 1-lb. (½-kg.)
loaf tin (preferably non-stick)
Preparation time: 20 minutes
Oven temperature: moderate
(350°F., 180°C., Gas Mark 4)
Cooking time: 30 minutes
Serves: 6

Imperial/Metric
2 rashers bacon
8 oz./225 g. cooked meat, chopped
1 small onion
2 oz./50 g. soft breadcrumbs
¼ pint/1½ dl. milk
1 teaspoon mixed herbs
½ teaspoon salt
pinch paprika pepper
ground black pepper
pinch celery salt
¼ pint/1½ dl. water
4 oz./100 g. cooked long-grain rice
1 small can tomatoes
1 oz./25 g. butter

American
2 bacon slices
1 cup chopped cooked meat
1 small onion
1 cup fresh soft bread crumbs
⅔ cup milk
1 teaspoon mixed herbs
½ teaspoon salt
pinch paprika pepper
ground black pepper
pinch celery salt
⅔ cup water
scant 1 cup cooked long-grain rice
1 small can tomatoes
2 tablespoons butter

Put the bacon and meat through a mincer. Soak the breadcrumbs in the milk, then add the minced meat together with herbs, salt, paprika, black pepper and celery salt to taste. Stir in the water. Turn the mixture into the loaf tin. Spread the top with cooked rice and pour over the sieved tomatoes. Dot with small knobs of the butter and cook in the centre of the preheated oven for about 30 minutes.

Soak the cabbage leaves in hot water to soften them.

Place a portion of filling in centre of each leaf and form into a neat parcel.

Pour liquidised sauce over the cabbage rolls.

Cabbage blankets

Main utensils: casserole dish,
liquidiser (optional)
Preparation time: about 25 minutes
Oven temperature: moderate
(325°F., 170°C., Gas Mark 3)
Cooking time: 1½ hours
Serves: 4

Imperial/Metric
8 oz./225 g. lean pork
8 oz./225 g. lean beef
1 onion
salt and pepper
2 oz./50 g. cooked long-grain rice
8 large cabbage leaves
Tomato sauce:
1 15-oz./425-g. can tomatoes
2 tablespoons vinegar
¼ teaspoon mixed herbs
few drops Tabasco sauce
¼ pint/1½ dl. water
1 teaspoon sugar

American
½ lb. lean pork
½ lb. lean beef
1 onion
salt and pepper
scant ½ cup long-grain rice
8 large cabbage leaves
Tomato sauce:
1 15-oz. can tomatoes
3 tablespoons vinegar
¼ teaspoon mixed herbs
few drops Tabasco sauce
⅔ cup water
1 teaspoon sugar

Chop the meat and onion finely, or mince it and place in a bowl with the seasoning and rice; mix the ingredients together. Soak the cabbage leaves in hot water to soften. Divide filling into eight and place one portion on each cabbage leaf. Form the cabbage leaves into neat parcels, tie with fine string and place in an ovenproof dish. Liquidise or sieve the tomatoes, add the other ingredients and pour over the cabbage parcels. Cover and cook in the centre of a preheated oven for about 1½ hours.

❄ These cabbage parcels can be frozen uncooked. Place the parcels and sauce in a foil tray. Cover, seal and label; cook from frozen state, allowing 30 minutes' extra cooking time.

Note: The stuffing for the cabbage leaves can be varied by using half rice and half breadcrumbs and binding it with a little beaten egg.

Veal birds

Main utensil: saucepan
(preferably non-stick)
Preparation time: 20 minutes
Cooking time: 10 minutes
Serves: 6

Imperial/Metric
8 oz./225 g. veal, minced
4 tablespoons white breadcrumbs
¼ pint/1½ dl. double cream
1 egg yolk
salt and pepper
1 cucumber
6 veal escalopes
3 tablespoons oil
1 oz./25 g. butter
Garnish:
parsley

American
1 cup ground veal
5 tablespoons fresh soft bread crumbs
⅔ cup whipping cream
1 egg yolk
salt and pepper
1 cucumber
6 veal scallops
4 tablespoons oil
2 tablespoons butter
Garnish:
parsley

Mix the minced veal, breadcrumbs, half the cream and the egg yolk in a bowl. Season with salt and pepper. Prepare the cucumber by peeling and cubing. Blanch in boiling water for 3–4 minutes, then drain.

Flatten the veal escalopes (or ask the butcher to do this for you). Divide the stuffing between the veal slices, roll up and secure with string or wooden cocktail sticks. Heat the oil and butter in a saucepan and fry the veal rolls until golden brown on all sides. Add the cucumber, reduce the heat, cover and simmer for 20 minutes. Place veal rolls on a serving dish and keep warm. Reduce the juices left in the pan by boiling in the open pan. Stir in the remaining cream and spoon the cream and cucumber sauce over the veal rolls. Garnish with parsley sprigs.

Variations
The veal birds may be stuffed with any of the following: Sausagemeat mixed with a pinch of tarragon and a little finely chopped onion. Garnish with sieved hard-boiled egg yolk.

Cooked long-grain rice mixed with small pieces of chicken, pimento, onion and crushed garlic.

Minced ham mixed with chopped asparagus. Garnish with asparagus tips.

Mushrooms with veal chops

Main utensils: frying pan,
flameproof casserole (preferably non-stick)
Preparation time: 5 minutes
Oven temperature: moderate (350°F., 180°C., Gas Mark 4)
Cooking time: about 20 minutes
Serves: 4

Imperial/Metric
4 veal chops
salt and pepper
1 teaspoon flour
4 tablespoons oil
1½ oz./40 g. butter
2 cloves garlic, crushed
10 oz./300 g. mushrooms
1 tablespoon brandy (optional)
2 tablespoons white wine or stock
3 tablespoons double cream
3 tablespoons chopped parsley

American
4 veal chops
salt and pepper
1 teaspoon flour
⅓ cup oil
3 tablespoons butter
2 cloves garlic, crushed
about 2 cups mushrooms
1 tablespoon brandy (optional)
3 tablespoons white wine or stock
4 tablespoons whipping cream
4 tablespoons chopped parsley

Sprinkle the veal chops with salt and pepper and dust with flour. Heat half the oil in a frying pan and sauté the chops for 3–4 minutes. Put the remaining oil and the butter in a flameproof casserole. Slice the mushrooms thickly, add to the casserole and sauté gently. Add the veal chops, pour over the heated brandy (if used) and ignite.

Add the wine or stock, cover and cook in a preheated moderate oven for about 20 minutes, depending on the thickness of the chops. Remove the chops to a serving dish, add the cream to the casserole and mix with the mushrooms. Pour over the chops and serve sprinkled with chopped parsley.

Poultry and game

To spit roast chicken (Illustrated opposite)

Place a chicken (or duck) evenly on the spit. Make sure it is well trussed as you want to avoid loose drumsticks or wings as this is when they tend to burn. If spit roasting more than one bird put the two birds on the spit the same way. (See line drawings of birds on spit.) It very often adds to the flavour, especially of frozen birds, to marinate them before cooking and then paint them with the marinade as they cook. Put some butter inside the chicken before cooking.

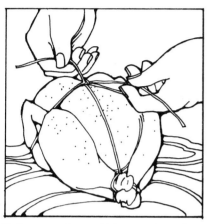

Before securing a chicken on the spit make sure it is well trussed to avoid loose drumsticks or wings which will tend to burn under the spit.

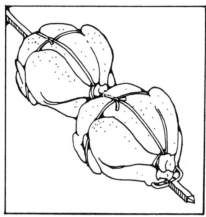

Secure the chicken with the weight evenly distributed to ensure that the spit can rotate. If roasting two small birds together put them on the spit the same way.

To improve the flavour of chicken it helps to brush it over with a marinade before and during spit roasting.

Marinade for chicken (Illustrated opposite)

Main utensil: liquidiser
Preparation time: few minutes

Imperial/Metric
1 small can tomatoes
$\frac{1}{4}$ pint/$1\frac{1}{2}$ dl. white wine
juice of $\frac{1}{2}$ lemon
few drops Worcestershire sauce
salt and pepper
1 clove garlic
1 small onion, chopped
few sprigs rosemary
1 bay leaf

American
1 small can tomatoes
$\frac{2}{3}$ cup white wine
juice of $\frac{1}{2}$ lemon
few drops Worcestershire sauce
salt and pepper
1 clove garlic
1 small onion, chopped
few sprigs rosemary
1 bay leaf

Blend the ingredients (except the herbs) in the liquidiser. Place the chicken to be marinated in a polythene bag and pour in the liquidised marinade. Add the herbs and secure the neck of the bag with a twist tie. Leave in the refrigerator for a few hours, or overnight.

Remove the chicken from the marinade and secure it on the spit. Spit roast, brushing the chicken with the marinade from time to time.

Spit roasting a whole, marinated chicken (see above)

Make the marinade for the chicken by blending the ingredients (except the herbs) in the liquidiser.

Place the chicken in a polythene bag and pour in the liquidised marinade. Add the herbs and secure the neck of the bag with a twist tie. Leave to marinate in the refrigerator for a few hours, or overnight.

Remove the chicken from the marinade and secure on the spit. Use the marinade to brush the chicken with while it is cooking on the spit.

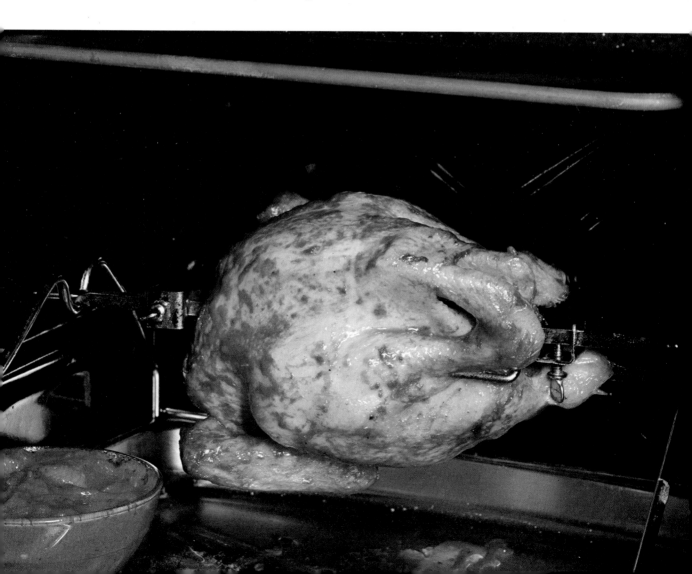

Chicken tandoori

Main utensil: roasting tin (preferably non-stick), skewers or a wire tray
Preparation time: 5 minutes, plus marinating time
Oven temperature: moderate (350°F., 160°C., Gas Mark 4)
Cooking time: 1½ hours
Serves: 4

Imperial/Metric	American
4 chicken quarters, skinned	4 chicken quarters, skinned
Marinade:	*Marinade:*
2 cartons natural yogurt	2 cartons unflavored yogurt
½ teaspoon ground ginger	½ teaspoon ground ginger
1 tablespoon paprika pepper	1 tablespoon paprika pepper
½ teaspoon garlic powder or 1 clove garlic, crushed	½ teaspoon garlic powder or 1 clove garlic, crushed
4 bay leaves	4 bay leaves
6 peppercorns	6 peppercorns
1 tablespoon tomato purée	1 tablespoon tomato paste
grated zest of 1 lemon	grated zest of 1 lemon
1 teaspoon salt	1 teaspoon salt
Garnish:	*Garnish:*
parsley sprigs	parsley sprigs

To make the marinade, place the yogurt in a bowl, add all the other ingredients and mix well. Add the chicken, making sure that the quarters are all completely covered with marinade. Cover tightly with foil and leave in the refrigerator for 5–6 hours, or overnight. Remove the bay leaves. Place the chicken on a wire rack in a roasting tin. (Alternatively, the chicken may be skewered and the ends of the skewers rested on the sides of the tin.) Brush each joint with the remaining marinade and cook in a preheated moderate oven for 1½ hours, basting from time to time with the marinade. Remove and serve on an oval dish, garnish with parsley and serve with a selection of salads or with green vegetables.

Chicken Marengo

Main utensils: frying pan, casserole dish (preferably non-stick)
Preparation time: 15 minutes
Oven temperature: moderate (350°F., 180°C., Gas Mark 4)
Cooking time: about 1 hour
Serves: 4

Imperial/Metric	American
3 ripe tomatoes	3 ripe tomatoes
1 oz./25 g. flour	¼ cup all-purpose flour
1½ teaspoons salt	1½ teaspoons salt
¼ teaspoon pepper	¼ teaspoon pepper
2 large or 4 medium chicken breasts	2 large or 4 medium chicken breasts
2 oz./50 g. butter	¼ cup butter
2 cloves garlic	2 cloves garlic
12 button mushrooms	12 button mushrooms
about ¾ pint white wine	1½ cups white wine
3 tablespoons brandy	scant ¼ cup brandy
¼ teaspoon thyme	¼ teaspoon thyme
sprig parsley	sprig parsley
1 bay leaf	1 bay leaf
Garnish:	*Garnish:*
chopped parsley	chopped parsley

Place the tomatoes in a bowl of boiling water for a few seconds; then remove them and peel off their skins. Cut into quarters. Blend the flour, salt and pepper together and use to coat the chicken breasts. Heat the butter in a frying pan and brown the chicken breasts on both sides; transfer to a casserole and chop the garlic finely and slice the mushrooms. Add the garlic to the casserole with the tomatoes, wine, brandy, thyme, parsley and bay leaf. Cover and cook in the centre of the preheated moderate oven for 30–40 minutes, turning the chicken breasts over halfway through the cooking time. Add the mushrooms and cook for a further 15 minutes. Remove the bay leaf and parsley sprig before serving garnished with chopped parsley.

Savoury chicken

Main utensils: frying pan with a lid
(preferably non-stick)
Preparation time: 10 minutes
Cooking time: 20 minutes
Serves: 4

Imperial/Metric
4 chicken breasts
2 oz./50 g. butter
1 clove garlic
3 teaspoons French mustard
1 tablespoon tomato purée
2 tablespoons white wine
4 tablespoons wine vinegar
2 tablespoons double cream
1 tablespoon Worcestershire sauce
salt and pepper

American
4 chicken breasts
¼ cup butter
1 clove garlic
3 teaspoons French mustard
1 tablespoon tomato paste
3 tablespoons white wine
⅓ cup wine vinegar
3 tablespoons whipping cream
1 tablespoon Worcestershire sauce
salt and pepper

Cut the chicken breasts into eight pieces, removing the bone and cook in the butter in a covered frying pan with the peeled garlic. Mix the mustard, tomato purée and white wine together with salt and pepper. When the chicken is cooked and golden brown, add the vinegar and cook until the pan is almost dry. Remove the chicken and keep warm on a serving dish. Pour the mixed mustard and tomato purée into a frying pan and reduce without covering the pan. Stir in the cream and Worcestershire sauce, then pour the sauce over the chicken just before serving.

Scottish hare pie

Main utensil: pie dish
Preparation time: 25 minutes, not
including making the pastry
Oven temperature: moderate
(350°F., 180°C., Gas Mark 4) then
hot (450°F., 230°C., Gas Mark 8)
Cooking time: 65 minutes
Serves: 4–6

Imperial/Metric
2 hind legs of hare
seasoned flour
8 oz./225 g. pork sausagemeat
4 thin bacon rashers
1 oz./25 g. chopped bacon
3 oz./75 g. browned breadcrumbs
1 tablespoon chopped onion
1 teaspoon crushed herbs
salt and celery salt to taste
paprika pepper and pepper to taste
1 egg, beaten
stock
8 oz./225 g. puff pastry (page 108)

American
2 hind legs of hare
seasoned flour
1 cup pork sausagemeat
4 thin slices bacon
2 tablespoons chopped bacon
generous ½ cup dry bread crumbs
1 tablespoon chopped onion
1 teaspoon crushed herbs
salt and celery salt to taste
paprika pepper and pepper to taste
1 egg, beaten
stock
½ lb. puff pastry (see page 108)

Remove the meat from the joints of hare and coat it in seasoned flour. Place in a pie dish with a pie funnel in the centre. With floured hands, shape the sausagemeat into marble-sized balls; form the bacon rashers into rolls and place, with the sausagemeat balls, in the pie dish. Mix together the chopped bacon, browned breadcrumbs, chopped onion, herbs and seasonings and moisten with a little of the beaten egg. Roll into small balls and place in the pie dish with the other ingredients. Pour in stock to come three-quarters of the way up the pie dish. Cover with foil and cook in the centre of a preheated moderate oven for 45 minutes, then remove and allow to cool. Increase the oven temperature to hot.

Roll out the pastry and use to cover the top of the pie (see page 109). Glaze with the remaining egg and bake near the top of the preheated hot oven for 20 minutes, until the pastry is golden brown and the filling hot.

Gipsy stew

Main utensils: frying pan,
flameproof casserole (preferably
non-stick)
Preparation time: 15 minutes
Cooking time: 2 hours
Serves: 4–5

Imperial/Metric
1 large rabbit
8 rashers bacon
2 tablespoons oil
seasoned flour
4 small potatoes
2 small onions
¾ pint/4½ dl. stock or water

American
1 large rabbit
8 bacon slices
3 tablespoons oil
seasoned flour
4 small potatoes
2 small onions
scant 2 cups stock or water

Cut the rabbit into joints. Fry the bacon in the oil until lightly brown, then remove from the pan. Dip the rabbit joints in flour seasoned with salt and pepper, then fry in the bacon fat and oil until brown all over. Place the joints in a flameproof casserole, in alternate layers, with the bacon, sliced potatoes and sliced onions. Dredge with a little flour. Add the stock or water. Cover and simmer for 2 hours.
❊ This dish freezes well. Check the seasoning on reheating.

A guide to vegetables and salads

It is now possible to buy a wide selection of vegetables throughout the year and, for freezer owners, the choice of vegetables, from freezer food centres and other outlets is enormous. Vegetables should be treated with reverence—the Continental cook lavishes care and attention on her vegetables to produce such delights as ratatouille and fennel au gratin.

Remember not to overcook vegetables—there is nothing more distressing than to see a dish of soggy cabbage or cauliflower. For the best results cook vegetables in the minimum amount of boiling salted water until *just* tender. They can also be cooked slowly in butter and oil in a fairly deep frying pan.

Most herbs blend well with vegetables—basil and tarragon with tomatoes, savory with broad beans, chervil, chives, garlic, marjoram, mint, sorrel and tarragon can all be used in salads.

The following chart gives preparation and cooking instructions for most vegetables and blanching times for freezing vegetables. If you own a freezer and grow your own vegetables, or can buy them at a reasonable price when they are in season and in good condition, it is certainly worth freezing them down—the flavour of home-frozen vegetables is really out of this world!

The types of salads which can be served are endless and there is more to a salad than a few lettuce leaves, chunks of cucumber and squashy tomatoes. Mayonnaise and dressings do a lot to enliven a salad and it's always a good idea to have a bottle of French dressing ready mixed in the store cupboard; making mayonnaise in a liquidiser is no trouble at all and it's so much better (and cheaper) than the bottled variety.

Vegetable	Preparation	Cooking time in boiling salted water	Blanching time for freezing
Asparagus	Wash, trim and tie in bundles.	10–15 minutes. Serve with hollandaise sauce (see page 44).	3 minutes
Aubergines	Slice thinly, sprinkle with salt; rinse, drain and dry after 30 minutes.	Cook slices in butter and oil for about 20 minutes. Serve with soured cream.	4 minutes
Avocados	Halve and remove stone. Serve with French dressing (see page 90).		To freeze, purée the flesh and add lemon juice and seasoning.
Broad beans	Pod	15–20 minutes. Serve with parsley sauce (see page 92).	3 minutes
Runner beans	Remove strings and slice.	10–15 minutes	2 minutes
Broccoli	Trim and break into spears.	10–15 minutes. Serve sprinkled with freshly grated nutmeg.	4 minutes
Brussels sprouts	Trim and cut a cross in the base of each.	10–15 minutes	4 minutes
Cabbage	Trim and shred.	10 minutes	1½ minutes
Carrots	Trim, scrape and slice (baby carrots can be cooked whole).	15–20 minutes	4 minutes

Vegetable	Preparation	Cooking time in boiling salted water	Blanching time for freezing
Cauliflower	Trim and break into sprigs.	10–15 minutes. Serve with a béchamel or cheese sauce (see page 92).	3 minutes
Celery	Trim and cut into short lengths.	10 minutes. Serve with a sprinkling of nutmeg and a béchamel sauce (see page 92).	3 minutes
Celeriac	Trim and slice.	10–15 minutes. Serve with a parsley or cheese sauce (see page 92).	2 minutes
Chicory	Remove outer leaves and blanch in boiling water.	15–20 minutes	Unsuitable for freezing
Corn-on-the-cob	Remove leaves and silks.	20–25 minutes. Serve with ground black pepper and melted butter.	5 minutes for medium-sized ones.
Courgettes	Slice	Cook in melted butter for 15–20 minutes.	1 minute
Fennel	Trim and halve.	25–30 minutes	3 minutes
Globe artichokes	Remove outer leaves.	Add 1 teaspoon lemon juice to the cooking water – 25–30 minutes. Serve with melted butter or French dressing (see page 90).	10 minutes
Jerusalem artichokes	Peel and place in water with lemon juice or vinegar added.	Simmer for 10–15 minutes.	Freeze as a purée.
Leeks	Trim and slice. Wash well.	10–15 minutes. Serve with a béchamel sauce (see page 92).	2 minutes
Marrow	Peel, slice and remove seeds.	10–15 minutes.	3 minutes
Parsnips	Trim, peel and slice. (Leave small ones whole.)	15–20 minutes, or boil for 5 minutes, drain and roast round a joint of beef.	2 minutes
Peas	Shell	10–15 minutes. Add a sprig of mint and sugar, if liked, to the boiling water.	1 minute
Spinach	Wash well.	Cook *without* water in a non-stick pan over medium heat for 10–15 minutes. Sprinkle with grated nutmeg.	2 minutes

Fennel au gratin

Main utensil: saucepan
(preferably non-stick)
Preparation time: 20 minutes,
including blanching time
Cooking time: about 20 minutes
Serves: 4

Imperial/Metric
4 fennel bulbs
2 oz./50 g. butter
1 oz./25 g. flour
½ pint/3 dl. milk
salt and pepper
2 oz./50 g. Cheddar cheese, grated
2 tablespoons dried breadcrumbs

American
4 fennel bulbs
¼ cup butter
¼ cup all-purpose flour
1¼ cups milk
salt and pepper
½ cup grated Cheddar cheese
3 tablespoons dry bread crumbs

Trim the outer leaves from the fennel and blanch the bulbs in boiling salted water for 10 minutes. Drain, dry on absorbent paper and cut into quarters. Melt the butter in a saucepan and sauté the fennel for 15–20 minutes, until tender. Remove, place in an ovenproof dish and keep hot. Stir the flour into the fat remaining in the pan and cook for 2–3 minutes, stirring. Remove from the heat and gradually stir in the milk. Return to the heat and bring to the boil, stirring; cook for 1–2 minutes. Stir in the seasoning and half the cheese and allow it to melt. Pour the sauce over the fennel, sprinkle with the remaining cheese and the breadcrumbs. Brown under a hot grill and serve.

Sweet-sour beans

Main utensils: saucepan, frying pan
(preferably non-stick)
Preparation time: 10 minutes
Serves: 4

Imperial/Metric
1 lb./½ kg. French or runner beans
4 rashers back bacon
1 onion, chopped
1 tablespoon wine vinegar
1 tablespoon castor sugar
ground black pepper

American
1 lb. green beans
4 rashers Canadian-style bacon
1 onion, chopped
1 tablespoon wine vinegar
1 tablespoon granulated sugar
ground black pepper

Prepare the beans and cook in boiling salted water until just tender. Rind the bacon and chop it finely. Place it in a frying pan over a low heat and cook until the fat runs out, then add the chopped onion and cook until the bacon is crisp and the onion softened. Drain the beans (reserve the cooking liquid) and mix with the bacon and onion; place in a serving dish. To the frying pan add the vinegar, sugar, black pepper and ½ pint (3 dl.) of the bean liquid. Bring to the boil, stirring and mixing in any juices in the pan. Pour over the beans and serve.

Ratatouille (Illustrated opposite)

Main utensil: frying pan
(preferably non-stick)
Preparation time: 15 minutes, not
including time for salting the
aubergines
Cooking time: about 30 minutes
Serves: 5–6

Imperial/Metric
3 medium aubergines
salt
3 tablespoons oil
3 onions, sliced
1 clove garlic, crushed
1 green pepper, seeded and sliced

1 red pepper, seeded and sliced

4 courgettes, sliced
6 ripe tomatoes, skinned and sliced
black pepper
pinch basil
Garnish:
chopped parsley

American
3 medium eggplants
salt
scant ¼ cup oil
3 onions, sliced
1 clove garlic, crushed
1 green sweet pepper, seeded and
sliced
1 red sweet pepper, seeded and
sliced
4 zucchini, sliced
6 ripe tomatoes, skinned and sliced
black pepper
pinch basil
Garnish:
chopped parsley

Slice the aubergines and arrange the slices in a shallow dish. Sprinkle with salt and leave aside for 30 minutes. Rinse thoroughly and dry on absorbent paper.

Heat the oil in a frying pan and add the prepared onions, garlic and peppers. Fry over a moderate heat to soften the vegetables, but do not allow them to brown. Add the aubergines, courgettes, tomatoes, seasoning and basil. Cover and cook gently for about 20 minutes. Turn into a serving dish and serve sprinkled with chopped parsley.

❊ Ratatouille can be frozen, but omit the garlic for freezing and add it at the reheating stage.

Ratatouille (see above)

Ratatouille is a vegetable dish containing aubergines, peppers, tomatoes, garlic, onions and courgettes cooked together in olive oil.

Slice the aubergines thinly and spread out on a plate; sprinkle with salt and leave aside. After 30 minutes, rinse away the salt and dry the aubergine slices – this removes the bitter flavour from the aubergines. Skin the tomatoes by placing them in a bowl and pouring over boiling water.

The prepared vegetables are cooked in olive oil in a frying pan until softened. Season well with salt and freshly ground black pepper.

Baked jacket potatoes

Main utensil: roasting tin
(preferably non-stick)
Preparation time: few minutes
Oven temperature: moderately hot
(375°F., 190°C., Gas Mark 5)
Cooking time: about 1 hour
Serves: 4

Imperial/Metric
4 medium potatoes
oil

American
4 medium potatoes
oil

Scrub the potatoes, prick with a fork and rub lightly with oil. Place in a roasting tin and cook in the centre of the moderately hot oven until cooked (about 1 hour).

Cut a cross on top of each potato and press together. Serve with soured cream and chive dressing (see page 92).

Alternatively, the potatoes can be halved, the cooked potato scooped out into a basin and mixed with grated cheese, cottage cheese, chopped ham or cooked bacon and seasoning and spooned back into the potato cases. Dot with butter and reheat in the oven for a few minutes.

Cream-baked potatoes

Main utensil: shallow ovenproof
dish
Preparation time: 10 minutes
Oven temperature: moderate
(325°F., 170°C., Gas Mark 3)
Cooking time: about 1 hour
Serves: 4

Imperial/Metric
1½ lb./about ¾ kg. potatoes
2 oz./50 g. butter
1 clove garlic, crushed
salt and pepper
pinch ground nutmeg
2 oz./50 g. Cheddar or Gruyère
cheese, grated
½ pint/3 dl. single cream
Garnish:
chopped chives

American
1½ lb. potatoes
¼ cup butter
1 clove garlic, crushed
salt and pepper
pinch ground nutmeg
½ cup grated Cheddar or Gruyère
cheese
1¼ cups coffee cream
Garnish:
chopped chives

Peel the potatoes and cut into wafer thin slices. Dry on absorbent paper and arrange in layers with the butter, melted and mixed with the garlic, the seasonings and the grated cheese in a shallow ovenproof dish. Pour over the cream and bake in the top of a preheated moderate oven for about 1 hour, until the potatoes are soft and the top golden brown. Garnish with chopped chives and serve from the dish.

Cauliflower polonaise

Main utensils: saucepan, frying
pan (preferably non-stick)
Preparation time: few minutes
Cooking time: 10–15 minutes
Serves: 4

Imperial/Metric
1 cauliflower
2 tablespoons fresh breadcrumbs
2 oz./50 g. butter
Garnish:
1 hard-boiled egg yolk
chopped parsley

American
1 cauliflower
3 tablespoons fresh bread crumbs
¼ cup butter
Garnish:
1 hard-cooked egg yolk
chopped parsley

Prepare the cauliflower and break into sprigs. Cook in boiling salted water (with some of the young green leaves added) until *just* tender. Meanwhile cook the breadcrumbs in the heated butter until golden brown. Drain the cauli-flower and place in a serving dish. Pour over the butter and crumbs and serve sprinkled with the sieved egg yolk and chopped parsley.

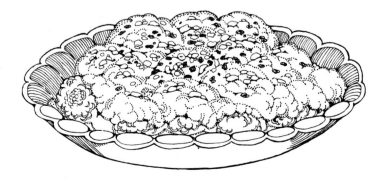

Celery and ham au gratin

Main utensil: ovenproof dish
Preparation time: 10 minutes
Oven temperature: moderately hot
(375°F., 190°C., Gas Mark 5)
Cooking time: 20 minutes
Serves: 4

Imperial/Metric
1 large can celery hearts
4 slices cooked ham
½ pint/3 dl. cheese sauce (see page 92)
2 tablespoons grated Parmesan cheese
few browned breadcrumbs

American
1 large can celery hearts
4 slices cooked ham
1¼ cups cheese sauce (see page 92)

3 tablespoons grated Parmesan cheese
few dry bread crumbs

Butter an ovenproof dish. Drain the celery hearts and wrap a piece of ham around each celery heart; secure with a wooden cocktail stick, if necessary, and place in the ovenproof dish. Pour over the cheese sauce, sprinkle with the Parmesan cheese and cook in a preheated moderately hot oven for 20 minutes. Sprinkle the top with breadcrumbs and brown under a hot grill.

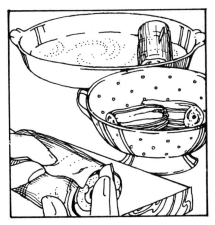

Wrap a piece of ham around each drained celery heart and secure with a wooden cocktail stick. Place in a greased ovenproof dish.

Pour over the cheese sauce.

Sprinkle over the Parmesan cheese and cook in a moderately hot oven for 20 minutes. Top with the breadcrumbs and brown under a hot grill.

Spiced red cabbage

Main utensils: frying pan
(preferably non-stick), ovenproof dish
Preparation time: 10 minutes
Oven temperature: moderate
(350°F., 180°C., Gas Mark 4)
Cooking time: about 45 minutes
Serves: 4

Imperial/Metric
1 small red cabbage
2 oz./50 g. butter
1 onion, chopped
2 cooking apples
3 tablespoons wine vinegar
2 tablespoons brown sugar
salt and pepper

American
1 small red cabbage
¼ cup butter
1 onion, chopped
2 baking apples
4 tablespoons wine vinegar
3 tablespoons brown sugar
salt and pepper

Cut the cabbage into quarters, discard the core and shred finely. Heat half the butter in a frying pan and fry the onion until softened but not browned. Peel, core and slice the apples. Arrange layers of cabbage, onion and apple in an ovenproof dish. Add the remaining butter, the vinegar, sugar and seasoning. Cover and cook in a preheated moderate oven for about 45 minutes, until the cabbage is tender. Serve from the dish.

Lettuce-braised peas

Main utensil: saucepan
  (preferably non-stick)
Preparation time: 15 minutes
Cooking time: about 30 minutes
Serves: 4

Imperial/Metric
1 lettuce
1½ lb./700 g. peas
6 button onions
few sprigs parsley
2 oz./50 g. butter
4 tablespoons water
salt and pepper
pinch castor sugar

American
1 lettuce
1½ lb. peas
6 small white onions
few sprigs parsley
¼ cup butter
⅓ cup water
salt and pepper
pinch granulated sugar

Wash the lettuce (discard the outer leaves), drain and dry with absorbent paper. Shell the peas and peel the onions. Place the lettuce leaves in the bottom of a saucepan. Put the peas, onions and parsley on top. Add the butter, water, seasoning and sugar; bring to the boil over a moderate heat, then lower the heat, cover the pan and cook gently for about 30 minutes, until the peas and onions are tender and the liquid has evaporated. (If there is still some liquid in the pan cook for a few more minutes without the lid on the pan.) Remove the parsley sprigs and transfer the vegetables to a hot dish.

Stuffed aubergines

Main utensil: saucepan (preferably non-stick)
Preparation time: 20 minutes
Oven temperature: moderate
  (350°F., 180°C., Gas Mark 4)
Cooking time: about 1 hour
Serves: 4

Imperial/Metric
2 large aubergines
2 tablespoons oil
Filling:
2 oz./50 g. butter
1 onion, finely chopped
4 oz./100 g. long-grain rice
½ pint/3 dl. chicken stock
1 tablespoon tomato purée
4 oz./100 g. mushrooms, sliced
salt and pepper

American
2 large eggplants
3 tablespoons oil
Filling:
¼ cup butter
1 onion, finely chopped
½ cup long-grain rice
1¼ cups chicken stock
1 tablespoon tomato paste
1 cup sliced mushrooms
salt and pepper

Cut the aubergines in half, horizontally, scoop out the flesh and chop half of it finely. Heat the butter in a saucepan and sauté the onion until softened but not browned. Stir in the rice and cook for 1–2 minutes. Add the chicken stock, tomato purée and mushrooms; bring to the boil and then simmer until the rice is tender and all the stock absorbed. Season well with salt and pepper and stir in the chopped aubergine flesh. Use this mixture to fill the aubergine halves. Place in an ovenproof dish, pour over the 2 tablespoons oil, cover with a lid or foil and cook in the preheated moderate oven for 45 minutes–1 hour. Serve hot.

Bubble and squeak

Main utensil: frying pan
  (preferably non-stick)
Preparation time: few minutes
Cooking time: about 15 minutes
Serves: 4

Imperial/Metric
1 lb./½ kg. cooked potatoes
1 lb./½ kg. cooked cabbage
salt and pepper
2 oz./50 g. butter or dripping
1 onion, chopped

American
1 lb. cooked potatoes
1 lb. cooked cabbage
salt and pepper
¼ cup butter or drippings
1 onion, chopped

Mix together the cooked potatoes and cabbage and season, if necessary. Heat the fat in a frying pan and cook the onion until softened. Stir in the cooked vegetables and cook over a moderate heat until beginning to brown; keep turning the vegetables until hot through and nicely browned—this takes about 15 minutes.

Creamed spinach

Main utensils: 2 saucepans
   (preferably non-stick)
Preparation time: 10 minutes
Cooking time: 15 minutes
Serves: 4

Imperial/Metric
2 lb./1 kg. spinach
2 oz./50 g. butter
1 tablespoon flour
¼ pint/1½ dl. plus 4 tablespoons
  milk
salt and pepper
pinch grated nutmeg
squeeze lemon juice
2 tablespoons cream

American
2 lb. spinach
¼ cup butter
1 tablespoon all-purpose flour
1 cup milk

salt and pepper
pinch grated nutmeg
squeeze lemon juice
3 tablespoons cream

Wash the spinach well, shake dry and place in a saucepan without any additional liquid. Cover and cook over a moderate heat until tender. Remove the lid and allow the liquid to boil away, then stir in half the butter and keep the spinach hot. Heat the remaining butter in a small saucepan, stir in the flour and cook over a moderate heat for 1–2 minutes. Off the heat, stir in the milk. Return the pan to the heat and, stirring, bring to the boil and cook until thickened. Season well and stir in a pinch of grated nutmeg. Stir in the spinach with the lemon juice and cream; cook over a moderate heat for a few minutes but do not allow to boil.

Carrot and raisin salad

Main utensil: shredder attachment
  or hand grater
Preparation time: 5 minutes
Serves: 4

Imperial/Metric
4 large carrots
3 oz./75 g. raisins
2 oz./50 g. walnuts or hazelnuts,
  chopped
salt and pepper
grated rind of 1 lemon
1 tablespoon lemon juice
1 carton soured cream

American
4 large carrots
½ cup raisins
½ cup chopped walnuts or
  hazelnuts
salt and pepper
grated rind of 1 lemon
1 tablespoon lemon juice
1 carton sour cream

Scrape the carrots and shred them either with a hand grater or using the shredder attachment to your mixer. Place the shredded carrots in a bowl and toss with the raisins, nuts, seasoning, lemon rind and juice. Chill lightly and spoon over the soured cream before serving.

Rice and corn salad (Illustrated on page 135)

Main utensil: saucepan
  (preferably non-stick)
Preparation time: 5 minutes
Serves: 4

Imperial/Metric
6 oz./175 g. long-grain rice
1 green pepper, seeded and
  chopped
2 sticks celery, chopped
few black olives
1 small can sweetcorn
pinch grated nutmeg
salt and pepper
4 tablespoons French dressing
  (see page 90)

American
about 1 cup long-grain rice
1 green sweet pepper, seeded and
  chopped
2 stalks celery, chopped
few ripe olives
1 small can kernel corn
pinch grated nutmeg
salt and pepper
⅓ cup French dressing (see page 90)

Cook the rice in boiling salted water until just tender. Drain and rinse cold water through the grains to separate them. Mix the rice with the green pepper, celery, olives and drained sweetcorn. Season with nutmeg and salt and pepper and toss in French dressing just before serving. If liked, serve in a lettuce-lined bowl.

Apple and nut salad

Main utensil: liquidiser (optional)
Preparation time: 5 minutes
Serves: 4

Imperial/Metric
3 red-skinned dessert apples
3 green-skinned dessert apples
juice of 1 lemon
1 head celery
2 oz./50 g. walnuts
salt and pepper
mayonnaise or French dressing
   (see page 90)

American
3 red-skinned dessert apples
3 green-skinned dessert apples
juice of 1 lemon
1 head celery
½ cup walnuts
salt and pepper
mayonnaise or French dressing
   (see page 90)

Quarter and core the apples; chop into cubes, place in a bowl and sprinkle with lemon juice. Wash and cut the celery into small pieces and place with the apples. Chop the walnuts and put with the other prepared ingredients.

(If liked, all these ingredients can be prepared in the liquidiser, adding a few at a time to the goblet.) Add salt and pepper to taste and toss all the ingredients together with mayonnaise or French dressing.

Tomato salad (Illustrated on page 135)

Main utensil: bowl
Preparation time: 10 minutes
Serves: 4

Imperial/Metric
1 lb./½ kg. firm tomatoes
salt and pepper
2 tablespoons French dressing
   (see page 00)
chopped chives and other chopped
   fresh herbs, as available

American
1 lb. firm tomatoes
salt and pepper
3 tablespoons French dressing
   (see page 00)
chopped chives and other chopped
   fresh herbs, as available

Place the tomatoes in a bowl and pour over boiling water. Leave for 2–3 minutes, then transfer to a bowl of cold water. Remove the skins from the tomatoes and slice thinly.

Arrange on a serving dish and sprinkle with salt and pepper. Just before serving spoon over the French dressing and sprinkle with the chopped herbs.

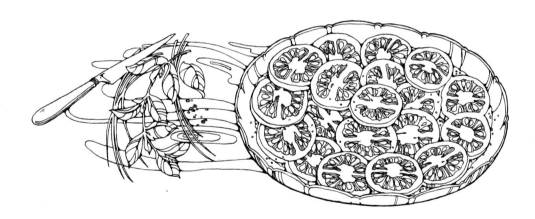

Pasta and tuna salad

Main utensil: saucepan
   (preferably non-stick)
Preparation time: about 45 minutes,
   including preparing the pasta
Serves: 4

Imperial/Metric
6 oz./175 g. pasta bows or shells
1 7-oz./200-g. can tuna
2 oz./50 g. stuffed olives
salt and pepper
French dressing (see page 90)
Garnish:
chopped parsley

American
6 oz. pasta bows or shells
1 7-oz. can tuna
about ½ cup stuffed olives
salt and pepper
French dressing (see page 90)
Garnish:
chopped parsley

Cook the pasta in boiling salted water until just tender. Drain well and rinse cold water through the pasta. Drain well and dry on absorbent paper. Drain the tuna and flake it into fairly large pieces. Mix together the pasta, tuna, olives and seasoning. Toss lightly in French dressing and serve sprinkled with chopped parsley.

Spinach slaw

Main utensil: shredder attachment
Preparation time: 10 minutes
Serves: 6

Imperial/Metric
1 lb./450 g. fresh spinach leaves
1 lb./450 g. white cabbage
2 red-skinned apples
juice of 2 lemons
salt and pepper
mustard dressing (see page 90)

American
1 lb. fresh spinach leaves
1 lb. white cabbage
2 red-skinned apples
juice of 2 lemons
salt and pepper
mustard dressing (see page 90)

Wash the spinach well. Drain well and dry with absorbent paper. Chop the spinach, and shred the cabbage, using a shredder attachment, if available. Core and slice the apples and toss in the lemon juice. Mix the spinach and cabbage together, sprinkle with salt and pepper and toss in mustard dressing. Place in a serving dish and arrange the apple slices round the edge.

Salad Niçoise

Main utensil: bowl
Preparation time: 15 minutes
Serves: 4

Imperial/Metric
3 tomatoes
½ cucumber
8 oz./225 g. cooked French beans
1 green pepper
1 clove garlic
1 crisp lettuce
1 onion, cut into rings
1 7-oz./200-g. can tuna fish, flaked
2 hard-boiled eggs, quartered
few black olives
French dressing (see page 90)

American
3 tomatoes
½ cucumber
½ lb. cooked green beans
1 green sweet pepper
1 clove garlic
1 crisp lettuce
1 onion, cut into rings
1 7-oz. can tuna fish, flaked
2 hard-cooked eggs, quartered
few ripe olives
French dressing (see page 90)

Skin and quarter the tomatoes and slice the cucumber and beans. Seed and slice the pepper. Rub all round the inside of a salad bowl with the cut clove of garlic and line the bowl with the lettuce leaves. Mix the other ingredients together in another bowl and toss them in French dressing. Spoon these ingredients into the lettuce-lined bowl and serve at once.

Green salad

Main utensil: salad bowl
Preparation time: 10 minutes
Serves: 4–6

Imperial/Metric
1 clove garlic
¼ cucumber
1 lettuce
1 bunch watercress
chopped parsley, chives or other
    fresh herbs
French dressing (see page 90)
salt and ground black pepper

American
1 clove garlic
¼ cucumber
1 lettuce
1 bunch watercress
chopped parsley, chives or other
    fresh herbs
French dressing (see page 90)
salt and ground black pepper

Cut the clove of garlic and rub the cut side all round the inside of a deep salad bowl. Cut the cucumber (peeled, if liked) into wafer-thin slices. Wash the lettuce leaves, drain and pat dry with absorbent paper. Wash and dry the watercress. Place the prepared salad ingredients in the salad bowl. Sprinkle with the chopped herbs, French dressing, salt and freshly ground black pepper, just before serving.

Dressings and sauces

Mayonnaise (Illustrated opposite)

Main utensil: liquidiser
Preparation time: few minutes
Makes: ½ pint (3 dl.)

Imperial/Metric	American
1 whole egg	1 whole egg
salt and pepper	salt and pepper
¼ teaspoon dry mustard	¼ teaspoon mustard powder
2 tablespoons wine vinegar	3 tablespoons wine vinegar
½ pint/3 dl. olive oil	1¼ cups olive oil

Do not take an egg straight out of the refrigerator and use it for mayonnaise. Have it at room temperature along with the other ingredients.

Place the egg, seasonings and half the vinegar in the liquidiser goblet; put the top on and let the machine run for a few seconds to blend the ingredients. Remove the centre from the liquidiser lid and (with the machine running) slowly pour in half the oil. Add the remaining vinegar and allow it to blend in, then add the remaining oil.

Variations

Garlic mayonnaise Add 1 crushed small clove of garlic.
Herb mayonnaise Add a mixture of chopped chervil, parsley and chives.
Chantilly mayonnaise Use lemon juice in place of the wine vinegar and blend 4 tablespoons double cream into the thickened mayonnaise.
Note: To store mayonnaise, keep it in an airtight container (a Tupperware container is ideal) in the refrigerator.

To make mayonnaise without a liquidiser use 2 egg *yolks*. Place them in a bowl with the seasonings and mix the ingredients together with a whisk or wooden spoon. Beating all the time, add the oil *drop by drop*. When the mayonnaise thickens beat in half the vinegar, then the remaining oil and vinegar.

French dressing (Illustrated opposite)

Main utensil: liquidiser
Preparation time: few seconds
Makes: about ½ pint (3 dl.)

Imperial/Metric	American
½ pint vegetable oil	1¼ cups vegetable oil
5 tablespoons wine vinegar	⅓ cup wine vinegar
¼ teaspoon French mustard	¼ teaspoon French mustard
pinch salt	pinch salt
ground black pepper	ground black pepper
pinch sugar	pinch sugar

Put all the ingredients into the liquidiser goblet and run the machine for a few seconds to blend the ingredients together.

Store in a screw-topped jar in the refrigerator. Shake well before using.

Variations

Herb dressing Add 1 teaspoon each chopped shallot and gherkins and 2 tablespoons chopped fresh parsley, thyme, sage and marjoram, mixed, as available.
Mustard dressing Use 1 teaspoon French mustard.
Roquefort dressing Add 2 tablespoons crumbled blue cheese to the dressing.
Garlic dressing Add 1 crushed clove of garlic.
Tomato dressing Add 2 tablespoons tomato ketchup to the dressing.

Herb dressing, tomato dressing and mayonnaise (see above)

Thousand island dressing

Main utensil: bowl
Preparation time: 10 minutes
Makes: ½ pint (3 dl.)

Imperial/Metric	American
½ pint/3 dl. mayonnaise (see page 90)	1¼ cups mayonnaise (see page 90)
3 tablespoons tomato ketchup	4 tablespoons tomato catsup
2 tablespoons chopped stuffed olives	3 tablespoons chopped stuffed olives
1 tablespoon chopped green pepper	1 tablespoon chopped green sweet pepper
1 tablespoon chopped chives	1 tablespoon chopped chives
2 teaspoons chopped parsley	2 teaspoons chopped parsley
1 hard-boiled egg, chopped	1 hard-cooked egg, chopped

Place the mayonnaise in a bowl and blend in the other ingredients.

This dressing can be served with salads, fish, egg and vegetable dishes.

Soured cream and chive dressing

Main utensil: bowl or liquidiser
Preparation time: few minutes
Makes: about ¼ pint (1½ dl.)

Imperial/Metric	American
¼ pint/1½ dl. soured cream	⅔ cup sour cream
2 tablespoons cottage cheese	3 tablespoons cottage cheese
salt and cayenne pepper	salt and cayenne pepper
pinch dry mustard	pinch mustard powder
1 tablespoon chopped chives	1 tablespoon chopped chives

Mix all the ingredients together and chill before serving with jacket potatoes or a tomato or cucumber salad.

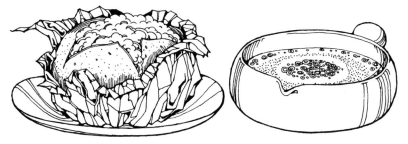

Béchamel sauce

Main utensil: saucepan (preferably non-stick)
Preparation time: 10 minutes
Makes: ½ pint (3 dl.)

Imperial/Metric	American
½ pint/3 dl. milk	1¼ cups milk
1 bay leaf	1 bay leaf
1 onion	1 onion
2–3 peppercorns	2–3 peppercorns
pinch nutmeg	pinch nutmeg
1 oz./25 g. butter	2 tablespoons butter
1 oz./25 g. flour	¼ cup all-purpose flour
2 tablespoons single cream	3 tablespoons coffee cream
salt and pepper	salt and pepper

Place the milk, bay leaf, onion, peppercorns and nutmeg in a saucepan. Very slowly bring to the boil, remove from the heat, cover and leave aside to infuse for about 5 minutes, then strain.

Melt the butter in a saucepan and stir in the flour. Cook for 1–2 minutes. Off the heat, gradually blend in the flavoured milk. Return to the heat, bring to the boil, stirring and cook for 2–3 minutes. Stir in the cream and seasoning to taste.

Variations

Cheese sauce Stir 2 oz. (50 g.) grated cheese into the sauce, before adding the cream. Add a pinch of dry mustard and cayenne pepper with the seasoning.

Mushroom sauce Mix in 2 oz. (50 g.) sliced mushrooms, sautéed in butter.

Parsley sauce Add 2 tablespoons finely chopped parsley to the basic sauce just before serving.

Onion sauce Add 1 onion, finely chopped and cooked slowly in butter, to the basic sauce.

A guide to puddings and desserts

Puddings and desserts are still a very popular part of every-day menus. The sweet course is an excellent way to ensure that all the members of the family have their quota of milk and eggs. With the price of meat and fish soaring it may become necessary to serve smaller portions of the expensive items and make up with nourishing pudding and sweets.

Lack of time prevents many people from venturing on making many pudding and sweets, but freezer owners can make up pies, crumbles, soufflés and cheesecakes well in advance and always have a pudding to serve. Beware of freezing custard mixtures as they tend to separate and become watery. Meringues make a delicious sweet with fruit and cream and can be stored (unfilled) in an airtight box. Choux pastry (see page 110) will also keep well in the freezer or, for a shorter time, in an airtight box. However, this is one part of the menu one has to cut back on when anyone has a weight problem, but many fruit sweets can be made using artificial sweeteners for those who just can't resist the sweet course!

Do remember the balance of your meal; if you have had a soup or starter to begin with and a substantial main course make sure the sweet is very light. Light supper meals such as flans, salads or grills can be followed by a slightly more substantial pudding.

Apple cream almond flan

Main utensils: flan ring, baking tray, saucepan (preferably non-stick), apple corer
Preparation time: 20 minutes
Oven temperature: moderately hot (375°F., 190°C., Gas Mark 5)
Cooking time: 30 minutes
Serves: 4–6

Imperial/Metric
1 7-inch (18-cm) flan case, made with flan pastry (see page 105)
2 large cooking apples
2 oz./50 g. brown sugar
1 teaspoon ground cinnamon
1 tablespoon ground almonds
2 tablespoons water
Topping:
2 5-oz./150-g. cartons soured cream

American
1 7-inch pie shell, made with flan pastry (see page 105)
2 large baking apples
¼ cup brown sugar
1 teaspoon ground cinnamon
1 tablespoon ground almonds
3 tablespoons water
Topping:
2 5-oz. cartons sour cream

Bake the pastry case blind as described on page 111. Peel, core and slice the apples. Place in a saucepan then add sugar, cinnamon, ground almonds and water. Cover and cook over a gentle heat until soft. Allow to cool and arrange the filling in the flan case then cover with the soured cream, smoothing the surface with a palette knife. If there are any strips of pastry left over decorate flan with a lattice of pastry by cutting thin strips and placing across the flan. Bake near the top of the preheated moderately hot oven for 20–25 minutes, until pastry is golden brown.

Rice pudding

Main utensils: saucepan (preferably non-stick), pie dish
Preparation time: 20 minutes
Oven temperature: moderate (350°F., 180°C., Gas Mark 4)
Cooking time: about 30 minutes
Serves: 4

Imperial/Metric
2 tablespoons round-grain rice
¼ pint/1½ dl. water
1 pint/6 dl. milk
1 small piece cinnamon stick
pinch salt
grated rind of 1 lemon
2 tablespoons granulated sugar
2 eggs, separated

American
3 tablespoons round-grain rice
⅔ cup water
2½ cups milk
1 small piece cinnamon stick
pinch salt
grated rind of 1 lemon
3 tablespoons granulated sugar
2 eggs, separated

Wash the rice and put in a saucepan with the water; bring to the boil, cover and simmer until the water is absorbed. Add the milk, cinnamon, salt, and lemon rind and simmer slowly until the rice is almost cooked, stirring from time to time with a wooden spoon. Remove from the heat and allow to cool slightly then stir in the sugar and egg yolks. Whip the egg whites stiffly and stir into the rice mixture. Butter a pie dish and spoon in the rice mixture. Bake near the top of the preheated moderate oven for 30 minutes, until the top of the pudding is nicely browned.

Apple delight meringue

Main utensils: saucepan (preferably non-stick), apple corer, whisk or mixer
Preparation time: 20 minutes
Oven temperature: moderate (350°F., 170°C., Gas Mark 4)
Cooking time: 25 minutes

Imperial/Metric
3 oz./75 g. granulated sugar
¼ pint/1½ dl. water
juice of 1 lemon
2 large or 4 medium cooking apples
1 teaspoon cinnamon
2 eggs, separated
½ 5-oz./150-g. carton soured cream
2 oz./50 g. castor sugar
Decoration:
glacé cherries
almond slivers
angelica

American
6 tablespoons granulated sugar
⅔ cup water
juice of 1 lemon
2 large or 4 medium baking apples
1 teaspoon cinnamon
2 eggs, separated
½ 5-oz. carton sour cream
¼ cup granulated sugar
Decoration:
candied cherries
almond slivers
candied angelica

Dissolve the granulated sugar slowly into water to make a syrup then boil rapidly for about 1 minute. Add half the lemon juice to the syrup. Peel, core and cut the apples into eight pieces and poach gently in the syrup, without allowing the liquid to boil. When the apples are tender, but still retain their shape, remove them from the syrup and place in individual ovenproof dishes. Sprinkle with the remaining lemon juice then the cinnamon. Mix the egg yolks with the soured cream and divide between the dishes of apples. Whisk the egg whites until still then gradually beat in the castor sugar, a little at a time, and pipe or spoon on top of the apples and custard. Decorate with cherries, almonds and angelica and bake in the centre of the preheated moderate oven until pale golden, about 15 minutes.

Blackberry and apple crumble

Main utensil: ovenproof dish
Preparation time: 20 minutes
Oven temperature: moderately hot (375°F., 190°C., Gas Mark 5)
Cooking time: 25 minutes
Serves: 4

Imperial/Metric
12 oz./350 g. cooking apples
1 teaspoon allspice
4 oz./100 g. granulated sugar
8 oz./225 g. blackberries
6 oz./150 g. plain flour
pinch salt
3 oz./75 g. butter
4 tablespoons brown sugar

American
¾ lb. baking apples
1 teaspoon allspice
½ cup granulated sugar
½ lb. blackberries
1½ cups all-purpose flour
pinch salt
6 tablespoons butter
5 tablespoons brown sugar

Peel core and slice the apples; place in an ovenproof dish sprinkle with the allspice and some of the granulated sugar. Put the blackberries onto the apples and sprinkle with remaining granulated sugar. Sieve the flour into a bowl with the salt; add the butter and rub into the flour until the mixture resembles breadcrumbs. Stir in half the brown sugar. Sprinkle the crumb mixture on top of the fruit and lastly sprinkle with remaining brown sugar.

Bake in the centre of a preheated moderately hot oven until the crumb mixture is golden brown and the brown sugar is slightly bubbling—about 25 minutes. Serve with whipped cream.

⁜ This dish freezes well, uncooked.

Cassata (see page 27)

Pour the thickened egg yolk mixture onto the melted chocolate and whisk the two mixtures together until well blended. Stir in the lightly whipped cream.

Line the sides and bottom of the loaf tin with the firmed chocolate mixture. A palette knife is best for smoothing the chocolate ice cream into the loaf tin. If the mixture in the tin has become too soft return it to the freezer before putting in the fruit water ice.

Fill the space left in the centre with the cream filling and return the cassata to the freezer until solid. To serve turn onto a dish, decorate with cream, cherries and angelica and cut in slices.

Golden apricot pudding

Main utensils: 8-inch (20-cm.) ovenproof dish, saucepan (preferably non-stick)
Preparation time: 20 minutes
Oven temperature: moderate (350°F., 180°C., Gas Mark 4)
Cooking time: 1 hour
Serves: 6

Imperial/Metric	American
1 lb./450 g. fresh apricots	1 lb. fresh apricots
¼ pint/1½ dl. water	⅔ cup water
4 oz./100 g. soft brown sugar	½ cup brown sugar
Topping:	*Topping:*
3 oz./75 g. butter	6 tablespoons butter
3 oz./75 g. sugar	6 tablespoons sugar
4 oz./100 g. self-raising flour	1 cup all-purpose flour sifted with 1 teaspoon baking powder
4 tablespoons milk	⅓ cup milk
3 egg whites	3 egg whites
1 tablespoon chopped nuts	1 tablespoon chopped nuts
Golden sauce:	*Golden sauce:*
3 egg yolks	3 egg yolks
1 oz./25 g. castor sugar	2 tablespoons sugar
3 tablespoons apricot juice	scant ¼ cup apricot juice
1 teaspoon lemon juice	1 teaspoon lemon juice

Halve and stone the apricots and stew lightly with the water and sugar until just tender. Drain off and keep the stewing liquid. Put fruit into a well buttered ovenproof dish. Cream the butter and sugar together until light and fluffy. Fold in sieved flour and milk. Whisk egg whites and gently fold in creamed mixture. Spread over fruit, sprinkle with chopped nuts and bake in the centre of the preheated oven for 1 hour. Ten minutes before serving blend egg yolks and sugar together and slowly stir in apricot juice and lemon juice in a basin over simmering water. Whisk until light and foamy. Serve at once with the apricot pudding.

Christmas pudding

Main utensils: 3 2-lb. (1-kg.) pudding basins, steamer or large saucepans (preferably non-stick)
Preparation time: 45 minutes
Cooking time: 10 hours
Serves: 12–14

Imperial/Metric	American
8 oz./225 g. plain flour	2 cups all-purpose flour
8 oz./225 g. fresh breadcrumbs	4 cups fresh bread crumbs
1 lb./450 g. shredded suet	3 cups shredded suet
1 lb./450 g. soft brown sugar	2 cups soft brown sugar
12 oz./350 g. sultanas	2 cups seedless white raisins
8 oz./225 g. raisins	1⅓ cups raisins
8 oz./225 g. candied peel	1⅓ cups candied peel
12 oz./350 g. currants	2 cups currants
2 oz./50 g. almonds, chopped	½ cup chopped almonds
grated rind of 2 lemons	grated rind of 2 lemons
juice of 1 lemon	juice of 1 lemon
1 teaspoon mixed spice	1 teaspoon mixed spice
1 teaspoon salt	1 teaspoon salt
4 tablespoons orange marmalade	5 tablespoons orange marmalade
6 large eggs	6 eggs
4 tablespoons rum or brandy	⅓ cup rum or brandy
½ pint/3 dl. stout	1¼ cups dark beer
½ teaspoon bicarbonate of soda	½ teaspoon baking soda

Place the flour, breadcrumbs, shredded suet, sugar, sultanas, raisins, candied peel, currants, almonds, grated lemon rind and juice, mixed spice and salt in a large mixing bowl. Make a well in the centre and add the marmalade and the well beaten eggs, mixing gradually into the dry ingredients. Add the rum or brandy and mix in well. Heat the stout in a saucepan, stir in the bicarbonate of soda and while the mixture is still frothy pour it into other ingredients and mix well together. Spoon into the pudding basins; cover well with greaseproof and foil and secure with string. Boil for about 8 hours.

Make these puddings well in advance of Christmas to allow time for them to mature. Before storing, cover with clean greaseproof paper covers and foil. Boil for 2 hours before serving.

Note: Alternatively, cook in a pressure cooker.

Cassata (Illustrated on page 95)

Main utensils: whisk, saucepan, 1-lb. (½-kg.) loaf tin, preferably non-stick, liquidiser
Preparation time: 30 minutes, not including freezing time
Serves: 6–8

Imperial/Metric	American
Chocolate ice cream:	*Chocolate ice cream:*
3 egg yolks	3 egg yolks
2½ oz./65 g. castor sugar	generous ¼ cup granulated sugar
½ pint/3 dl. milk	1¼ cups milk
4 oz./100 g. plain chocolate	¾ cup semi-sweet chocolate pieces
4 tablespoons double cream	5 tablespoons whipping cream
Strawberry or raspberry water ice:	*Strawberry or raspberry water ice:*
1½ lb./½ kg. strawberries or raspberries	1½ lb. strawberries or raspberries
4 oz./100 g. sugar	½ cup granulated sugar
6 tablespoons water	½ cup water
juice of 1 lemon	juice of 1 lemon
Cream filling:	*Cream filling:*
¼ pint/1½ dl. double cream	⅔ cup whipping cream
2 teaspoons chopped angelica	2 teaspoons chopped candied angelica
1 tablespoon chopped almonds	1 tablespoon chopped almonds
1 tablespoon chopped glacé cherries	1 tablespoon chopped candied cherries

Beat the egg yolks and sugar together with a small whisk then gently pour on milk and heat to just below boiling. Strain the liquid into a clean saucepan and cook on a low heat until the mixture is slightly thickened and coats the back of a wooden spoon. Allow to cool. Meanwhile, melt the chocolate in a bowl over a saucepan of boiling water, or in a double saucepan. Whisk the egg mixture into the chocolate, mixing well, then fold in the lightly whipped cream. Pour into an ice tray and put into the refrigerator, at its coldest setting, or the freezer and allow to become firm but not solid. Stir from time to time, during freezing.

Cook the strawberries or raspberries with the sugar for 5 minutes. Allow to cool. Sieve or liquidise the fruit and add the lemon juice. Pour into ice tray and refrigerate until firm but not solid. Stir occasionally, during freezing.

Method for assembling the cassata: chill the loaf tin (for a 2-lb. (½-kg.) loaf tin as shown in picture make double quantities of all three mixtures); line sides and bottom with the firmed chocolate ice cream and then pack a layer of strawberry or raspberry water ice over the chocolate, leaving a space in the middle. Fill the space left with the cream filling, made by whipping the cream and stirring in the angelica, almonds and cherries. Put any extra ice cream left over on the top. Freeze until solid then remove from the tin by passing it under cold water. Decorate with whipped cream, cherries and angelica and cut in slices to serve.

To vary the strawberry or raspberry water ice add ¼ pint (1½ dl.) lightly whipped double cream and partially freeze the mixture.

Chocolate cheesecake (Illustrated on page 103)

Main utensils: liquidiser, (optional), 8-inch (20-cm.) spring form pan, or cake tin (preferably non-stick)
Preparation time: 20 minutes
Serves: 10

Imperial/Metric	American
8 oz./225 g. chocolate-coated digestive biscuits	½ lb. chocolate-coated semi-sweet cookies
4 oz./100 g. butter, melted	½ cup butter, melted
Filling:	*Filling:*
8 oz./225 g. cream cheese	1 cup cream cheese
4 oz./100 g. castor sugar	½ cup granulated sugar
1 teaspoon vanilla essence	1 teaspoon vanilla extract
4 oz./100 g. plain chocolate	4 squares semi-sweet chocolate
2 eggs, separated	2 eggs, separated
½ pint/3 dl. double cream	1¼ cups whipping cream
Decoration:	*Decoration:*
crushed chocolate flake bar	crushed chocolate flake bar

Crush the biscuits finely by blending in a liquidiser, or place them in a polythene bag and crush with a rolling pin. Place the crushed biscuits in a bowl and add the melted butter. Mix well. Press the crumb mixture over the base and around the sides of the spring form pan and place in the refrigerator for 1 hour.

Beat the cream cheese until smooth, then stir in half the sugar and the vanilla essence. Allow the chocolate to melt in a bowl, over a pan of hot water. Cool slightly then beat into the cream cheese mixture together with the lightly beaten egg yolks. Beat the egg whites until stiff and fold in the remaining sugar; fold this mixture into the cream cheese mixture. Finally fold in the lightly whipped cream. Turn the filling into the prepared biscuit crust and refrigerate until set. To serve, turn out and decorate with crushed chocolate flake bar.

Grapefruit cheesecake (Illustrated on page 103)

Main utensils: liquidiser (optional), 8-inch (20-cm.) spring form pan, or cake tin (preferably non-stick)
Preparation time: 20 minutes
Serves: 10

Imperial/Metric
4 oz./100 g. digestive biscuits
2 oz./50 g. butter, melted
Filling:
12 oz./350 g. cream or curd cheese
2 large grapefruit
1 lemon
6 oz./175 g. castor sugar
2 eggs
½ oz./15 g. gelatine
3 tablespoons water
½ pint/3 dl. double cream
Decoration:
whipped cream
grapefruit segments
few grapes

American
¼ lb. graham crackers
¼ cup butter, melted
Filling:
1½ cups cream or curd cheese
2 large grapefruit
1 lemon
¾ cup granulated sugar
2 eggs
2 envelopes gelatin
scant ¼ cup water
1¼ cups whipping cream
Decoration:
whipped cream
grapefruit segments
few grapes

Crush the biscuits finely by blending in a liquidiser, or place them in a polythene bag and crush with a rolling pin. Place the crushed biscuits in a bowl and mix in the melted butter. Press the biscuit crumb mixture over the base of the spring form pan and place in the refrigerator until firm. Press the cheese through a fine sieve (or liquidise it). Grate the rind from one of the grapefruits and the lemon; squeeze the juice from the lemon. Peel the grapefruits, remove all the white pith and chop the fruit; reserve any grapefruit juice. Place the sugar, 3 tablespoons fruit juice and the egg yolks in a bowl. Place over a pan of hot water and whisk the mixture until thick and creamy.

Dissolve the gelatine in the water and fold it into the whisked mixture. Whip the egg whites and cream until fairly stiff. Blend the cheese with the fruit, juices and rinds and fold into the gelatine mixture. Finally fold in the whipped egg whites and cream. Spoon the mixture into the prepared tin. Chill in the refrigerator for several hours and serve decorated with whipped cream, grapefruit segments and a few grapes.

Raspberry cheesecake (Illustrated opposite and on page 103)

Main utensils: liquidiser (optional), 8-inch (20-cm.) spring form pan, or cake tin (preferably non-stick)
Preparation time: 15 minutes
Serves: 8–10

Imperial/Metric
4 oz./100 g. digestive biscuits
2 oz./50 g. butter, melted
Filling:
8 oz./225 g. frozen raspberries, defrosted
4 oz./100 g. castor sugar
8 oz./225 g. cream cheese
½ oz./15 g. gelatine
3 tablespoons water
½ pint/3 dl. double cream
2 egg whites
Decoration:
¼ pint/1½ dl. double cream
few raspberries

American
¼ cup graham crackers
¼ cup butter, melted
Filling:
1½ cups frozen raspberries, defrosted
½ cup granulated sugar
1 cup cream cheese
2 envelopes gelatin
scant ¼ cup water
1¼ cups whipping cream
2 egg whites
Decoration:
⅔ cup whipping cream
few raspberries

Crush the biscuits fully by blending in a liquidiser, or place them in a polythene bag and crush with a rolling pin. Place the crushed biscuits in a bowl and mix in the melted butter. Press the biscuit crumb mixture over the base of the spring form pan and place in the refrigerator until firm. Liquidise the raspberries with the sugar then press the mixture through a nylon sieve; mix the fruit purée with the softened cream cheese. Dissolve the gelatine in the water, then add to the cheese mixture. Lightly whip the cream and beat the egg whites until stiff. Fold the cream and egg whites into the cheese mixture. Spoon over the crumb base and return to the refrigerator for several hours, or overnight. Serve decorated with whipped cream and raspberries.

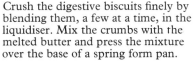

Crush the digestive biscuits finely by blending them, a few at a time, in the liquidiser. Mix the crumbs with the melted butter and press the mixture over the base of a spring form pan.

Sieve the liquidised raspberry mixture and mix with the softened cream cheese. Add the dissolved gelatine to the raspberry and cheese mixture.

Lightly whip the cream and whisk the egg whites until stiff. Fold the cream into the raspberry mixture and finally, fold in the whisked egg whites. Spoon the mixture into the spring form pan and leave to set.

Milanaise soufflé

Main utensils: 6-inch (15-cm.)
  soufflé dish, whisk
Preparation time: 20 minutes
Serves: 6

Imperial/Metric	American
4 eggs	4 eggs
5 oz./150 g. castor sugar	$\frac{2}{3}$ cup granulated sugar
2 lemons	2 lemons
$\frac{1}{2}$ oz./15 g. gelatine	2 envelopes gelatin
$\frac{1}{4}$ pint/1$\frac{1}{2}$ dl. water	$\frac{2}{3}$ cup water
$\frac{1}{2}$ pint/3 dl. double cream	1$\frac{1}{4}$ cups whipping cream
Decoration:	*Decoration:*
chopped nuts	chopped nuts
$\frac{1}{4}$ pint/1$\frac{1}{2}$ dl. double cream	$\frac{2}{3}$ cup whipping cream

Secure a double band of greaseproof paper, to come about 2 inches (5 cm.) above the top of the dish, around the outside of the dish and brush all round the inside lightly with oil.

Separate the eggs and place the yolks and sugar in a bowl with the finely grated lemon rind and strained juice. Whisk together (over a pan of hot water, if using a hand whisk) until the mixture is thick and creamy in colour—the whisk should leave a trail in the mixture. Soften the gelatine in the water then dissolve it over a low heat.

Whisk the egg whites until stiff and lightly whip the cream. Whisk the dissolved gelatine into the egg yolk mixture, then fold in the cream; finally fold in the stiffly whisked egg white. Turn the mixture into the prepared soufflé dish, or into individual dishes and leave in a cool place to set.

To serve the soufflé, carefully remove the band of greaseproof from the outside of the dish. Press chopped nuts into the sides of the soufflé and decorate the top edge with a piping of whipped cream.

Meringue 1

This mixture is usually used for meringue shells which are filled with whipped cream, or as a topping for pies.

Main utensils: baking trays
(preferably non-stick), whisk or
mixer, piping bag and nozzle
Preparation time: 10 minutes
Oven temperature: very cool (250°F.,
130°C., Gas Mark ½)
Cooking time: 1 hour 30 minutes

Imperial/Metric
4 egg whites
8 oz./225 g. castor sugar
pinch salt
½ pint/3 dl. double cream

American
4 egg whites
1 cup sugar
pinch salt
1¼ cups whipping cream

Prepare two baking trays by lightly brushing with oil and then dredging with flour. Alternatively line the baking sheets with non-stick silicone paper. Put the egg whites in the mixer bowl and beat until quite stiff, the mixture should stand up in peaks. Whisk in 4 teaspoons sugar until the mixture becomes more glossy. Sprinkle the remaining sugar into the mixture and fold in with a metal spoon. Shape the meringue mixture into shells with two spoons and place on prepared baking trays. For a more professional finish put the meringue mixture into a piping bag with a plain nozzle and pipe into rounds. Dredge with castor sugar and bake in the oven for about 1 hour, changing the trays round to avoid the meringues becoming brown.

After about 1 hour the meringues will be set; lift them gently from the trays with a palette knife, press the flat bottom to form a hollow, then return to the oven to dry for a further 15–20 minutes. Cool on a wire tray. Fill with whipped cream and sandwich together in pairs just before serving.

Meringue 2

This is a firmer type of meringue which is hard work to make by hand but is quickly done with the mixer. It is really easier to handle than the softer mixture and even an inexperienced cook will find it easy to pipe as it holds firm for longer even in a warm kitchen.

Main utensils: baking trays
(preferably non-stick), whisk or
mixer, piping bag and nozzle
Preparation time: 10 minutes
Oven temperature: very cool (250°F.,
130°C., Gas Mark ½)
Cooking time: 50 minutes

Imperial/Metric
4 egg whites
8½ oz./240 g. icing sugar
pinch salt
2 drops vanilla essence

American
4 egg whites
2 cups sifted confectioners' sugar
pinch salt
2 drops vanilla extract

Prepare the baking trays as in the previous recipe. Put the egg whites in the mixer bowl and whisk until foaming but not quite stiff. Add the icing sugar 1 tablespoon at a time until the mixture is stiff and shiny. To test, lift a little mixture up and if ready it should retain its shape as it falls back onto the mixture. Put the mixture into a piping bag with a large plain pipe and pipe onto the baking trays. Bake in the oven for about 50 minutes, until dried out. Alternatively pipe into a large basket. Fill with fruit and cream or ice cream and fruit and serve as a dessert.

Hazelnut meringue gâteau

Main utensils: 2 8-inch (20-cm.)
sandwich tins (preferably
non-stick), mixer or whisk,
liquidiser (optional)
Preparation time: 10 minutes
Oven temperature: cool (275°F.,
140°C., Gas Mark 1)
Cooking time: 60 minutes
Serves: 6

Imperial/Metric
4 egg whites
9 oz./250 g. castor sugar
4 oz./100 g. hazelnuts
Decoration:
½ pint/3 dl. double cream
8 hazelnuts

American
4 egg whites
1 cup plus 2 tablespoons sugar
¾ cup hazelnuts
Decoration:
1¼ cups whipping cream
8 hazelnuts

Lightly grease and line the sandwich tins with greaseproof paper. Make the meringue as directed for meringue 1. Put the hazelnuts in the liquidiser and blend until finely chopped. Fold into the meringue mixture after the sugar, divide the mixture between the tins, and dry out in the preheated oven for about 60 minutes.

Allow to cool and fill with whipped cream which can be flavoured with a few drops of vanilla essence or brandy. Decorate the top with piped cream rosettes topped with a hazelnut.

Meringue swans (Illustrated on page 103)

Make up a batch of meringue 2 and pipe out in ovals with walls onto prepared baking trays, as shown in the line drawings. Pipe the heads separately on a baking tray (preferably lined with rice paper) by piping an S shape. Dry out in a cool oven. Allow to cool then fill the baskets with fruit and whipped cream, and put the heads in position.

To make meringue swans, pipe the meringue out in small oval shapes onto a silicone paper-lined baking tray.

Pipe two layers around the outside of each oval to form a wall.

On a separate baking tray (preferably lined with rice paper) pipe the meringue out into small S shapes. Dry the meringue out in a cool oven. Fill the baskets with cream and fruit and put the heads in position—see colour picture on page 103.

Chocolate mousse

Main utensils: double saucepan, hand mixer, individual dishes
Preparation time: 10 minutes
Serves: 4

Imperial/Metric
4 oz./100 g. plain chocolate
4 eggs
2 tablespoons Grand Marnier
4 oz./100 g. castor sugar
1 teaspoon grated orange rind

American
¾ cup semi-sweet chocolate pieces
4 eggs
3 tablespoons Grand Marnier
½ cup granulated sugar
1 teaspoon grated orange rind

Melt the chocolate in a double saucepan over hot water; separate the egg yolks from the whites and mix the liqueur with the egg yolks. Stir the sugar into the chocolate mixture. Add the egg yolk mixture gradually to the chocolate. Allow to cool slightly. Add the orange rind to the chocolate mixture and beat up the egg whites until light and fluffy. Gently stir the egg whites into the chocolate mixture until the two are well mixed. Spoon into individual dishes and serve chilled.

Syllabub

Main utensil: mixer or whisk
Preparation time: 5 minutes
Serves: 4

Imperial/Metric
¾ pint/4½ dl. double cream
2 egg whites
4 tablespoons castor sugar
¼ pint/1½ dl. sweet sherry
1 tablespoon brandy
grated rind of 1 lemon or orange

American
scant 2 cups heavy cream
2 egg whites
5 tablespoons granulated sugar
⅔ cup sweet sherry
1 tablespoon brandy
grated rind of 1 lemon or orange

Whip the cream very slightly with a fork, beat the egg whites until frothy then add with sugar to the cream and continue whisking until the mixture is thick and frothy, gradually adding sherry and brandy. Serve in individual glasses and sprinkle the top with grated lemon or orange rind.

Fresh blackcurrant yogurt sorbet

Main utensils: liquidiser, cake tin (preferably non-stick) or polythene container
Preparation time: 10 minutes
Serves: 4

Imperial/Metric	American
8 oz./225 g. cooked blackcurrants	½ lb. cooked black currants
2 5-oz./125-g. cartons natural yogurt	2 5-oz. cartons unflavored yogurt
juice of ½ lemon	juice of ½ lemon
non-fattening liquid sweetener to taste	non-fattening liquid sweetener to taste
½ oz./15 g. gelatine	2 envelopes gelatin
4 tablespoons water	⅓ cup water
2 egg whites	2 egg whites

Adjust the refrigerator to lowest setting. Purée the blackcurrants in the liquidiser (or press through a sieve). Combine the purée, yogurt and lemon juice in a bowl. Sweeten with non-fattening liquid sweetener to taste. Dissolve the gelatine, in the water, in a basin placed over a pan of hot water. When dissolved, stir into purée mixture. When mixture begins to set fold in egg whites beaten until just stiff. Pour into a cake tin or polythene container and freeze.

Summer pudding

Main utensil: 1-pint (½-litre) pudding basin
Preparation time: 15 minutes
Serves: 4

Imperial/Metric	American
1 lb./450 g. raspberries, strawberries or blackberries	1 lb. raspberries, strawberries or blackberries
4 oz./100 g. red or blackcurrants	¼ lb. red or black currants
1 tablespoon lemon juice	1 tablespoon lemon juice
1 tablespoon water	1 tablespoon water
4 oz./100 g. sugar	½ cup sugar
8 slices stale bread, crusts removed	8 slices stale bread, crusts removed

Prepare the fruit and cook with lemon juice, water and sugar for a few minutes, until softened. Line a pudding basin with fingers of sliced bread. Make sure the bread is fitted together well so that the fruit juice will not seep through. Fill with the fruit and a little juice then cover the top with bread fingers. Cover the dish with a plate or saucer and put a weight on top and allow to chill in the refrigerator overnight. Turn out and serve with extra fruit juice and whipped cream.
❅ Freeze summer puddings if you have an abundance of fruit in the summer.

Soften the prepared fruit in a pan with lemon juice, water and sugar. Line a pudding basin with fingers of sliced bread, making sure that the bread fits together well so that the fruit juice will not seep through.

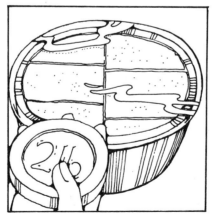

Fill the bread-lined basin with the fruit and a little of the juice; cover with bread fingers, then cover with a plate or saucer and weight down.

Allow the pudding to chill in the refrigerator overnight, then turn out onto a dish.

Grapefruit cheesecake, raspberry cheesecake, chocolate cheesecake, meringue swans, éclairs and cream puffs (see pages 98, 97, 101, 113)

A guide to baking

A guide to pastry

Shortcrust pastry

This is the most versatile of all pastries; it should be crisp and light in texture and free from cracks or bubbles. It can be used for both sweet and savoury dishes—pies, flans, tartlets, pasties and turnovers.

When making shortcrust pastry, the flour (always plain) and the salt should be sieved to aerate the mixture. When rubbing the fat into the flour lift your hands, as high as possible out of the bowl, to incorporate more air. The fat used can be any of the following: butter, margarine, cooking fat or lard, or half butter or margarine and half white fat. The amount of liquid used is very important—too much liquid produces a tough pastry; too little produces a dry and crumbly dough which is difficult to handle. Flours vary in the amount of liquid they will absorb, but 2 tablespoons to 8 oz. (225 g.) flour is usually sufficient. When adding the water to the rubbed-in mixture ensure that it is cold. Also, try and keep all your utensils and your hands as cold as possible for pastry making.

When rolling out the shortcrust dough, be careful not to sprinkle too much flour onto the surface or the rolling pin as this extra flour could destroy the balance of the recipe and produce too dry a dough. All that is necessary is a light sprinkling to prevent the pastry sticking. It is important to use short light strokes when rolling out the dough and roll in one direction only. Even if you use baking equipment which has not been coated to give a non-stick surface it is not necessary to grease it for shortcrust pastry recipes.

In this book, when a recipe states '8 oz. (225 g.) shortcrust or puff pastry' it refers to pastry made with 8 oz. (225 g.) flour etc., not the made-up weight of the dough.

Main utensils: sieve, mixing bowl	Imperial/Metric	American
Preparation time: 5 minutes	8 oz./225 g. plain flour	2 cups all-purpose flour
Oven temperature: see individual recipes	½ teaspoon salt	½ teaspoon salt
	4 oz./110 g. fat	¼ cup fat
Cooking time: see individual recipes	2 tablespoons water	3 tablespoons water

Sieve the flour and salt into a mixing bowl. Cut the fat into quarters and rub it into the flour and salt until the mixture resembles fine breadcrumbs. Add the water and mix with a round-bladed knife until the mixture begins to hold together.

Using your fingertips gather the mixture together, leaving the bowl clean. Turn onto a lightly floured board and knead lightly until the dough is smooth.

Making shortcrust pastry in a mixer

Follow the manufacturer's instructions for putting the bowl and beaters firmly in position. Sieve the flour and salt into the bowl. Cut up the fat and place with the flour. Turn the mixer on to a low speed until the fat and flour are blended together. Switch the mixer off and scrape any loose flour from the sides of the bowl and mix again until the mixture resembles fine breadcrumbs.

Turn off the machine and add the water. Switch on to a low speed again to mix the ingredients together. Turn off the machine and gather the mixture together with your fingertips to form a dough.

Cheese pastry can also be made in a mixer. Follow the instructions above; mix in the cheese at the breadcrumb stage.

Cheese pastry

Main utensils: sieve, mixing bowl
Preparation time: 5 minutes
Oven temperature: see individual recipes
Cooking time: see individual recipes

Imperial/Metric	American
8 oz./225 g. plain flour	2 cups all-purpose flour
½ teaspoon salt	½ teaspoon salt
pinch dry mustard	pinch dry mustard
pinch cayenne pepper	pinch cayenne pepper
3 oz./75 g. fat	6 tablespoons fat
2 oz./50 g. cheese, grated	½ cup grated cheese
2 tablespoons cold water	3 tablespoons cold water

Follow the method for shortcrust pastry (see page 104), sieving the added seasonings with the flour and salt. Stir the grated cheese into the breadcrumb-like mixture before adding the liquid.

Fork-mix pastry

This pastry is very quick to make and can be used in place of shortcrust pastry in a recipe. For successful fork-mix pastry it is essential to use a soft margarine.

Main utensils: mixing bowl, fork
Preparation time: few minutes
Oven temperature: see individual recipes
Cooking time: see individual recipes

Imperial/Metric	American
5 oz./125 g. soft margarine	½ cup plus 2 tablespoons soft margarine
8 oz./225 g. plain flour	2 cups all-purpose flour
2 tablespoons water	3 tablespoons water

Put the margarine, half the sieved flour and the water in a mixing bowl. Mix with a fork until the ingredients are blended together. Stir in the remaining flour to form a dough. Turn onto a lightly floured board and knead until the dough is smooth.

Flan pastry

This is a sweet pastry, richer than shortcrust and is used for sweet flan dishes. It can be made in a mixing bowl, but the correct way to make it is on a flat, cold surface (preferably marble) as shown in the step by step pictures overleaf. Butter is the best fat to use for this type of pastry.

Main utensils: sieve, marble slab
Preparation time: 5 minutes
Oven temperature: see individual recipes
Cooking time: see individual recipes

Imperial/Metric	American
4 oz./100 g. plain flour	1 cup all-purpose flour
2 oz./50 g. butter	¼ cup butter
2 oz./50 g. castor sugar	¼ cup granulated sugar
1 large egg yolk	1 egg yolk

Sieve the flour onto the working surface. Make a well in the centre and add the butter, sugar and egg yolk. Work the butter, sugar and egg yolk together with the fingertips; now mix in the flour and work the mixture to form a dough. Knead lightly, into a ball, and place in a polythene bag. Leave in the refrigerator for at least 30 minutes before being rolled out as directed in the individual recipes.

Flan pastry should be made, if possible, on a marble slab. Sieve the flour onto the marble. Make a well in the centre and add the butter (in one piece), sugar and egg yolk.

Work the butter, sugar and egg yolk together with your fingertips, then draw in the flour and work the mixture with your hands to form a dough. Place the dough in a polythene bag and leave it in the refrigerator for at least 30 minutes before rolling it out.

Flaky pastry

Many housewives shy away from this pastry, thinking it is difficult to make—it calls for patience and a light touch with a rolling pin, but it is certainly not difficult. Your patience and skill will be rewarded with a beautifully crisp, light and delicate pastry. Flaky pastry is used for savoury pies, sausage rolls, cream horns, fruit and cream slices, Eccles cakes, etc.

Flaky pastry uses more fat to flour than shortcrust pastry and the object, when making the dough, is to capture as much air as possible between the layers of fat and dough, to produce as light a pastry as possible. That is why the fat is dotted over the dough in small knobs and the rolling and folding processes are repeated. At each stage, more fat and more air is rolled in and more layers added. Another way in which air is trapped into the layers of the dough is when the edges of the folded dough are sealed. All pastry benefits from being rested in a cool place (or refrigerator) before

being baked, but with flaky pastry it is essential that this is done. It is also necessary to rest the dough in a cool place between the rollings and foldings—this enables the fat to become firm again. Before leaving the dough to rest, place it in a polythene bag, to prevent a skin forming.

For successful flaky pastry it is better to use a harder type of fat or a mixture of butter and a hard-type white fat. (The softer fats, although excellent for cake making, are not quite as good for making flaky pastry.)

As with shortcrust pastry, keep all utensils as cool as possible. Greasing of baking equipment is unnecessary, but it does help to dampen the baking tray; the steam, during the initial baking, will help to give the pastry a lift. Before baking, the oven should always be preheated, but it is particularly important to do this when baking flaky pastry.

Main utensils: sieve, bowl
Preparation time: about 2 hours, including resting time
Oven temperature: see individual recipes
Cooking time: see individual recipes

Imperial/Metric
8 oz./225 g. plain flour
$\frac{1}{2}$ teaspoon salt
6 oz./175 g. fat
7 tablespoons cold water

American
2 cups all-purpose flour
$\frac{1}{2}$ teaspoon salt
$\frac{3}{4}$ cup shortening
generous $\frac{1}{2}$ cup cold water

Sieve the flour and salt into a bowl. Divide the fat into quarters and rub one-quarter into the sieved flour and salt, until the mixture resembles breadcrumbs. Add the water and mix with a round-bladed knife to form a soft dough. Turn onto a lightly floured board and knead lightly to remove all the cracks. Place the dough in a polythene bag and leave in the refrigerator or a cool place to rest for 20 minutes.

Roll out the dough to a rectangular shape, about a $\frac{1}{4}$ inch ($\frac{1}{2}$ cm.) thick, and three times as long as it is wide. Take one portion of the remaining fat and dot it in small knobs over the top two-thirds of the dough and to within a $\frac{1}{2}$ inch (1 cm.) of the edges. Bring the bottom third of the dough

up and the top third down to cover the centre third. Press the edges firmly with a rolling pin to seal. Cover the dough as before, and leave it to rest until firm to the touch.

Half turn the dough, so that the fold is on the right hand side. Repeat the rolling, dotting with fat and folding processes twice more. After the pastry has rested until it is firm to the touch it is ready to use as directed in the individual recipes. Flaky pastry can be made the day before it is required, provided it is placed in a polythene bag and stored in the refrigerator.

☼ Flaky pastry can be frozen unbaked. Allow the dough to thaw before using.

Sieve the flour and salt into a bowl. Divide the fat into four pieces and rub one-quarter of it into sieved flour, until the mixture resembles fine breadcrumbs. Add the water and mix, with a round-bladed knife, to form a soft dough.

Turn the dough onto a lightly floured surface and knead it to remove all the cracks and form a smooth dough. Place the dough in a polythene bag and leave it in the refrigerator for 20 minutes.

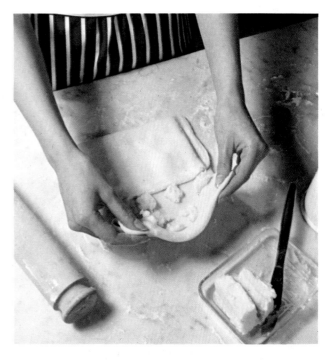

After resting the dough, roll it out to a rectangular shape three times as long as it is wide. Dot one portion of the remaining fat over the top two-thirds of the dough.

Bring the bottom third of the dough up and the top third down to cover the centre third. Press the edges firmly with a rolling pin to seal. Cover and leave to rest before repeating the rolling, dotting and folding processes with the remaining portions of fat.

Puff pastry

In this type of pastry equal quantities of fat and flour are used. Use iced water to make the dough and also add a squeeze of lemon juice. If possible, use butter for making puff pastry which should be firm but not soft. Avoid making puff pastry on a very hot day, or when the kitchen is very hot as the rolling will become difficult and the results will not be too good.

Rolling puff pastry requires some practice; give the dough quick, short rolls—avoid pushing the pin along the dough as this tends to push the butter out. With each rolling, the dough should become thinner and thinner. The first two or three rollings need care to ensure that the butter does not come through and stick to the surface or the rolling pin. Beware of using too much flour on the rolling surface or pin otherwise the equal proportions will be altered.

Main utensils: sieve, bowl
Preparation time: about 2 hours, including resting time
Oven temperature: see individual recipes
Cooking time: see individual recipes

Imperial/Metric	American
6 oz./175 g. plain flour	1½ cups all-purpose flour
pinch salt	pinch salt
6 oz./175 g. butter	¾ cup butter
about ¼ pint/1½ dl. iced water	about ⅔ cup iced water
squeeze lemon juice	squeeze lemon juice

Sieve the flour and salt into a bowl. Rub in 1 oz. (25 g.) of the butter. Add the water and lemon juice and mix, with a round-bladed knife, to form a firm dough. Roll out the dough to a rectangle about ½ inch (1 cm.) thick. Place the butter, in a whole slab and shaped roughly to an 8-oz. (225-g.) block, in the centre of one half of the dough. Fold over the other half to enclose the butter and press the edges together. Cover and place in the refrigerator for 15 minutes.

Roll out the dough, with the sealed ends towards you, to a rectangle slightly larger than the previous one; fold into three. Turn the dough so that the open edge faces you and roll out again, to a still slightly larger rectangle. Repeat the process twice more, so that altogether the dough has six turns of rolling and resting. If the dough still appears streaky give it another roll and turn. Place in a polythene bag and leave in the refrigerator for 15 minutes before using as directed in the individual recipes. Puff pastry dough can be kept, covered, in the refrigerator for up to 2 days.

❄ Puff pastry can be frozen unbaked. Allow the dough to thaw before using.

Rough puff pastry

This pastry is similar to puff pastry, the method of making is slightly similar but the proportion of fat to flour is less. It can be used in place of puff pastry. For best results use a hard margarine, butter or a mixture of white fat (not lard) and butter or margarine.

Main utensils: sieve, bowl
Preparation time: about 1½ hours, including resting time
Oven temperature: see individual recipes
Cooking time: see individual recipes

Imperial/Metric	American
8 oz./225 g. plain flour	2 cups all-purpose flour
pinch salt	pinch salt
6 oz./175 g. fat	¾ cup shortening
6–8 tablespoons cold water	½–⅔ cup cold water

Sieve the flour and salt into a mixing bowl. Cut the fat into small pieces and add to the sieved flour mixture. Toss lightly with the fingertips so that each piece of fat is coated with flour *but not broken up*. Add 6 tablespoons of the water and mix together with a round-bladed knife to form a soft dough (add the remaining water if necessary to take up any loose flour in the bowl). Gather the dough together and turn onto a lightly floured board. Sprinkle lightly with flour. Roll out to a piece twice as long as it is wide. Fold into three by bringing the bottom third upwards and the top third down to cover it. Lightly press the three open edges with the rolling pin to seal.

Turn the dough round so that the right hand edge is facing you and roll out to a slightly smaller oblong than before. Fold and seal the edges as before, place the dough in a polythene bag and put it in the refrigerator for 20 minutes. Repeat the rolling and folding processes twice more. Cover and leave to rest for 20 minutes before using as directed in the individual recipes.

❄ Rough puff pastry can be frozen unbaked. Allow the dough to thaw before using.

Suet pastry

This is an easy pastry to make and can be used for sweet and savoury dishes—fruit layer puddings, meat puddings, dumplings etc. It should be light and spongy in texture, not wet and leathery.

Unlike other pastries, suet pastry needs some form of raising agent, so self-raising flour is usually used (or plain flour and baking powder). The best suet to use is that which surrounds beef kidneys—it should be grated before using. A good alternative is the ready-shredded package suet.

	Imperial/Metric	American
Main utensils: sieve, bowl	8 oz./225 g. self-raising flour or plain flour and 2 teaspoons baking powder	2 cups all-purpose flour and 2 teaspoons baking powder
Preparation time: few minutes		
Cooking time: see individual recipes	½ teaspoon salt	½ teaspoon salt
	4 oz./110 g. shredded suet	scant 1 cup finely chopped suet
	¼ pint/1½ dl. cold water	⅔ cup cold water

Sieve the flour (and baking powder, if used) into a mixing bowl. Stir in the shredded suet and add the water. Mix with a round-bladed knife to form a soft dough. Turn onto a lightly floured board, sprinkle with a little flour and knead and shape into a ball. Cover the dough with the upturned mixing bowl and leave it to rest for about 10 minutes, before using as directed in the recipes.

Hot water crust pastry (See step by step pictures on pages 72 and 73)

This is the pastry used for raised game and pork pies and is prepared in a very different way from the other pastries. Hot water crust must be moulded while it is still warm and can be handled a little more roughly than the other pastries. It is not difficult to make, but care must be taken when moulding it to ensure that there are no cracks through which the meat juices could escape during baking. The best fat to use for hot water crust is lard or a white fat.

	Imperial/Metric	American
Main utensils: sieve, bowl, saucepan	12 oz./350 g. plain flour	3 cups all-purpose flour
Preparation time: 5 minutes	½ teaspoon salt	½ teaspoon salt
Oven temperature: see individual recipes	4 oz./100 g. lard	½ cup lard
	¼ pint/1½ dl. water	⅔ cup water
Cooking time: see individual recipes		

Sieve the flour and salt into a mixing bowl. Place the lard and water in a saucepan and put over a moderate heat. Bring gradually to the boil and then pour into the centre of the sieved flour mixture. Beat the mixture with a wooden spoon until it clings together. Turn onto a lightly floured board and knead until smooth. This dough must be moulded while it is still warm. Keep any dough which you put aside for a lid under an upturned basin to keep it warm.

Crumb crust pastry

This type of pastry is used for lining flan cases and as a base for cheesecakes. It can be made from digestive, semi-sweet or ginger biscuits, or breakfast cereals.

	Imperial/Metric	American
Main utensils: liquidiser, saucepan (preferably non-stick)	6 oz./175 g. biscuit crumbs	2 cups graham cracker crumbs
Preparation time: few minutes	3 oz./75 g. butter	6 tablespoons butter
Oven temperature: see individual recipes	3 oz./75 g. castor sugar	6 tablespoons granulated sugar
Cooking time: see individual recipes		

Crush the biscuits finely (a liquidiser can be used; put the biscuits into the goblet, a few at a time, and switch on until they are reduced to crumbs). Melt the butter in a saucepan, remove from the heat and stir in the crumbs and sugar. Blend well together. Press the mixture into an 8-inch (20-cm.) flan dish or sandwich tin (or shaped foil dishes for freezing).

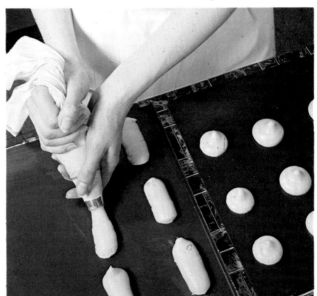

Bring the water and butter or margarine to the boil over a moderate heat. Stir in the sieved flour and beat the mixture, with a wooden spoon, over the heat until it forms a ball and leaves the sides of the pan clean.

Remove from the heat and beat in the eggs, one at a time, beating well after the addition of each egg. When ready, the choux paste should be soft with no traces of egg in the mixture.

Spoon the choux paste into a piping bag fitted with a plain tube and pipe the mixture onto baking trays (preferably non-stick) into the required shapes.

Choux pastry

A very light pastry with a crisp texture. This pastry is used for éclairs, choux buns, savoury puffs, gougère etc. and surprisingly enough it is not difficult to make. To incorporate as much air as possible into the mixture it must be thoroughly beaten with a wooden spoon after the addition of each egg. Plain flour is always used for choux pastry. Thorough cooking is important for this type of pastry—if it is not sufficiently cooked it will collapse when taken from the oven.

Main utensil: saucepan (preferably non-stick)
Preparation time: 5 minutes
Oven temperature: see individual recipes
Cooking time: see individual recipes

Imperial/Metric
2½ oz./65 g. plain flour

¼ pint/1½ dl. water
2 oz./50 g. butter or margarine
2 eggs

American
½ cup plus 2 tablespoons all-purpose flour
⅔ cup water
¼ cup butter or margarine
2 eggs

Sieve the flour. Put the water and butter or margarine in a pan and bring to the boil over a moderate heat (as soon as the mixture boils remove it from the heat to prevent any evaporation of the liquid). Stir in the sieved flour, return to a low heat and cook, beating with a wooden spoon, until the mixture forms a ball and leaves the sides of the pan clean. Remove from the heat and beat in the eggs, one at a time, beating well after the addition of each egg. The choux pastry is now ready to be used as directed in the recipes.
  Choux pastry can be frozen either baked or unbaked.

To line a flan ring

Place the flan ring (a fluted one is usually used for sweet flans and a plain one for savoury flans) on a baking tray—a non-stick one for ease. Roll out the pastry a $\frac{1}{4}$ inch ($\frac{1}{2}$ cm.) thick and 2 inches (5 cm.) larger than the flan ring. Lift the pastry on the rolling pin, transfer it to the ring and ease the pastry into the shape, using your fingertips, without pulling or stretching it—this will cause it to shrink back during baking. Roll across the top of the ring (from the centre out to each side) with the rolling pin to cut off the surplus pastry.

A fluted flan dish is lined in the same way, but there is no need to stand it on a baking tray.

Roll out the flan pastry to a circle a little larger than the flan ring. Place the flan ring on a baking tray. Lift the pastry on the rolling pin, transfer it to the ring and ease the pastry into the shape, using your fingertips, without pulling or stretching it.

To cut off surplus pastry, roll pin across the top of the ring from the centre out to each side. To bake the flan case blind, line it with greaseproof paper and fill with baking beans. After 15 minutes' baking remove the flan ring, paper and beans and bake the pastry shell for a further 10–15 minutes.

To bake a flan case blind

Line the flan case with a circle of greaseproof paper and fill it with baking beans, rice or crusts of stale bread. Cook, on the second shelf from the top, in a preheated moderately hot oven (400°F., 200°C., Gas Mark 6) for 15 minutes. Remove the greaseproof paper, beans and flan ring and return the pastry shell to the oven and bake for a further 10–15 minutes, after which time the flan case will be fully baked. When cold

the flan case can be filled with fresh, canned or frozen fruit, or a prepared savoury filling. Often a flan case is baked blind for 15 minutes, a filling is added and then the flan is returned to a slightly lower oven; this prevents the filling making the pastry soggy.

Baking in a flan dish enables you to serve the flan from the dish in which it was cooked.

To freeze unbaked pies

Do not glaze the pie or cut a steam vent. Wrap in freezer foil or place in a polythene bag. Seal, label and freeze. Before baking (frozen or defrosted) brush with beaten egg or milk and cut a steam vent.
Note: It is most important to allow the filling of a pie to cool before covering it with the pastry. A hot filling causes the pastry to become soggy underneath.

To freeze unbaked and baked pastry cases

It is much more useful to have a selection of unbaked and baked pastry cases frozen than it is to freeze a piece of shortcrust dough. When freezing unbaked pastry cases, line shaped foil dishes so that your flan dishes and pie plates are not out of commission for weeks on end. Wrap the cases in freezer foil; seal and label. Baked pastry cases are a little fragile so must be stored carefully to avoid being damaged.

Glazes for savoury and sweet pies

To give an attractive finish, the surface of a pie or tart is usually glazed before baking. A savoury pie can be brushed with egg yolk (for a very shiny finish given to raised pies), beaten egg, milk or a mixture of beaten egg and milk. A sweet pie does not have such a shiny glaze and is usually brushed with water and sprinkled with castor sugar before baking. If liked, more sugar, or icing sugar if preferred, can be sprinkled over while the pie is cooling.

Fruit, in a flan, is also given a glaze mainly to keep it moist and attractive looking. In this case a glaze is made with fruit juice or water and arrowroot; boiled, sieved jam can be used as an alternative. Choose a flavour of jam that will blend with the fruit in the flan.

To cover a pie or line a pie plate

Roll out the pastry to a shape 2 inches (5 cm.) larger than the pie dish. Cut off a strip 1 inch (2·5 cm.) wide all round the edge; brush the pie dish edge with water and fit on the strip; brush the strip with water. Lift the remaining pastry on the rolling pin and transfer it to the pie dish. Press the edges firmly together and trim neatly. Knock up the pastry edges by making a series of shallow cuts round the edge of the pastry with a knife held horizontally. Flute the edges by making indentations between the thumb and forefinger.

To make pastry decorations

Leaves Make them from the pastry trimmings by rolling the trimmings out and cutting into strips. Cut the strips, at an angle, into diamond-shaped pieces. With the back of the knife mark veins on the leaves.
Decorative bud Form a piece of pastry into a small ball. Roll out two small pastry rounds and cover the ball with them, bringing the loose ends together underneath and pressing them firmly to seal. With a sharp knife cut a cross in the top of the pastry ball; open out and turn back the cut segments.

Shortcrust and cheese pastry recipes

Raisin and cider tart

Main utensils: saucepan
  (preferably non-stick), 9-inch
  (23-cm.) ovenproof plate
Preparation time: 10 minutes, not
  including making the pastry
Oven temperature: moderately hot
  (400°F., 200°C., Gas Mark 6)
Cooking time: about 30 minutes
Serves: 6

Imperial/Metric
4 teaspoons cornflour
½ pint/3 dl. sweet cider
12 oz./350 g. raisins
2 oz./50 g. castor sugar
12 oz./350 g. shortcrust pastry
  (see page 104)
beaten egg white to glaze

American
4 teaspoons cornstarch
1¼ cups sweet cider
2 cups raisins
¼ cup granulated sugar
¾ lb. shortcrust pastry (see page 104)

beaten egg white to glaze

Blend the cornflour with a little of the cider. Put the raisins, blended cornflour, remaining cider and half the sugar in a saucepan. Place over a low heat and bring to the boil, stirring. Cook for 1–2 minutes, stirring all the time. Remove from the heat and leave aside to cool.

Roll out half the pastry and use to line the 9-inch (23-cm.) ovenproof plate. Spread the raisin filling over the pastry-lined plate; roll out the remaining pastry, dampen the pastry edge on the plate and cover with the pastry lid. Flake and flute the edges, brush with beaten egg white and sprinkle with the remaining sugar. Make a steam vent and bake near the top of the oven for about 30 minutes. Serve hot or cold, with cream.

Macaroon tartlets

Main utensils: patty tins
  (preferably non-stick), fluted
  cutter
Preparation time: 20 minutes, not
  including making the pastry
Oven temperature: moderately hot
  (400°F., 200°C., Gas Mark 6)
Cooking time: about 25 minutes
Makes: 18

Imperial/Metric
6 oz./175 g. shortcrust pastry
  (see page 104)
1 tablespoon sieved jam
2 egg whites
2 oz./50 g. ground almonds
4 oz./100 g. castor sugar
few drops almond essence

American
6 oz. shortcrust pastry (see page 104)

1 tablespoon sieved jam
2 egg whites
½ cup ground almonds
½ cup granulated sugar
few drops almond extract

Roll out the pastry fairly thinly and cut out 18 rounds, using a fluted cutter. Line the patty tins with the pastry rounds. Spoon a little of the jam into the bottom of each pastry-lined tin. Place the remaining ingredients in a basin and whisk them together until well mixed and frothy. Three-quarters fill each tart with the almond mixture. From the pastry trimmings cut small strips and place two, crossways, on each tart. Bake near the top of the oven for about 25 minutes, until the pastry is light golden brown and the filling risen and set.

Veal and bacon pie

Main utensils: 1½-pint (about
  1-litre) pie dish, baking tray
  (preferably non-stick)
Preparation time: 20 minutes, not
  including making the pastry
Oven temperature: moderately hot
  (400°F., 200°C., Gas Mark 6)
Cooking time: about 1 hour 10
  minutes
Serves: 6

Imperial/Metric
1¼ lb./600 g. pie veal
4 oz./100 g. bacon
1 teaspoon grated lemon rind
little thyme
1 small onion, chopped
salt and pepper
¼ pint/1½ dl. stock
1 hard-boiled egg
8 oz./225 g. shortcrust pastry
  (see page 104)
beaten egg to glaze

American
1¼ lb. pie veal
¼ lb. bacon slices
1 teaspoon grated lemon rind
little thyme
1 small onion, chopped
salt and pepper
⅔ cup stock
1 hard-cooked egg
½ lb. shortcrust pastry (see page 104)

beaten egg to glaze

Trim the veal and chop the bacon. Mix with the lemon rind, thyme, onion and seasoning. Place in the pie dish and pour in the stock. Slice the egg and arrange over the filling.

Roll out the pastry and use to cover the pie. Flake and flute the edges, decorate with pastry leaves made from the trimmings, brush the top with beaten egg and make a steam vent. Place on a baking tray and bake near the top of the oven for about 40 minutes. Lower the heat to moderate (350°F., 180°C., Gas Mark 4) and bake for a further 30 minutes, covering the pastry with foil, if necessary, to prevent it from becoming too brown.

Cheese and apple pie

Main utensils: 1-pint (about ½-litre) pie dish, baking tray (preferably non-stick)
Preparation time: 15 minutes, not including making the pastry
Oven temperature: moderately hot (400°F., 200°C., Gas Mark 6)
Cooking time: 25 minutes
Serves: 6

Imperial/Metric
8 oz./225 g. cheese pastry (see page 105)
4 oz./100 g. Cheddar cheese
4 oz./100 g. castor sugar
pinch salt
1 oz./25 g. plain flour
¼ teaspoon ground cinnamon
grated rind of 1 lemon
1 lb./½ kg. cooking apples
castor sugar to sprinkle

American
½ lb. cheese pastry (see page 105)
¼ lb. Cheddar cheese
½ cup granulated sugar
pinch salt
¼ cup all-purpose flour
¼ teaspoon ground cinnamon
grated rind of 1 lemon
1 lb. baking apples
granulated sugar to sprinkle

Roll out the pastry and use to line the pie dish. Cut the cheese into cubes and mix with the sugar, salt, flour, cinnamon and lemon rind. Peel, core and slice the apples. Cover the bottom of the pastry-lined dish with a layer of prepared apples and add half the cheese mixture. Fill the dish in this way, ending with a layer of apples. Roll out the pastry trimmings and cut into strips; use to make a lattice work over the filling. Sprinkle with castor sugar, place the pie dish on a baking tray and bake near the top of the oven for 25 minutes. Cover with a piece of foil to prevent the pie from becoming too brown and bake for about a further 10 minutes. Serve hot.

Flaky, puff and rough puff pastry recipes

Cream horns (Illustrated on page 115)

Main utensils: cream horn tins, baking tray (preferably non-stick)
Preparation time: 20 minutes, not including making the pastry
Oven temperature: hot (425°F., 220°C., Gas Mark 7)
Cooking time: 20 minutes
Makes: 8

Imperial/Metric
8 oz./225 g. flaky pastry (see page 106)
milk and castor sugar to glaze
Filling:
about 2 oz./50 g. jam
¼ pint/1½ dl. double cream

American
½ lb. flaky pastry (see page 106)
milk and granulated sugar to glaze
Filling:
about 3 tablespoons jam
⅔ cup whipping cream

Roll out the pastry to an oblong about 10 inches (26 cm.) by 13 inches (32·5 cm.) and cut into 1-inch (2·5-cm.) wide strips about 12 inches (30 cm.) long. Brush one edge of each strip with water. Wind the pastry strips around the outside of the greased horn tins, beginning at the pointed end, and overlapping the dampened edge of each new turn of the pastry.

Place on a baking tray with the pastry ends underneath and leave to rest in the refrigerator for at least 15 minutes.

Bake near the top of the preheated oven for 15 minutes. Remove from the oven, brush with milk and sprinkle with sugar and return to the oven to bake for a further 5 minutes. (Watch carefully to see that the open ends of the cream horns do not burn.) Cool slightly, then remove from the tins and cool on a wire tray. When cold pipe (or spoon) a little jam into each and fill with whipped cream.
Note: Serve fairly soon, when filled, as the filling tends to make the pastry soft.

Fruit border (Illustrated opposite)

Main utensils: baking tray, small
   saucepan (preferably non-stick)
Preparation time: 10 minutes, not
   including making the pastry
Oven temperature: hot (425°F.,
   220°C., Gas Mark 7)
Cooking time: about 20 minutes
Serves: 6–8

Imperial/Metric	**American**
8 oz./225 g. flaky pastry (see page 106)	½ lb. flaky pastry (see page 106)
milk to glaze	milk to glaze
4–6 fresh peaches	4–6 fresh peaches
1 tablespoon apricot or peach jam	1 tablespoon apricot or peach jam
2 teaspoons water	2 teaspoons water

Roll out the pastry to a rectangle about 10 inches (26 cm.) by 6 inches (15 cm.). Cut a 1-inch (2·5-cm.) strip off each side; place the pastry rectangle on a baking tray and prick all over with a fork. Brush the edges with milk. Carefully place the pastry strips on the edges of the rectangle and press gently to secure the strips. Leave to rest in the refrigerator for about 20 minutes. Mark a diamond pattern, with the blade of a knife, on the strips and brush with milk. Bake near the top of the preheated oven for 15–20 minutes; cool on a wire tray.

Peel the peaches, if liked, and cut them into thin slices. Arrange the peach slices in the pastry case. Heat the jam with the water then sieve it. Brush the fruit slices with the jam glaze. Serve cold with cream.
Note: Other fresh fruit, frozen fruit or drained canned fruit can be used in place of the peaches. A mixture of fruits also makes an attractive filling.

Cream and raspberry layer (Illustrated opposite)

Main utensil: baking tray
   (preferably non-stick)
Preparation time: 10 minutes, not
   including making the pastry
Oven temperature: hot (425°F.,
   220°C., Gas Mark 7)
Cooking time: about 10 minutes
Serves: 6

Imperial/Metric	**American**
6 oz./175 g. puff or flaky pastry (see pages 108, 106)	6 oz. puff or flaky pastry (see pages 108, 106)
½ pint/3 dl. double cream	1¼ cups whipping cream
4 oz./100 g. fresh raspberries	about 1 cup fresh raspberries
icing sugar to sprinkle	confectioners' sugar to sprinkle

Divide the pastry in half and roll out each piece to a strip about 4 inches (10 cm.) wide and as long as possible. Trim the edges neatly, place on a baking tray and prick all over with a fork. Leave to rest in the refrigerator for 20 minutes. Bake near the top of the oven for 10–12 minutes, until risen and a light golden brown colour. Cool on a wire tray.

Just before serving, whip the cream until thickened and spread or pipe over one of the layers. Arrange the raspberries on the cream and top with the other pastry layer. Dust the top with sieved icing sugar.

Sausage rolls (Illustrated opposite)

Main utensil: baking tray
   (preferably non-stick)
Preparation time: 10 minutes, not
   including making the pastry
Oven temperature: very hot (450°F.,
   230°C., Gas Mark 8)
Cooking time: 20–25 minutes
Makes: 14–16

Imperial/Metric	**American**
8 oz./225 g. flaky pastry (see page 106)	½ lb. flaky pastry (see page 106)
8 oz./225 g. sausage meat	½ lb. sausage meat
beaten egg to glaze	beaten egg to glaze

Roll out the pastry to an oblong 14 inches (36 cm.) by 10 inches (26 cm.). Cut in half, lengthways, making two long strips. Form the sausage meat into two rolls, each one about 14 inches (36 cm.) in length. Place the sausage meat on the front half of each strip, brush one of the long edges with water and fold the pastry over the sausage meat. Seal the edges together and flake with the back of a knife. Cut each length into seven or eight sausage rolls and make three diagonal cuts across the top of each. Place on a baking tray and leave in the refrigerator for at least 15 minutes. Brush with beaten egg and bake near the top of the pre-heated oven for 20–25 minutes. Serve hot or cold.

Boeuf en croûte, sausage rolls, vol-au-vent, bouchées, cream horns, fruit border and cream and raspberry layer (see pages 116, 114, 113)

Boeuf en croûte (Illustrated on page 115)

Main utensils: roasting tin, frying pan (preferably non-stick)
Preparation time: 15 minutes, not including making the pastry
Oven temperature: hot (425°F., 220°C., Gas Mark 7)
Cooking time: 45 minutes
Serves: 6

Imperial/Metric
1 piece beef fillet (about 2 lb./ 1 kg.)
2 oz./50 g. butter
salt and pepper
1 onion, chopped
4 oz./100 g. mushrooms, chopped
1 tablespoon tomato purée
8 oz./225 g. flaky, puff or rough puff pastry (see pages 106, 108)
beaten egg to glaze
Garnish:
watercress

American
1 piece beef tenderloin (about 2 lb.)
¼ cup butter
salt and pepper
1 onion, chopped
1 cup chopped mushrooms
1 tablespoon tomato paste
½ lb. flaky, puff or rough puff pastry (see pages 106, 108)
beaten egg to glaze
Garnish:
watercress

Trim the fillet, place in a roasting tin and spread half the butter over the meat. Season well and place in the centre of the hot oven for about 15 minutes, to seal the meat. Tip any juices from the meat into a frying pan and heat with the remaining butter. Sauté the chopped onion and mushrooms for 3–4 minutes, until softened. Stir in the tomato purée and seasoning.

Roll out the pastry to an oblong large enough to completely enclose the meat. Place the cooled fillet in the centre of the pastry, spread with the onion and mushroom mixture. Brush the edges with water, bring them together to make a parcel. Seal all edges and place on a baking tray with the joins underneath. Make leaves from any trimmings; glaze the pastry with beaten egg and put the leaves in position. Bake near the top of the oven for about 30 minutes. The pastry should be golden brown and crisp and the meat rare; serve garnished with watercress. A crisp green salad goes well with this dish which is equally good served hot or cold.

Vol-au-vent cases (Illustrated on page 115)

Main utensils: baking tray (preferably non-stick), pastry cutters
Preparation time: 10 minutes, not including making the pastry
Oven temperature: hot (425°F., 220°C., Gas Mark 7)
Cooking time: about 20 minutes
Makes: 8

Imperial/Metric
8 oz./225 g. puff pastry (see page 108)
beaten egg to glaze

American
½ lb. puff pastry (see page 108)
beaten egg to glaze

Roll out the pastry to a ½-inch (1-cm.) thickness and cut into rounds using a 2½-inch (6-cm.) floured plain cutter. With a smaller cutter, cut through the centre of each round, almost to the bottom; do not remove the pastry from the centre. Place the rounds on a dampened baking tray. Leave to rest in the refrigerator for 20 minutes. Brush the tops with beaten egg and bake near the top of the oven for about 20 minutes, until well risen. Allow to cool slightly, then remove the cut-out centre pieces from each case, leaving a complete pastry shell. Keep the tops to use as lids and scrape out and discard any soft dough with the handle of a teaspoon.

Note: Bouchée cases are made in the same way, but they are much smaller and served with various fillings, as a cocktail or party snack. If liked, you can make large oval vol-au-vent cases, to serve three or four, using an oval cardboard shape as a guide.

Fillings for vol-au-vent and bouchée cases

Kidney and mushroom Soak 2–3 lambs' kidneys in salted water. Drain and cut into small pieces. Fry in heated oil for 2–3 minutes with a few sliced mushrooms added. Season to taste, add 1 tablespoon red wine and cook until it has evaporated. Spoon into the hot cases and place the lids at an angle to show the filling.

Mushroom and bacon Stir 4 oz. (100 g.) sliced sautéed mushrooms and 2 bacon rashers, chopped and fried, into ½ pint (3 dl.) well seasoned white sauce.

Prawn and egg Stir 4 oz. (100 g.) prepared prawns and 1 chopped hard-boiled egg into ½ pint (3 dl.) well seasoned white sauce. Use whole prawns to garnish, if liked.

Cheese Make a thick cheese sauce and season it well with cayenne pepper and dry mustard. Use as a filling for bouchées and garnish with parsley and small pieces of black olive.

Note: It is easier to pipe certain fillings into bouchée cases. Try softened cream cheese mixed with chopped chives, small pineapple pieces or tomato purée, sieved or liquidised cottage cheese.

Suet pastry recipes

West Country apple dumplings

Main utensil: saucepan	Imperial/Metric	American
(preferably non-stick)	2 oz./50 g. butter	¼ cup butter
Preparation time: 10 minutes, not	2 oz./50 g. soft brown sugar	¼ cup brown sugar
including making the pastry	1 tablespoon brandy	1 tablespoon brandy
Cooking time: 35 minutes	4 medium cooking apples	4 medium baking apples
Serves: 4	8 oz./225 g. suet pastry (see page 109)	½ lb. suet pastry (see page 109)
	castor sugar to sprinkle	granulated sugar to sprinkle

Mix together the butter, brown sugar and brandy and set aside for the filling. Peel and core the apples. Divide the pastry into four and roll out each piece to a round large enough to completely cover the apple. Place an apple on each pastry round and fill the centre with some of the filling. Brush the edges of each round with water and enclose the apple in pastry by bringing the edges to the top of the apple and moulding them to seal. Wrap each dumpling in a piece of foil, twist to seal tightly and place the dumplings in a pan of boiling water. Cover and boil for 35 minutes, replenishing the pan with more boiling water if necessary.

To serve the dumplings, remove them from the foil and sprinkle with castor sugar. Serve hot.

Bacon and onion roll

Main utensil: saucepan	Imperial/Metric	American
(preferably non-stick)	8 oz./225 g. streaky bacon	½ lb. bacon slices
Preparation time: 10 minutes, not	1 large onion	1 large onion
including making the pastry	8 oz./225 g. suet pastry (see page 109)	½ lb. suet pastry (see page 109)
Cooking time: 2 hours	2 sage leaves, chopped, or pinch dried mixed herbs	2 sage leaves, chopped, or pinch dried mixed herbs
Serves: 4	pepper	pepper

Rind and chop the bacon and chop the onion finely. Roll out the pastry to a rectangle about 10 inches (26 cm.) by 8 inches (20 cm.). Spoon on the prepared bacon and onion and sprinkle with the herbs and pepper. Roll up the pastry from the longer side and wrap loosely, but securely, in a piece of foil. Twist the ends to seal. Put into a pan of boiling water, cover with a lid, and boil steadily for 2 hours, replenishing the pan with more boiling water to keep the roll covered. To serve, remove the foil and place the roll on a serving dish.

Choux pastry recipes

Cream puffs (Illustrated on page 103)

Main utensils: saucepan, 2 baking	Imperial/Metric	American
trays (preferably non-stick)	2½ oz./65 g. choux pastry (see page 110)	2½ oz. choux pastry (see page 110)
Preparation time: 15 minutes	¼ pint/1½ dl. double cream	⅔ cup whipping cream
Oven temperature: hot (425°F.,	icing sugar to sprinkle	confectioners' sugar to sprinkle
220°C., Gas Mark 7)		
Cooking time: about 35 minutes		
Makes: 12–14		

Spoon the choux pastry into a piping bag fitted with a large plain tube. Pipe round shapes of the choux pastry, well apart, onto the baking trays. Bake on the second and third shelves from the top of the preheated hot oven for 15 minutes. Lower the heat to moderately hot (375°F., 190°C., Gas Mark 5) and bake for a further 20–25 minutes, until the puffs are crisp, dry and well risen. Cool on a wire tray. When cold, make a slit in the side of each and spoon or pipe in a little whipped cream. Dust the top with icing sugar and serve.

Variations

Eclairs (Illustrated on page 103) Make and bake the choux pastry as directed for cream puffs, but pipe the mixture into 3-inch (7·5-cm.) lengths onto the baking trays. When cold, fill with whipped cream and coat the tops with chocolate or coffee glacé icing (see page 134).

Profiteroles Make the choux pastry and pipe small balls of it onto baking trays. Bake until well risen and crisp; cool on a wire tray. Slit the base of each profiterole and fill with whipped cream. Pile into a serving dish, or individual dishes and just before serving spoon over a little chocolate sauce, made by melting 2 oz. (50 g.) plain chocolate in a basin over hot water. Mix in 2 tablespoons golden syrup, 1 oz. (25 g.) butter and 1 teaspoon brandy and beat until smooth and glossy. (Or use a double saucepan.)

To freeze baked choux pastry shapes, allow them to cool, then pack and seal. Fill when defrosted.

Gougère

Main utensils: saucepan (preferably non-stick), medium ovenproof dish
Preparation time: 20 minutes, including making the pastry
Oven temperature: moderately hot (400°F., 200°C., Gas Mark 6)
Cooking time: 40–45 minutes
Serves: 4

Imperial/Metric
2½ oz./65 g. choux pastry (see page 110)
Filling:
1 oz./25 g. butter
4 oz./100 g. cooked chicken, finely chopped
1 onion, chopped
1 tablespoon flour
2 oz./50 g. mushrooms, chopped
1 tablespoon tomato purée
¼ pint/1½ dl. chicken stock
salt and pepper
pinch rosemary
2 oz./50 g. cheese, grated
2 tablespoons browned breadcrumbs

American
2½ oz. choux pastry (see page 110)
Filling:
2 tablespoons butter
½ cup finely chopped cooked chicken
1 onion, chopped
1 tablespoon all-purpose flour
½ cup chopped mushrooms
1 tablespoon tomato paste
⅔ cup chicken stock
salt and pepper
pinch rosemary
½ cup grated cheese
3 tablespoons dry bread crumbs

To make the filling, heat the butter in a saucepan and sauté the chicken and onion until softened, but not brown. Stir in the flour and cook for 1–2 minutes. Add the mushrooms, tomato purée, stock, salt, pepper and rosemary. Stirring, bring to the boil; lower the heat and cook gently until thickened and the liquid has reduced.

Spoon or pipe the choux paste, in a circle, inside an ovenproof dish. Carefully spoon the chicken filling into the centre, sprinkle over the grated cheese and browned breadcrumbs. Bake in the centre of the preheated moderately hot oven for 40–45 minutes, until the choux paste is well risen and golden brown. Sprinkle with chopped parsley and serve at once.

Cheese aigrettes

Main utensil: deep fat fryer (preferably non-stick)
Preparation time: 10 minutes, including making the pastry
Cooking time: few minutes
Serves: 6

Imperial/Metric
2½ oz./65 g. choux pastry (see page 110)
pinch cayenne pepper
salt and pepper
1 oz./25 g. grated Parmesan cheese
3 oz./75 g. Cheddar cheese, finely grated
fat or oil for deep frying

American
2½ oz. choux pastry (see page 110)
pinch cayenne pepper
salt and pepper
¼ cup grated Parmesan cheese
¾ cup finely grated Cheddar cheese
shortening or oil for deep frying

Make the choux pastry and beat in cayenne pepper, salt and pepper to taste. Beat in the grated Parmesan cheese and 2 oz. (50 g.) of the Cheddar cheese. Heat the fat or oil and drop in teaspoonfuls of the mixture, a few at a time.

Fry for a few minutes, turning them if necessary to brown evenly, until brown and well risen. Remove with a draining spoon and drain on absorbent paper. Arrange on a dish, sprinkle with the remaining cheese and serve at once.

Curry puffs

Main utensil: baking tray (preferably non-stick)
Preparation time: 15 minutes, including making the pastry
Oven temperature: moderately hot (400°F., 200°C., Gas Mark 6)
Cooking time: 40 minutes
Makes: about 16

Imperial/Metric
2½ oz./65 g. choux pastry (see page 110)
1–2 tablespoons curry powder
pinch paprika pepper
Filling:
4 oz./100 g. cream cheese
2 oz./50 g. butter
1 oz./25 g. walnuts, finely chopped

American
2½ oz. choux pastry (see page 110)
2 tablespoons curry powder
pinch paprika pepper
Filling:
½ cup cream cheese
¼ cup butter
¼ cup finely chopped walnuts

Make the choux pastry, beating in the curry powder and paprika pepper with the flour. Pipe or spoon the paste, in small rounds, onto baking trays. Bake near the top of the oven for 20 minutes. Lower the heat to moderate (325°F., 170°C., Gas Mark 3) and bake for a further 20 minutes. Make a small hole in the side of each puff and leave them to cool on a wire tray.

To make the filling, beat together the cream cheese, butter and walnuts. Cut each choux puff in half and sandwich together with some of the filling. Arrange on a dish and garnish with a sprinkling of paprika pepper.
Note: Serve these curry puffs fairly soon after they have been filled as the filling tends to make the choux pastry soft.

A selection of loaves and rolls (see pages 120, 121)

A guide to yeast cookery

Prepare the dried yeast by placing it with the sugar and half the warm water in a jug and leaving it in a warm place until frothy. Rub the butter or margarine into the sieved flour and salt. Mix in the yeast liquid and remaining water to form a dough.

Turn the dough onto a floured surface and knead it thoroughly until it is elastic and no longer sticky. Cover and leave to rise.

Turn out the risen dough and knock out the air bubbles. It is now ready to be shaped in various ways and put to prove, or to be put in a polythene bag, sealed and labelled for freezing.

Contrary to many housewives' belief, cooking with yeast is not difficult. It may be a little time consuming (but with the introduction of short-time doughs even those of you with little time to spare can have no excuse for not baking with yeast), but you can do other jobs in the kitchen while the dough is rising. Another bonus to yeast cookery is that unbaked and baked dough freezes well, so when you are having a baking session do double, or even treble the amount and place some in the freezer.

When using yeast it must be remembered that it is a living organism and is killed by very high temperatures (or low ones) during the proving stages. When the loaf is baked the yeast is then killed by the oven temperature, but by then it has done its job of making the bread rise. The rising action can be slowed down by proving the dough in the refrigerator overnight.

For baking, yeast is available in two forms:
Fresh yeast which will keep for up to 1 month stored in an airtight container, or for about 5 days stored in a cool place. Fresh yeast can also be stored in the freezer.
Dried yeast is possibly more easy to obtain and can be kept for up to 6 months if the lid is replaced firmly on the tin and it is stored in a cool, dry place.

Note: Where a recipe gives an amount for fresh yeast, if using dried yeast use half the amount.

The choice of flour for bread making is important. It needs to be a strong flour with a high gluten content so that it will expand well, but hold its shape until set by the baking. Always use plain flour when cooking with yeast.

Terms used in yeast cookery
Sponging The action of the yeast when it is in contact with sugar and a warm liquid.
Kneading The action of pummelling the dough to make it smooth and elastic (see step by step pictures page 119). The dough must be kneaded until it feels firm and elastic and is no longer sticky—about 10 minutes.
Rising When mixed, the dough is left, covered, to rise until it has doubled in size. The rising times can be varied, to suit, with the temperature—45–60 minutes in a warm place; 2 hours at average room temperature; 12 hours in a cold room or larder and 24 hours in a refrigerator.
Proving The action of the shaped dough rising, before it is baked. Dough which is proving must be put in a warm place—the oven warming drawer for example.

Short-time doughs
This new, quick method of bread making uses ascorbic acid which cuts out the initial rising process and replaces it with a short rest period. Fresh yeast is better than the dried variety for short-time dough; dried yeast tends to give the bread too much of a yeast flavour.

To freeze bread
Unbaked Place the risen dough in an airtight container or a polythene bag; seal, label and freeze. Allow the dough to thaw out before shaping and baking. (Store for not longer than 4 weeks.)
Baked Wrap in freezer foil or place in a polythene bag. Seal, label and freeze.

Basic white bread

Main utensils: two 1-lb. (½-kg.) or one 2-lb. (1-kg.) loaf tins or baking trays (preferably non-stick)	Imperial/Metric	American
Preparation time: about 2 hours, depending on rising times	½ oz./15 g. fresh yeast or 2 teaspoons dried yeast	½ cake compressed yeast or 2 teaspoons active dry yeast
Oven temperature: hot (450°F., 230°C., Gas Mark 8)	1 teaspoon castor sugar	1 teaspoon granulated sugar
Cooking time: about 45 minutes (for loaves). About 25 minutes (for rolls)	½ pint/3 dl. warm water	1¼ cups warm water
Makes: two 1-lb. (½-kg.), or one 2-lb. (1-kg.) loaves, or 20 rolls	1 lb./450 g. plain flour	4 cups all-purpose flour
	2 teaspoons salt	2 teaspoons salt
	½ oz./15 g. butter or margarine	1 tablespoon butter or margarine
	beaten egg to glaze	beaten egg to glaze

Either blend the fresh yeast with the sugar and ¼ pint (1½ dl.) of the water, or place the dried yeast and sugar in ¼ pint (1½ dl.) of the water and leave in a warm place until frothy.

Sieve the flour and salt into a mixing bowl and rub in the butter or margarine. Mix in the yeast liquid and remaining water. Mix with a wooden spoon until the dough leaves the sides of the bowl clean. Turn the dough out and knead thoroughly until it is elastic and no longer sticky. Shape into a ball, place in a lightly oiled polythene bag and leave in a warm place for 45–60 minutes to rise (see notes on various rising times, above). Turn out the dough, knock out the air bubbles and shape to fit the tin or tins (or shape into rolls). Cover again with polythene and leave in a warm place to prove—until the dough rises to the top of the tin. Brush with beaten egg or milk and bake in the centre of the oven for 35–45 minutes. (It is a good idea to turn the loaf out of the tin onto a baking tray for the last 15 minutes' cooking time. This ensures that the loaf cooks underneath—cooked, it should sound hollow when tapped underneath.) Cool on a wire tray.
Note: The risen dough can also be shaped into any of the loaves shown in the picture on page 119.

Short-time enriched dough

Main utensils: baking tray, 1-lb. (½-kg.) loaf tin (preferably non-stick)
Preparation time: about 1¼ hours
Oven temperature: hot (450°F., 230°C., Gas Mark 8)
Cooking time: 45–50 minutes
Makes: 1 poppyseed twist and a 2-lb. (1-kg.) loaf

Imperial/Metric
1 lb./450 g. plain flour
1 teaspoon salt
1 teaspoon castor sugar
2 oz./50 g. butter
1 oz./25 g. fresh yeast
8 fl. oz./2½ dl. warm milk
25-mg. ascorbic acid tablet
1 egg
beaten egg to glaze

American
4 cups all-purpose flour
1 teaspoon salt
1 teaspoon granulated sugar
¼ cup butter
1 cake compressed yeast
1 cup warm milk
25-mg. ascorbic acid tablet
1 egg
beaten egg to glaze

Sieve the flour and salt into a mixing bowl. Stir in the sugar and rub in the butter. Blend the fresh yeast, milk and crushed ascorbic acid tablet together and pour into the dry ingredients together with the egg. Using a palette knife, work the mixture together to form a dough. Turn out and knead thoroughly—about 10 minutes. Place the dough in a lightly oiled polythene bag and leave to rest for 10 minutes.

Remove the dough from the bag and shape as required. Place the shapes on a baking tray, cover with polythene and leave to prove in a warm place for 45–50 minutes. Brush with beaten egg, sprinkle on the poppyseeds and bake in the centre of the oven for 45–50 minutes, until golden brown and hollow-sounding when tapped underneath. Cool on a wire tray.

Quick wholemeal bread

Main utensil: one 2-lb. (1-kg.) loaf tin (preferably non-stick)
Preparation time: 10 minutes, not including rising times
Oven temperature: hot (450°F., 230°C., Gas Mark 8)
Cooking time: 45–50 minutes
Makes: one 2-lb. (1-kg.) loaf

Imperial/Metric
12 oz./350 g. wholemeal flour
12 oz./350 g. plain flour, sieved
2 teaspoons castor sugar
1½ teaspoons salt
1 oz./25 g. fresh yeast
1 oz./25 g. butter, melted
¾ pint/scant ½ litre warm water

American
3 cups wholewheat flour
3 cups sifted all-purpose flour
2 teaspoons granulated sugar
1½ teaspoons salt
1 cake compressed yeast
2 tablespoons melted butter
scant 2 cups warm water

Put the flours, sugar and salt in a mixing bowl. Rub in the yeast with your fingertips. Add the melted butter together with the warm water and mix (using your hand) to form a soft dough. Turn out and knead to a shape to fit the loaf tin (or a 6-inch (15-cm.) non-stick, cake tin, or shape as

shown in the picture on page 119), place in the tin and put in a lightly oiled polythene bag. Leave to prove in a warm place for about 30 minutes, or until doubled in size. Bake in the centre of the preheated oven for 45–50 minutes. Turn out and cool on a wire tray.

Bun loaf

Main utensil: 2-lb. (1-kg.) loaf tin (preferably non-stick)
Preparation time: about 1½ hours, including rising time
Oven temperature: hot (425°F., 220°C., Gas Mark 7)
Cooking time: about 50 minutes
Makes: one 2-lb. (1-kg.) loaf

Imperial/Metric
10 oz./275 g. plain flour
½ teaspoon salt
½ oz./15 g. fresh yeast or ¼ oz./10 g. dried yeast
1 teaspoon sugar
2 eggs
½ pint/3 dl. warm milk and water mixed
8 oz./225 g. mixed dried fruit
Glaze:
2 tablespoons sugar
3 tablespoons water

American
2½ cups all-purpose flour
½ teaspoon salt
½ cake compressed yeast or ¼ oz. active dry yeast
1 teaspoon sugar
2 eggs
1¼ cups warm milk and water mixed
1⅓ cups mixed dried fruit
Glaze:
3 tablespoons sugar
scant ¼ cup water

Sieve the flour and salt into a mixing bowl. Cream the fresh yeast with the sugar (or place dried yeast, sugar and half the liquid in a bowl and leave in a warm place for about 10 minutes) and add the beaten eggs and liquid. Pour into the sieved flour mixture and mix to form a dough. Turn out and knead well. Cover with a piece of polythene and leave in a warm place to rise until doubled in bulk—about 40 minutes. Knead in the dried fruit and shape to fit a 2-lb. (1-kg.) loaf

tin. Place in the tin and leave to prove in a warm place until the dough reaches the top of the tin. Bake in the centre of the oven for 20 minutes, then reduce the heat to moderate (350°F., 180°C., Gas Mark 4) and bake for a further 25–30 minutes. Turn out of the tin and immediately brush the top with glaze made by dissolving the sugar in the water over a low heat and then boiling the mixture for 1–2 minutes.

Pizza (Illustrated opposite)

Main utensil: baking tray
(preferably non-stick)
Preparation time: 15 minutes, not
including making the dough
Oven temperature: hot (425°C.,
220°C., Gas Mark 7)
Cooking time: 25–30 minutes
Serves: 4

Imperial/Metric
8 oz./225 g. risen basic white
dough (see page 120)
olive oil
Topping:
1 tablespoon oil
1 small onion, chopped
1 clove garlic, crushed
1 8-oz./225-g. can tomatoes, drained
1–2 thyme leaves, chopped or
pinch oregano
salt and pepper
pinch castor sugar
1 tablespoon tomato purée
6 oz./175 g. cheese, thinly sliced
1 small can anchovy fillets, drained
black olives

American
½ lb. risen basic white dough
(see page 120)
olive oil
Topping:
1 tablespoon oil
1 small onion, chopped
1 clove garlic, crushed
1 ½-lb. can tomatoes, drained
1–2 thyme leaves, chopped or
pinch oregano
salt and pepper
pinch granulated sugar
1 tablespoon tomato paste
6 oz. cheese, thinly sliced
1 small can anchovy fillets, drained
ripe olives

Heat the oil in a frying pan and sauté the onion and garlic until softened but not browned. Stir in the drained tomatoes, herbs, seasoning, sugar and tomato purée. Cook over a low heat until thickened.

Roll out the dough to a 9-inch (23-cm.) round and place it on the baking tray. (Alternatively press the dough into a plain flan ring placed on a baking tray.) Brush with olive oil and spread with the cooled tomato mixture and top with the cheese slices. Garnish with the strips of anchovy fillets and black olives as shown in the picture. Leave in a warm place for about 15 minutes, then bake near the top of a preheated hot oven for 25–30 minutes.

Orange tea ring

Main utensil: baking tray
(preferably non-stick)
Preparation time: 20 minutes, not
including rising time
Oven temperature: moderately hot
(375°F., 190°C., Gas Mark 5)

Imperial/Metric
2 teaspoons dried yeast
5 tablespoons warm milk
½ teaspoon castor sugar
8 oz./225 g. plain flour
pinch salt
1 egg, beaten
1 oz./25 g. butter, melted
2 oz./50 g. brown sugar
2 oz./50 g. sultanas
grated rind of 1 orange
pinch cinnamon
Decoration:
2 oz./50 g. icing sugar
glacé cherries
angelica

American
2 teaspoons active dry yeast
6 tablespoons warm milk
½ teaspoon granulated sugar
2 cups all-purpose flour
pinch salt
1 egg, beaten
2 tablespoons melted butter
¼ cup brown sugar
½ cup seedless white raisins
grated rind of 1 orange
pinch cinnamon
Decoration:
½ cup sifted confectioners' sugar
candied cherries
candied angelica

In a bowl mix the yeast with the warm milk, castor sugar and 2 oz. (50 g.) of the flour. Leave to stand in a warm place until frothy, about 25 minutes.

Sieve the remaining flour with the salt. Add to the yeast liquid together with the egg and half the melted butter and mix well. Turn onto a floured board and knead well. Put inside a lightly oiled large polythene bag, tie the neck loosely and leave in a warm place until doubled in size. Remove from the polythene bag and roll out the dough to a rectangle 12 inches (30 cm.) by 9 inches (23 cm.); brush with the remaining butter and sprinkle over the brown sugar, sultanas, grated orange rind and cinnamon. Roll up as for a Swiss roll, from the longer edge, and seal the ends together to form a ring. Place on a baking tray and, with scissors, cut slashes at an angle 1 inch (2·5 cm.) apart and to within ½ inch (1 cm.) of the centre. Cover with lightly oiled polythene and leave to prove in a warm place for about 30 minutes. Bake in the centre of the preheated moderately hot oven for 30–35 minutes. Cool on a wire tray.

Sieve the icing sugar into a bowl and mix with a little water to give a coating consistency. Spoon the icing over the tea ring and decorate with glacé cherries and angelica. Leave to set before serving.

Pizza (see above)

Danish pastries

Main utensils: baking trays
   (preferably non-stick)
Preparation time: 30 minutes, not
   including rising and resting time
Oven temperature: moderately hot
   (400°F., 200°C., Gas Mark 6)
Cooking time: about 15 minutes
Makes: 12 of any shape

Imperial/Metric
1 teaspoon castor sugar
½ oz./15 g. dried yeast
7 tablespoons warm milk
1 egg, beaten
10 oz./275 g. plain flour
pinch salt
4½ oz./115 g. butter

American
1 teaspoon granulated sugar
½ oz. active dry yeast
½ cup warm milk
1 egg, beaten
2½ cups all-purpose flour
pinch salt
½ cup, plus 1 tablespoon butter

Place the 1 teaspoon castor sugar, dried yeast, warm milk and egg in a small bowl. Leave in a warm place until frothy, about 10 minutes.

Sieve the flour and salt into a bowl. Make a well in the centre of the flour mixture and tip in the yeast mixture. Mix to form a smooth dough.

Turn the dough onto a floured board, knead lightly and roll out to an oblong ¼ inch (½ cm.) thick. Form the butter into a block and set it in the centre of the dough. Fold and roll as for puff pastry (see page 108). Fold in three and roll out to an oblong again. Fold and leave in the refrigerator for 15 minutes. The pastry is now ready to be rolled out and shaped in any of the following ways:

Fruit pinwheels Roll out the dough thinly and cut into 4-inch (10-cm.) squares. Spread with 1 oz. (25 g.) softened butter mixed with a little soft brown sugar and a pinch of cinnamon; sprinkle with a few sultanas. Cut in halves, lengthwise and roll up each piece, from a shorter end, to form a thick roll. Cut into 1-inch (2·5-cm.) slices, place on a

baking tray, cover and leave to prove for about 20 minutes. Brush with beaten egg and bake near the top of the preheated moderately hot oven for about 15 minutes. Cool on a wire tray.

Windmills Roll out the dough thinly and cut into 4-inch (10-cm.) squares. Make diagonal cuts from each corner to within ½ inch (1 cm.) of the centre. Put a small piece of almond paste in the centre and fold alternate corners to the centre, overlapping each other; press firmly to seal. Prove and bake as above.

Crescents Roll out the dough to a large thin circle. Cut it into triangles, place a small piece of almond paste at the base of each triangle and roll up loosely, from the base. Shape into croissants, place on baking trays, prove and bake as above.

Note: If liked, the Danish pastries can be spread with a little glacé icing (see page 134) before serving.

❄ Baked Danish pastries (without any icing) freeze well. Before serving they can be heated in a moderate oven.

A guide to cake making

Basically, cakes are made from a mixture of fat, sugar, flour and eggs which are combined together in various ways giving the cake its characteristics. Different ingredients can be included to give additional flavour to the cake—chocolate, coffee, nuts, essences, dried fruit, citrus peel, coconut etc.

The creaming method
The fat and sugar are beaten together until the mixture is light in colour, fluffy in texture and the sugar granules have been dissolved. During creaming, air is incorporated into the mixture which is why a cake which has been insufficiently creamed will not rise adequately. A mixer certainly takes the hard work out of cake making and, when fitted on a stand, enables you to prepare the other ingredients for the cake. A mixer can be used for preparing all of the recipes in this section. The fat for creaming should be at normal room temperature—never so soft that it is on the point of oiliness.

The eggs should be added to the creamed mixture, one at a time and a little of the sieved flour added with each egg helps to prevent the mixture from curdling. When making cakes in the mixer scrape the mixture down from the sides of the bowl frequently so that it all becomes well mixed.

The flour should be folded into the mixture, very gently, using a metal tablespoon. The folding in should be done thoroughly but gently, to ensure that the flour is well mixed in, but not to knock out the air which has been previously incorporated. If adding the flour on the mixer have the machine on the lowest speed and be very careful not to over-mix the ingredients otherwise a heavy cake will be your result.

The rubbing-in method
The fat is rubbed into the flour until the mixture resembles fine breadcrumbs, then the remaining dry ingredients are mixed in and the eggs and any liquid are added.

The melting method
The method for making gingerbread; some fruit cakes can also be made using this method. The fat, sugar and syrup are heated gently until the fat has melted. The mixture is then allowed to cool and poured onto the dry ingredients in a bowl and beaten together, with the eggs.

The whisking method
The method used for Swiss rolls, fatless and Genoese sponges. The eggs and sugar are whisked together, over hot water, until light in colour and thick; the mixture is then whisked, away from the heat, to cool. A mixer is almost a must here, otherwise it can be a lengthy process with a hand whisk. A hand-held, cordless mixer really does comes into its own here as it can be taken to the cooker for the whisking over the hot water and back to the table for the further whisking to cool the mixture without any danger from a trailing length of flex. (See step by step pictures, page 130.)

With the whisking method the flour (and melted fat for a Genoese sponge) must be folded in carefully and quickly so that all the air incorporated during whisking is not lost. A whisked sponge must not sit around in a warm kitchen

once it has been mixed—put it into a preheated oven *straight away*.

Note: With some modern, soft fats, it is possible simply to mix all the ingredients together at one time. This method produces excellent results (the method is practically foolproof) but when using these recipes don't forget to add the extra raising agent—this is necessary to replace the air which would normally be incorporated during creaming.

Preparation of tins for baking
Unless you are using non-stick bakeware, tins need to be greased, floured or lined before baking, depending on the type of cake you are baking.

For *sandwich cakes* brush the tin with oil or melted fat and line the bottom of uncoated tins with greased greaseproof paper. (It is a good idea to have a supply of 7- and 8-inch (18- and 20-cm.) circles ready cut.) For *sponges* prepare the tin as for a sandwich cake and coat the insides with a sprinkling of flour. (Even when using non-stick bakeware it is recommended that you grease and flour the tin as there is no fat in the mixture.) For *Swiss rolls* grease the inside of the tin and line it with a single sheet of greaseproof paper to come a little way above the sides of the tin. Grease the paper. For *rich fruit cakes* line the inside and the bottom of the tin with greaseproof paper. Grease the paper. When baking very rich fruit cakes, such as a Christmas or wedding cake, it is necessary to protect the cake further by tying several thicknesses of newspaper around the outside of the tin and standing the tin on a baking tray on several sheets of newspaper.

It is a good idea, for any type of cooking, to preheat your oven, but it is particularly important for baking recipes so that the mixture is cooked at the same temperature throughout the baking time.

The best way of testing a cake to see if it is cooked is to press it lightly with your fingertips—the surface should be firm. To test a rich fruit cake, insert a *warmed* metal skewer into the centre of the cake. If it comes out with no uncooked mixture clinging to it the cake is ready. You can also 'listen' to a fruit cake—the singing noise it makes during baking will stop when it is cooked.

To prevent cakes from steaming they must be turned onto a wire tray to cool. Sponges and sandwich cakes should be turned out straight away but leave larger fruit cakes in the tin for about 5 minutes before turning out.

Note: If you do not have the size of square cake tin specified in a recipe, use a round one 1 inch (2·5 cm.) smaller in diameter.

Storage of cakes
Cakes, apart from fatless sponges, will keep quite well stored in an airtight tin. A sandwich cake will keep for up to a week. Rich fruit cakes can be kept for 2—3 months and, in fact, mature and have a richer flavour with storage. Gingerbreads store well and often improve with storage. All cakes freeze well. Place the cooked cake in a polythene bag or wrap in freezer foil. Seal, label and freeze. A cake piped with butter icing can also be frozen. It is best to open freeze it first, until firm, then place it in a polythene bag and withdraw the air before sealing.

Victoria sandwich cake (Illustrated opposite)

	Imperial/Metric	American
Main utensil: one 8-inch (20-cm.) or two 7-inch (19-cm.) sandwich tins (preferably non-stick) Preparation time: 10 minutes Oven temperature: moderate (325 °F., 170 °C., Gas Mark 3) Cooking time: about 35 minutes	4 oz./110 g. butter or margarine 4 oz./110 g. castor sugar 2 eggs 4 oz./110 g. self-raising flour, sieved	½ cup butter or margarine ½ cup granulated sugar 2 eggs 1 cup all-purpose flour sifted with 1 teaspoon baking powder

Cream the fat and sugar together until light and fluffy. Beat in the eggs, one at a time, adding a little of the sieved flour with the second. Using a metal tablespoon, gently fold in the remaining flour. Turn the mixture into tin or tins and smooth the top. Bake in the centre of the preheated moderate oven for 35–40 minutes for one 8-inch tin, or 25–30 minutes for two 7-inch tins. Turn out and cool on a wire tray. Sandwich the two cakes (or cut one in half through the centre) with jam and cream and dredge the top with icing sugar.

Ways to vary a sandwich cake
Chocolate Beat 1 tablespoon cocoa powder, blended with 2 tablespoons hot water and cooled, into the creamed fat and sugar.
Chocolate and sultana As for chocolate, above and fold in 2 oz. (50 g.) sultanas with the flour.
Coffee and walnut Beat in 1 tablespoon coffee essence with the eggs and fold in 2 oz. (50 g.) chopped walnuts with the flour.
Orange or lemon Beat in the finely grated rind of 1 orange or lemon with the eggs.

To make a Victoria sandwich cake the all-in-one way, use a soft margarine and add 1 teaspoon baking powder. Place all the ingredients in a bowl and beat them together with a wooden spoon until well mixed, about 3 minutes.

Ways to decorate a sandwich cake
Place a doily on top of the cake and dredge with sieved icing sugar. Carefully lift off the doily to leave a pattern of icing sugar on top of the cake.

Sandwich together with butter icing (see page 134), spread icing around the sides and then roll the sides in chopped nuts. Smooth butter icing over the top, mark a pattern with a fork and decorate the top edge with a piping of butter icing, and nuts.
Fill and decorate with fudge icing (see page 134).
Fill with lemon curd or jam and top with glacé icing (see page 134).
To make a fruit gâteau, sandwich together with whipped cream and fresh soft fruit (strawberries or raspberries) and top with more cream and fruit. If liked, the cake can be soaked with fruit juice or Kirsch.
Fill and decorate a chocolate cake with chocolate butter icing (see page 134) and roll the sides in chocolate vermicelli.
Fill and decorate an orange or lemon cake with orange or lemon butter icing (see page 134) and decorate with crystallised fruit slices.

Spiced honey loaf

	Imperial/Metric	American
Main utensil: 2-lb. (1-kg.) loaf tin (preferably non-stick) Preparation time: 10 minutes Oven temperature: moderate (350 °F., 180 °C., Gas Mark 4) Cooking time: about 1¼ hours	12 oz./350 g. self-raising flour 1 teaspoon salt 3 teaspoons mixed spice 4 oz./100 g. soft brown sugar 6 oz./175 g. clear honey 2 oz./50 g. butter 6 tablespoons milk *Topping:* 1 tablespoon clear honey 1 oz./25 g. hazelnuts, chopped	3 cups all-purpose flour sifted with 3 teaspoons baking powder 1 teaspoon salt 3 teaspoons mixed spice ½ cup brown sugar ½ cup clear honey ¼ cup butter ½ cup milk *Topping:* 1 tablespoon clear honey ¼ cup chopped hazelnuts

Sieve the flour, salt and mixed spice into a bowl. Stir in the sugar. Put the honey, butter and milk in a pan and place over a low heat to melt the butter. Allow to cool, then mix into the dry ingredients to form a fairly stiff dough. Turn the mixture into the tin and bake in the centre of the preheated moderate oven for about 1¼ hours. Turn out to cool on a wire tray and immediately brush the top with the honey and sprinkle with chopped hazelnuts. Serve sliced and spread with butter.

Victoria sandwich cake (see above)

When making a sandwich cake on the mixer, put the fat and sugar in the bowl and let the mixer run until the fat and sugar is light in colour and fluffy in texture. Switch off the machine and scrape the bowl down once or twice during creaming. Switch off the machine and add one of the eggs; run the machine until the egg is blended in. Add second egg, with a little of the flour.

Remove the mixer bowl from the stand and tip in the flour. Fold in the flour, using a metal tablespoon. (The flour can be mixed in by machine, but care must be taken not to overmix it otherwise a heavy cake will result.)

Bake the cake in the centre of a preheated moderate oven for 35–40 minutes. Turn out and leave to cool on a wire tray.

Banana and walnut loaf

Main utensil: 2-lb. (1-kg.) loaf tin
 (preferably non-stick)
Preparation time: 10 minutes
Oven temperature: moderate
 (350°F., 180°C., Gas Mark 4)
Cooking time: about 1¼ hours

Imperial/Metric
7 oz./200 g. self-raising flour

¼ teaspoon bicarbonate of soda
½ teaspoon salt
3 oz./75 g. butter
3 oz./75 g. castor sugar
2 eggs
1 lb./450 g. bananas, mashed
4 oz./100 g. walnuts

American
1¾ cups all-purpose flour sifted with
 1½ teaspoons baking powder
¼ teaspoon baking soda
½ teaspoon salt
6 tablespoons butter
6 tablespoons granulated sugar
2 eggs
1 lb. bananas, mashed
¼ lb. walnuts

Sieve the flour, bicarbonate of soda and salt together. Cream the butter and sugar together until light and fluffy. Beat in the eggs, one at a time, adding a little of the sieved flour mixture with the second, and the bananas. Chop the walnuts roughly (using a liquidiser, if available) and fold into the creamed mixture together with the remaining flour. Spoon the mixture into the tin and smooth the top. Bake in the centre of the preheated moderate oven for about 1¼ hours, until well risen and firm. Turn out and cool on a wire tray. The following day, slice and spread with butter.

Irish tea bread

Main utensil: 2-lb. (1-kg.) loaf tin
Preparation time: 5 minutes, plus
 overnight soaking of the fruit
Oven temperature: moderate (350°F.,
 180°C., Gas Mark 4)
Cooking time: about 1¾ hours

Imperial/Metric
¾ pint/scant ½ litre cold tea
 (without milk)
7 oz./200 g. soft brown sugar
12 oz./350 g. mixed dried fruit
10 oz./275 g. self-raising flour,
 sieved
1 egg, beaten

American
scant 2 cups cold tea (without milk)

scant 1 cup brown sugar
2 cups mixed dried fruit
2½ cups all-purpose flour sifted with
 2½ teaspoons baking powder
1 egg, beaten

Put the tea, sugar and fruit in a bowl. Cover and leave to soak overnight.

The following day mix the sieved flour and beaten egg into the soaked fruit mixture. Blend well and spoon into the tin and bake in the centre of the preheated moderate oven for about 1¾ hours. Turn out and cool on a wire tray. Cut in slices and spread with butter to serve.

Cut-and-come-again cake

Main utensil: 8-inch (20-cm.)
 square cake tin (preferably
 non-stick)
Preparation time: 10 minutes
Oven temperature: cool (300°F.,
 150°C., Gas Mark 2)
Cooking time: about 2 hours

Imperial/Metric
5 oz./150 g. butter
6 tablespoons golden syrup
8 oz./225 g. raisins
8 oz./225 g. currants
4 oz./110 g. sultanas

4 oz./110 g. stoned dates, chopped
4 oz./110 g. mixed chopped peel
generous ¼ pint (1½ dl.) milk
8 oz./225 g. plain flour
1 teaspoon mixed spice
1 teaspoon grated nutmeg
pinch salt
2 eggs, beaten
½ teaspoon bicarbonate of soda

American
½ cup plus 2 tablespoons butter
½ cup corn syrup
1⅓ cups raisins
1⅓ cups currants
scant 1 cup seedless white
 raisins
½ cup chopped, pitted dates
scant 1 cup mixed chopped peel
generous ⅔ cup milk
2 cups all-purpose flour
1 teaspoon mixed spice
1 teaspoon grated nutmeg
pinch salt
2 eggs, beaten
½ teaspoon baking soda

Place the butter, golden syrup, raisins, currants, sultanas, dates, chopped peel and milk in a saucepan. Bring to the boil slowly, to melt the butter then reduce the heat and allow the mixture to simmer for 2–3 minutes, stirring now and then. Remove from the heat and leave to cool.

Sieve the flour, mixed spice, nutmeg and salt into a mixing bowl. Make a well in the centre and add the eggs. Mix the bicarbonate of soda into the cooled fruit mixture, then mix into the ingredients in the bowl. Beat well to blend all the ingredients together. Spoon into the cake tin and bake in the centre of the preheated slow oven for about 2 hours; cover the top of the cake with a sheet of greaseproof paper towards the end of the cooking time to prevent it from becoming too brown. Turn out and cool on a wire tray.
Note: This is a cake which becomes more moist with keeping. Wrap it in foil or greaseproof paper and store in an airtight tin or polythene box.

Orange gingerbread

Main utensil: 8-inch (20-cm.) square cake tin (preferably non-stick)
Preparation time: 5 minutes
Oven temperature: moderate (325°F., 170°C., Gas Mark 3)
Cooking time: about 1 hour

Imperial/Metric
6 oz./175 g. golden syrup
3 oz./75 g. butter or margarine
8 oz./225 g. self-raising flour

3 teaspoons ground ginger
1 egg, beaten
8 oz./225 g. coarse-cut orange marmalade
2 tablespoons hot water

American
½ cup corn syrup
6 tablespoons butter or margarine
2 cups all-purpose flour sifted with 2 teaspoons baking powder
3 teaspoons ground ginger
1 egg, beaten
½ lb. coarse-cut orange marmalade
3 tablespoons hot water

Put the golden syrup and butter or margarine in a pan. Place over a low heat to melt the fat; remove from the heat and allow to cool.

Sieve the flour and ground ginger into a bowl, make a well in the centre and add the egg. Pour in the melted and cooled ingredients and mix, together with the marmalade and hot water, until well blended. Pour into the tin and bake in the centre of the preheated moderate oven for about 1 hour. Turn out and cool on a wire tray.

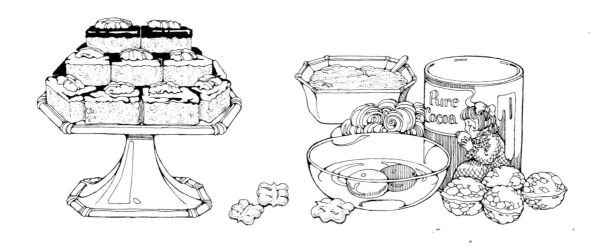

Chocolate brownies (Illustrated on page 131)

Main utensil: 8-inch (20-cm.) square cake tin (preferably non-stick)
Preparation time: 10 minutes
Oven temperature: moderate (350°F., 180°C., Gas Mark 4)
Cooking time: about 1 hour
Makes: 16 squares

Imperial/Metric
3 oz./75 g. self-raising flour

1½ oz./40 g. cocoa powder

4 oz./100 g. butter or margarine
8 oz./225 g. soft brown sugar
2 eggs, beaten
2 oz./50 g. walnuts, chopped
Chocolate icing:
1½ oz./40 g. butter or margarine
1 oz./25 g. cocoa powder
3 tablespoons evaporated milk
4 oz./100 g. icing sugar, sieved
walnut halves to decorate

American
¾ cup all-purpose flour sifted with ½ teaspoon baking powder
about ¼ cup unsweetened cocoa powder
½ cup butter or margarine
1 cup brown sugar
2 eggs, beaten
about ½ cup chopped walnuts
Chocolate icing:
3 tablespoons butter or margarine
¼ cup unsweetened cocoa powder
scant ¼ cup evaporated milk
1 cup sifted confectioners' sugar
walnut halves to decorate

Sieve the flour and cocoa powder together. Cream the fat and sugar until fluffy. Beat in the eggs, one at a time, adding a little of the sieved flour mixture with the second. Fold in the remaining flour together with the chopped walnuts. Spoon the mixture into the tin and smooth the top. Bake in the centre of the preheated moderate oven for about 1 hour. Turn out and cool on a wire tray.

To make the icing, melt the butter in a saucepan, mix in the cocoa powder and cook over a low heat for 1 minute, stirring. Remove from the heat and add the evaporated milk and sieved icing sugar. Beat to make a smooth and glossy consistency. Spread over the top of the brownies and decorate with walnut halves. When set cut into 16 squares.

Sponge flan

Main utensil: 8-inch (20-cm.)
  sponge flan tin (preferably
  non-stick), whisk
Preparation time: 15 minutes
Oven temperature: moderate
  (350°F., 180°C., Gas Mark 4)
Cooking time: 30 minutes

Imperial/Metric
3 eggs
3 oz./75 g. castor sugar
3 oz./75 g. plain flour
½ teaspoon baking powder

American
3 eggs
6 tablespoons granulated sugar
¾ cup all-purpose flour
½ teaspoon baking powder

Place the eggs and sugar in a large bowl. Place the bowl over a saucepan of hot water and whisk until the mixture is thick and light in colour. Remove the bowl from the saucepan and whisk for 3–4 minutes to cool the mixture. Sieve the flour and baking powder together, then sieve it onto the whisked eggs and sugar. Quickly and lightly fold it in, using a metal tablespoon. Spoon the mixture into a lightly oiled and floured (if liked) sponge flan tin. (Even when using non-stick bakeware it is recommended that the tin be lightly oiled, as there is no fat in this mixture.) Bake in the centre of the preheated moderately hot oven for about 30 minutes. Turn out and cool on a wire tray.

To serve, fill with sliced fresh or canned fruit and coat with a glaze (see page 111).

Variations

Genoese sponge Follow the basic recipe, but fold in 1 oz. (25 g.) melted butter with the flour. Bake the mixture in an 8-inch (20-cm.) or two 7-inch (19-cm.) sandwich tins. When cold sandwich together with jam and cream, or fruit and cream and top with castor sugar, icing sugar, or whipped cream and fruit.

Iced fancies (Illustrated opposite) Place the mixture in a Swiss roll tin and bake for 10–12 minutes only. When cold, cut into various shapes, rounds, squares or oblongs and put on a wire tray placed over a piece of greaseproof paper. Coat completely with glacé icing (see page 134) and decorate as shown or with chopped nuts, etc.

Place the eggs and sugar in a basin and whisk them together over hot water until thick and almost white in colour. The cordless mixer shown here is ideal as it can be used anywhere in the kitchen; it does not need to be plugged into a socket when in use.

Remove the bowl from the saucepan of hot water and continue whisking the mixture to cool it. Sieve in the flour and baking powder and very quickly and gently fold it into the whisked mixture.

Turn the mixture into the sponge flan tin and bake it in the centre of a preheated moderately hot oven for about 30 minutes. Turn out and cool on a wire tray. When cold the sponge flan can be filled with fresh or canned fruit.

A guide to scones and biscuits

Scones are very quick to make and are always welcome at teatime. The scone dough should not be over-handled otherwise tough and leathery scones will result. They can be made with the mixer in next to no time and the basic mixture can be varied in a number of ways. Sour milk helps to give scones a good lift.

Biscuits are always good to have in store. Cooked biscuits keep well in an airtight tin or Tupperware container. Uncooked biscuit dough can be formed into a roll, wrapped in freezer film and stored in the freezer. Cooked biscuits can also be kept in the freezer; make sure they are packed carefully, preferably with foil dividers, to avoid being damaged.

Iced fancies, chocolate brownies, Viennese fingers and Swiss buns (see pages 130, 129, 133)

Scones

Main utensil: baking tray
   (preferably non-stick)
Preparation time: 5 minutes
Oven temperature: hot (425°F.,
   220°C., Gas Mark 7)
Cooking time: 10–12 minutes
Makes: about 12

Imperial/Metric
8 oz./225 g. self-raising flour
1 teaspoon baking powder
2 oz./50 g. margarine
1 oz./25 g. castor sugar
7 tablespoons sour milk
milk to glaze

American
2 cups all-purpose flour
3 teaspoons baking powder
¼ cup margarine
2 tablespoons granulated sugar
generous ½ cup sour milk
milk to glaze

Sieve the flour and baking powder into a bowl. Rub in the margarine until the mixture resembles fine breadcrumbs. Stir in the sugar; add the milk and mix quickly with a round-bladed knife to form a soft dough. Knead very lightly, roll out and cut into rounds with a 2-inch (5-cm.) cutter. Place on a baking tray, brush the tops with milk and bake near the top of the preheated hot oven for 10–12 minutes. Cool on a wire tray and serve fresh.

Variations

Fruit scones Stir 4 oz. (100 g.) dried fruit into the rubbed-in mixture with the sugar.
Date and walnut scones Stir 2 oz. (50 g.) finely chopped dates and 1 oz. (25 g.) chopped walnuts into the rubbed-in mixture with the sugar.
Wholemeal scones Replace 4 oz. (100 g.) of the flour with 4 oz. (100 g.) wholemeal flour. Add a pinch more baking powder.

Cheese and bacon scones Omit the sugar and sieve 1 teaspoon dry mustard and a pinch of salt and cayenne pepper with the flour. Stir 4 oz. (100 g.) finely grated cheese and 2 chopped rashers lightly fried bacon into the rubbed-in mixture.

Dropped scones

Main utensil: frying pan
   (preferably non-stick) or girdle
Preparation time: few minutes,
   plus 15 minutes' standing time
Cooking time: few minutes
Makes: about 20

Imperial/Metric
8 oz./225 g. self-raising flour
2 teaspoons baking powder
1 oz./25 g. castor sugar
1 egg
generous ¼ pint/1½ dl. milk

American
2 cups all-purpose flour
4 teaspoons baking powder
2 tablespoons granulated sugar
1 egg
¾ cup milk

Sieve the flour and baking powder into a bowl. Stir in the sugar. Make a well in the centre, drop in the egg and add the milk. Beat with a wooden spoon, gradually drawing in the flour from the edges, until a smooth batter is formed. Leave to stand in a cool place for 15 minutes. Preheat gently a frying pan and rub *very lightly* with a small knob of cooking fat. Drop four tablespoonfuls of the batter into the pan; when the surface of each is covered with tiny bubbles, turn over and allow the underside to brown. Wrap in a clean tea towel placed on a wire tray while you are cooking the rest of the batter. Serve, as fresh as possible, with golden syrup, or butter and jam.

Florentines

Main utensil: baking trays
   (preferably non-stick)
Preparation time: 5 minutes
Oven temperature: moderate (325°F.,
   170°C., Gas Mark 3)
Cooking time: 10–15 minutes
Makes: about 30

Imperial/Metric
4 oz./100 g. demerara sugar
4 oz./100 g. butter or margarine
4 oz./100 g. golden syrup
4 oz./100 g. self-raising flour

2 oz./50 g. hazelnuts
2 oz./50 g. almonds
3 oz./75 g. glacé cherries, chopped
½ oz./15 g. angelica, chopped
8 oz./225 g. plain chocolate

American
½ cup brown sugar
½ cup butter or margarine
½ cup corn syrup
1 cup all-purpose flour sifted with
   1 teaspoon baking powder
½ cup hazelnuts
½ cup almonds
⅓ cup chopped candied cherries
½ oz. candied angelica
8 squares semi-sweet chocolate

Put the sugar, fat and golden syrup in a saucepan and place over a low heat to melt the ingredients. Remove from the heat and let the mixture cool slightly, then stir in the flour, nuts (chopped in the liquidiser), cherries and angelica. Place teaspoonfuls of the mixture, well apart, on baking trays and bake on the second and third shelves from the top of the preheated oven for 10–15 minutes. Cool slightly on the baking trays, then remove with a palette knife to a wire tray to finish cooling. (If some of the florentines become too hard to remove from the tray, return them to the oven for a couple of minutes to soften.)

Break up the chocolate and put it in a bowl placed over a pan of hot water to melt. When the florentines have cooled, spread the smooth side of each one with a layer of chocolate. When the chocolate has almost set, make ridged marks with the prongs of a fork.

Peanut cookies

Main utensil: baking trays
  (preferably non-stick)
Preparation time: 5 minutes
Oven temperature: moderate (350°F.,
  180°C., Gas Mark 4)
Cooking time: about 10 minutes
Makes: about 25

Imperial/Metric	American
5 oz./150 g. self-raising flour	1¼ cups all-purpose flour sifted with 1 teaspoon baking powder
¼ teaspoon ground cinnamon	¼ teaspoon ground cinnamon
4 oz./100 g. butter or margarine	½ cup butter or margarine
4 oz./100 g. soft brown sugar	½ cup brown sugar
4 teaspoons coffee essence	4 teaspoons strong black coffee
4 oz./100 g. salted peanuts, coarsely chopped	1 cup coarsely chopped salted peanuts

Sieve the flour and cinnamon together. Cream the fat and sugar together and beat in the coffee essence. Stir in the flour and peanuts to form a fairly soft dough. Form the mixture into small balls and place on baking trays. Flatten each cookie slightly with the prongs of a fork. Bake on the second and third shelves from the top of the preheated moderate oven for about 10 minutes. Cool on a wire tray.

Honey ginger snaps

Main utensils: baking trays
  (preferably non-stick), cream horn
  tins
Preparation time: 5 minutes
Oven temperature: moderately hot
  (375°F., 190°C., Gas Mark 5)
Cooking time: about 10 minutes
Makes: about 16

Imperial/Metric	American
2 oz./50 g. plain flour	½ cup all-purpose flour
½ teaspoon ground ginger	½ teaspoon ground ginger
2 oz./50 g. butter or margarine	¼ cup butter or margarine
2 oz./50 g. soft brown sugar	¼ cup brown sugar
2 tablespoons clear honey	3 tablespoons clear honey
1 tablespoon golden syrup	1 tablespoon corn syrup
1 tablespoon lemon juice	1 tablespoon lemon juice
Filling:	*Filling:*
whipped double cream	whipped cream

Sieve together the flour and ground ginger. Put the fat, sugar, honey and syrup in a saucepan and place over a low heat to melt the ingredients. Remove from the heat and mix in the sieved dry ingredients, together with the lemon juice. Drop teaspoonfuls of the mixture, well apart, on the baking trays and bake on the second and third shelves of the preheated moderately hot oven for about 10 minutes. Allow to cool slightly on the trays, then with a palette knife, lift the biscuits off and roll each one around the outside of a greased cream horn tin (or the handle of a wooden spoon). If you find that some of the honey ginger snaps have become difficult to remove from the trays, return them to the oven for about half a minute to soften.

When the biscuits have cooled, remove them from the cream horn tins and just before serving fill with whipped cream.

Viennese fingers (Illustrated on page 131)

Main utensil: baking tray
  (preferably non-stick)
Preparation time: 10 minutes
Oven temperature: moderate (350°F.,
  180°C., Gas Mark 4)
Cooking time: about 15 minutes
Makes: about 8

Imperial/Metric	American
4 oz./100 g. butter	½ cup butter
1½ oz./40 g. icing sugar, sieved	generous ¼ cup sifted confectioners' sugar
4 oz./100 g. plain flour	1 cup all-purpose flour
Filling and decoration:	*Filling and decoration:*
butter icing (see page 134)	butter icing (see page 134)
2 oz./50 g. plain chocolate	2 squares semi-sweet chocolate

Soften the butter then mix in the icing sugar and beat together until very soft and light. Stir in the flour and spoon the mixture into a piping bag fitted with a star tube. Pipe the mixture, in fingers, onto a baking tray. Bake in the centre of the preheated moderate oven for about 15 minutes (do not let them brown). Cool on a wire tray.

Sandwich the fingers together in pairs with butter icing. Melt the chocolate in a bowl over hot water and dip each end of the Viennese fingers in chocolate; leave to set.

Note: This mixture can also be piped into paper bun cases and baked for 15–20 minutes. To serve, sprinkle the tops with sieved icing sugar and place a glacé cherry in the centre of each one—these are known as Swiss buns.

Icings

Butter icing

Main utensil: mixing bowl
Preparation time: 5 minutes
Makes: sufficient to fill, coat sides
    and top of an 8-inch (20-cm.)
    sandwich cake

Imperial/Metric
3 oz./75 g. butter
8 oz./225 g. icing sugar, sieved
2–3 tablespoons milk

American
6 tablespoons butter
2 cups sifted confectioners' sugar
scant ¼ cup milk

Soften the butter and beat in the icing sugar and milk to form a fairly soft consistency.

Variations

Coffee Replace 1 tablespoon of milk with 1 tablespoon coffee essence.
Chocolate Blend 2 tablespoons cocoa powder with 2 tablespoons hot water. Use 1 tablespoon less icing sugar and 1–2 tablespoons milk.

Orange or lemon Replace the milk with orange or lemon juice or squash. Add finely grated orange or lemon rind.
Peppermint Add a few drops of peppermint essence and green food colouring.

Glacé icing

Main utensil: mixing bowl
Preparation time: few minutes
Makes: sufficient to ice the top of an
    8-inch (20-cm.) sandwich cake, or
    to coat about 10 small cakes

Imperial/Metric
4 oz./100 g. icing sugar, sieved
1–2 tablespoons warm water

American
1 cup sifted confectioners' sugar
about 2 tablespoons warm water

Mix the icing sugar with the warm water to give a smooth icing. (Cover the icing with a damp tea towel if you are not using it immediately.)

Variations

Orange or lemon Use orange or lemon juice or squash in place of the water.
Coffee Use coffee essence in place of the water.

Chocolate Sieve 1 tablespoon cocoa powder with the icing sugar. Add a little extra water.

Fudge icing

Main utensil: mixing bowl
Preparation time: 10 minutes
Makes: sufficient to fill and coat the
    top of an 8-inch (20-cm.)
    sandwich cake

Imperial/Metric
2 oz./50 g. butter
3 tablespoons milk
8 oz./225 g. icing sugar, sieved

American
¼ cup butter
scant ¼ cup milk
2 cups sifted confectioners' sugar

Put the butter and milk to melt in a bowl placed over a pan of hot water. Remove from the heat and gradually beat in the icing sugar. Continue beating until the icing has cooled and thickened to a spreading consistency.
Note: Fudge icing can be varied in the same way as butter icing.

Ten-minute frosting

Main utensil: mixer with whisks
    attached
Preparation time: 10 minutes
Makes: sufficient to coat top and
    sides of a deep 8-inch (20-cm.)
    cake

Imperial/Metric
1 egg white
6 oz./175 g. icing sugar, sieved
1 tablespoon golden syrup
3 tablespoons water
pinch salt
squeeze lemon juice

American
1 egg white
1⅓ cups sifted confectioners' sugar
1 tablespoon corn syrup
scant ¼ cup water
pinch salt
squeeze lemon juice

Place all the ingredients in a mixing bowl. Stand the bowl over a pan of hot water and whisk with the mixer for about 10 minutes, until the mixture stands in peaks. Remove from the heat and continue whisking until the frosting is cool. Use at once to cover the cake, swirling the frosting with a small palette knife.

Spinach flan, quiche Lorraine, tomato salad and rice and corn salad (see pages 140, 88, 87)

A guide to eggs and cheese

Eggs and cheese are surely two of the most necessary items on any shopping list. Both are a source of first class protein and cheaper than most fish and meat. We feel that there are so many things to make with eggs and cheese that no home need ever have boring repetitious menus if these ingredients are exploited to the full. From delicious savoury flans, salads and soufflés to toasted sandwiches, and fruit and cheese to round off a dinner party the combinations seem endless and should be explored to the full by anyone seeking either economy or sheer variety.

Most egg and cheese dishes are fairly quick and simple to make so if you have tended to ignore this branch of cookery do try it now as it is well worthwhile. A supply of grated cheese and whole pieces can be stored successfully in the freezer ready for use. For slimmers, the cheese with the lowest calories is Dutch Edam.

Egg cheese cakes

Main utensil: deep fat fryer with basket (preferably non-stick)
Preparation time: few minutes
Cooking time: few minutes for each cake
Serves: 4

Imperial/Metric	American
6 eggs, beaten	6 eggs, beaten
1 onion, chopped	1 onion, chopped
2 oz./50 g. plain flour	½ cup all-purpose flour
1 teaspoon baking powder	1 teaspoon baking powder
½ teaspoon salt	½ teaspoon salt
8 oz./225 g. cheese, cubed	2 cups cubed cheese

Place all the ingredients in a bowl and mix well together. Heat fat or oil for deep frying and drop tablespoonfuls of the cheese batter mixture into the fat. Fry for a few minutes, until golden brown. Drain on absorbent paper and serve with tomato sauce (see page 58).

French omelette

Main utensil: omelette pan or frying pan (preferably non-stick)
Preparation time: few minutes
Cooking time: few minutes
Serves: 2

Imperial/Metric	American
6 eggs	6 eggs
¾ teaspoon salt	¾ teaspoon salt
dash pepper	dash pepper
1½ oz./40 g. butter	3 tablespoons butter

Beat eggs just enough to mix the whites and yolks; add the salt and pepper. Heat the butter in the pan, pour a little of it into the beaten eggs and reheat the remainder. Turn the eggs into the pan and as the mixture cooks on the bottom and sides, prick it with a fork so that the egg on top will penetrate the cooked surface and run under the sides. While the eggs are still soft, but thickened, fold over, and allow underside to brown. Turn onto a hot dish and serve at once.

Puffy omelette

Main utensil: omelette pan or frying pan (preferably non-stick)
Preparation time: 5 minutes
Cooking time: few minutes
Serves: 3

Imperial/Metric	American
6 eggs, separated	6 eggs, separated
6 tablespoons hot water	½ cup hot water
¾ teaspoon salt, pepper	¾ teaspoon salt, pepper
1 oz./25 g. butter	2 tablespoons butter

Beat egg whites until stiff. Beat yolks until thick and lemon coloured, add the hot water and mix together; season to taste. Fold yolks and stiffly beaten whites together. Melt the butter in an omelette pan and tilt the pan so that the sides are greased. Turn the egg mixture into the pan, cover and cook over low heat until it is puffy and light brown underneath, then place under a preheated moderate grill for a few minutes, until the top is dry. Loosen the edges of the omelette, cut through the centre, slip a spatula or flexible knife under side next to handle on pan, fold one half over the other half and press lightly to make it stay in place; slip the omelette onto a hot plate and serve at once.

Cheese fondue (Illustrated on page 138)

Main utensils: fondue set
Preparation time: 15 minutes
Cooking time: about 15 minutes
Serves: 4

Imperial/Metric	**American**
8 oz./225 g. Gruyère cheese	½ lb. Gruyère cheese
8 oz./225 g. Emmenthal cheese	½ lb. Emmenthal cheese
1 teaspoon cornflour	1 teaspoon cornstarch
1 clove garlic	1 clove garlic
½ pint/3 dl. dry white wine	1¼ cups dry white wine
2 tablespoons Kirsch	3 tablespoons Kirsch
1 teaspoon salt	1 teaspoon salt
freshly ground black pepper	freshly ground black pepper
freshly grated nutmeg	freshly grated nutmeg
cubes French bread	cubes French bread

A fondue can make an informal buffet party go with a swing.

Grate the cheese coarsely and add the cornflour. Rub all around the inside of the fondue pot with the cut clove of garlic. Pour in the wine and allow to heat slowly, but do not let it boil. When it is hot gradually add the cheese, stirring all the time over a very low heat until the cheese has melted and is smoothly mixed with the wine. Add the Kirsch, salt, and pepper and sprinkle with freshly grated nutmeg. Serve the fondue with cubes of French bread which are speared on the forks and dipped into the delicious fondue.

Spinach roulade

Main utensils: mixer or whisk, liquidiser, saucepan, Swiss roll tin (preferably non-stick), greaseproof paper
Preparation time: 15 minutes
Oven temperature: moderately hot (400°F., 200°C., Gas Mark 6)
Cooking time: about 10 minutes
Serves: 4–6

Imperial/Metric	**American**
4 eggs	4 eggs
1 8-oz./225-g. packet frozen chopped spinach	1 8-oz. package frozen spinach
½ oz./15 g. butter	1 tablespoon butter
salt and pepper	salt and pepper
1 tablespoon Parmesan cheese	1 tablespoon Parmesan cheese
Filling:	*Filling:*
6 oz./150 g. mushrooms	1½ cups sliced mushrooms
½ oz./15 g. butter	1 tablespoon butter
1 tablespoon flour	1 tablespoon flour
salt and pepper	salt and pepper
¼ pint/1½ dl. milk	⅔ cup milk
grated nutmeg	grated nutmeg
2 tablespoons double cream	3 tablespoons whipping cream

Strictly speaking a special paper case is used for a roulade but it is just as simple to line a 12- (30-) by 8-inch (20-cm.) Swiss roll tin as for a Swiss roll with oiled greaseproof paper. Allow 1½-inch (3·5-cm.) side pieces and cut into each corner carefully so that one piece can be folded over the other to form a neat mitre. Brush the paper with oil.

Separate the eggs. Cook the spinach as directed on the packet, drain, and blend in the liquidiser, then add the butter, seasoning, cheese and egg yolks one at a time. In the mixer whisk up the egg whites until white and peaky and fold into the spinach mixture with a metal spoon. Turn into the prepared tin and bake on the top shelf of a moderately hot oven for about 10 minutes, or until firm to the touch.

Wash and slice the mushrooms and sauté in the melted butter in a saucepan. Remove from the heat and add the flour. Season and stir in the milk and nutmeg. Return to the heat, stir until thick, and add the cream when the mixture is again removed from the heat. Turn the spinach roulade onto a sheet of greaseproof paper, spread with the mushroom filling, and roll up. It can then be sliced as a first course, or larger portions make a delicious main course.

Variation

Meat and fish fillings can be used in place of mushroom.

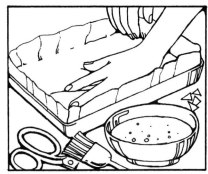

Line a Swiss roll tin with greaseproof paper.

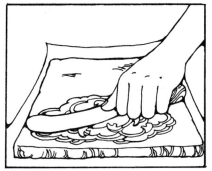

Turn the cooked roulade out onto a sheet of greaseproof paper and spread with the mushroom filling.

With the help of the greaseproof paper roll up the roulade.

Cheese soufflé (Illustrated opposite)

Main utensils: 7-inch (19-cm.)
soufflé dish, saucepan (preferably
non-stick)
Preparation time: 10–15 minutes
Oven temperature: moderately hot
(375°F., 190°C., Gas Mark 5)
Cooking time: 25–30 minutes
Serves: 4

Imperial/Metric
1½ oz./40 g. butter
1 oz./25 g. flour
scant ½ pint/3 dl. milk
salt
cayenne pepper
1 teaspoon made mustard
4 oz./100 g. cheese, grated
4 egg yolks
5 egg whites

American
3 tablespoons butter
¼ cup all-purpose flour
1 cup milk
salt
cayenne pepper
1 teaspoon made mustard
1 cup grated cheese
4 egg yolks
5 egg whites

Prepare the soufflé dish by brushing with oil or rubbing over well with a butter paper. Make a roux by melting the butter in a saucepan, add the flour and stir over the heat for 2–3 minutes. Off the heat add the milk gradually with the seasonings and stir until well blended. Return to the heat and cook, stirring until thickened. Transfer the mixture to a bowl and add the egg yolks one at a time, then stir in the grated cheese. Whisk the egg whites until just stiff then fold gradually into the cheese mixture with a metal tablespoon.

Pour into the prepared soufflé dish and bake in the centre of the preheated oven for 25–30 minutes. Serve immediately.

Individual cheese soufflés can be made in ramekin dishes and served as a first course. These require only 10–15 minutes' cooking time.

Variation

2–4 oz. (50–100 g.) chopped spinach or cooked ham can be used in place of some of the cheese.

Below : Cheese fondue (see page 137)

Opposite : Cheese soufflé

Melt the butter in a pan. Stir in the flour and cook the roux over a moderate heat, stirring. Remove from the heat and stir in the milk; add the seasonings. Return to the heat and cook, stirring, until thickened.

Transfer to a mixing bowl and beat the egg yolks into the thickened sauce.

Stir in the grated cheese, then fold in the whisked egg whites. Spoon the mixture into the greased soufflé dish and bake in a moderately hot oven for 25–30 minutes. A soufflé must be served immediately it is cooked, as when it is taken out of the oven it starts to collapse.

Spinach flan (Illustrated on page 135)

Main utensils: flan ring, baking tray (preferably non-stick)
Preparation time: 10 minutes, not including making the pastry
Oven temperature: moderately hot (400°F., 200°C., Gas Mark 6) then moderate (350°F., 180°C., Gas Mark 4)
Cooking time: about 50 minutes
Serves: 4–6

Imperial/Metric
6 oz./175 g. shortcrust pastry (see page 104)
Filling:
1 1-lb./450-g. packet frozen chopped spinach or 2 lb./1 kg. fresh spinach
2 oz./50 g. cheese, grated
2 eggs
¼ pint/1½ dl. double cream
salt and pepper

American
6 oz. shortcrust pastry (see page 104)
Filling:
1 1-lb. package frozen chopped spinach or 2 lb. fresh spinach
½ cup grated cheese
2 eggs
⅔ cup whipping cream
salt and pepper

Roll out the pastry and use to line a 7–8-inch (18–20-cm.) flan tin or plate (see page 00). Prick the bottom of the pastry, line with paper and fill with baking beans. Bake blind on the second shelf of the oven for 15 minutes. Reduce the oven temperature to moderate. Meanwhile cook the spinach or heat the frozen, add a knob of butter and turn into a mixing bowl. Add the grated cheese, keeping back 1 tablespoon for the top, the eggs, cream, salt and pepper. Remove the baking beans from the flan case and fill with the filling; sprinkle with remaining cheese. Return to the centre of the oven and cook at the reduced temperature for 35 minutes, or until set.

❊ This flan and the following ones freeze well.

Variations

Quiche Lorraine (Illustrated on page 135)

Imperial/Metric
1 egg
1 egg yolk
1 oz./25 g. cheese, grated
¼ pint/1½ dl. milk
½ oz./15 g. butter
2–3 rashers lean bacon, diced
1 small onion, chopped

American
1 egg
1 egg yolk
¼ cup grated cheese
⅔ cup milk
1 tablespoon butter
2–3 bacon slices, diced
1 small onion, chopped

Mix the first four ingredients together in a bowl. Melt the butter in a frying pan and fry the bacon until cooked; add the onion and cook until it is pale golden. Add to the egg mixture, turn into the partly-baked flan case and cook as above. (If liked 1 tablespoon cream may be added to the egg mixture.)

Onion flan

Imperial/Metric
1 lb./450 g. onions
1½ oz./40 g. butter
1 tablespoon oil
2 eggs
¼ pint/1½ dl. double cream

American
1 lb. onions
3 tablespoons butter
1 tablespoon oil
2 eggs
⅔ cup whipping cream

Cut the peeled onions into rings and sauté in a frying pan in the butter and oil—do not allow the onions to brown. Beat the eggs with the cream and season well. Arrange the onions in the partly-baked flan case and pour over the egg mixture; cook as for spinach flan.

Bacon and tomato flan

Imperial/Metric
2 eggs
2 tablespoons milk or single cream
salt and pepper
3 rashers bacon
2 medium tomatoes

American
2 eggs
3 tablespoons milk or coffee cream
salt and pepper
3 bacon slices
2 medium tomatoes

Mix the eggs, milk or cream, salt and pepper in a bowl. Fry the chopped bacon for a few minutes. Remove the skin from the tomatoes by dipping them in hot water; cut into thick slices. Place the bacon in the partly-baked flan case, pour over the egg mixture and arrange the sliced tomatoes on the top. Cook as above and garnish with sprigs of parsley.

A guide to pressure cooking

Most housewives are short of time and this is when a pressure cooker really comes into its own. The busy mum, the working housewife or the bachelor girl will all find what a splendid piece of kitchen equipment a pressure cooker can be. There is nothing difficult or complicated about using a pressure cooker; it is an appliance, which if you bear certain rules in mind, can save you time and expense and give very good results to the food which is cooked in it.

Another bonus to owning a pressure cooker is that it can also be used as an ordinary saucepan and will give you a good-sized saucepan which you will find useful on many occasions. There is a particularly good pressure cooker available which has a non-stick interior surface.

When using recipes from other chapters of this book for pressure cooking it may be necessary to cut down the amount of liquid used as there is no evaporation of liquid in a pressure cooker; also a little less seasoning may be necessary.

When making soups and stews in a pressure cooker the initial frying of the meat and vegetables is done in the cooker (treating it as an ordinary pan), the liquid is added, the lid is fixed in position and the cooker is brought up to pressure. If necessary the soup or stew should be thickened *at the end* of the cooking time, preferably by whisking in small pieces of beurre manié (see page 18).

When making jam or marmalade in a pressure cooker the fruit or peel is softened under pressure and the preserve is cooked in the open pan after the sugar has been added.

Advantages of using a pressure cooker

1 It saves time and expense as the food is cooked at a higher temperature than normal and therefore cooks more quickly.
2 It is a conservative method of cooking, retaining all the natural goodness of the food. Vegetables cooked in a pressure cooker retain a higher percentage of that very elusive vitamin—vitamin C.
3 The cheaper cuts of meat, which need long, slow cooking to tenderise the coarse fibres, can be cooked in a pressure cooker in a fraction of the time it takes normally.
4 More than one vegetable can be cooked at the same time, thus giving you a greater variety yet it needs only the minimum amount of fuel to cook them.
5 Last but not least—a pressure cooker cuts out a lot of washing up of pans, casserole dishes etc.; and the non-stick lining in the pressure cooker makes even washing up less of a chore.

Suitable foods for pressure cooking

Many types of food can be cooked in a pressure cooker but it is most suitable for cooking soups, stews and vegetables and for jam and marmalade making. A pressure cooker can be used in conjunction with other appliances, and cut down on time-consuming stages; for example, the ingredients for a soup can be cooked in the pressure cooker and blended in the liquidiser giving you a delicious soup in next to no time, which if made in the traditional way could take anything up to a couple of hours. Any extra soup could be frozen for use at a later date.

Reducing the pressure

At the end of the cooking period the pressure, which has built up inside the cooker in order to cook the food in record time, must be reduced before the pressure weight and the lid can be removed. This can be done in two ways: either take the cooker to the sink and let cold water run over it (do not let the water run over the automatic air vent); or allow the pressure to reduce at room temperature.
Note: If you cook by electricity or solid fuel, when the pressure cooking time is up and you have switched off the heat carefully move the pressure cooker from the heat. This is necessary because the residual heat would allow the contents in the pressure cooker to go on cooking.

Rules for pressure cooking

1 Always read the manufacturer's booklet carefully, and check the amount of liquid, pressure weight and timing necessary for each recipe.
2 Never fill the cooker more than two-thirds full (or half full with liquids such as stock, soups, etc. and for preserving).
3 Reduce the pressure as indicated in the recipe *before* removing the pressure weight.
4 After use, store the pressure weight in a safe place and wash and dry the cooker.

Pot-roasting in a pressure cooker

This method of cooking the less choice cuts of meat (silverside, topside etc.) produces excellent results—none of the flavour and goodness of the meat is lost and it makes the meat tender. Do not choose a piece of meat too big for the cooker—the joints must never extend above the pan.

It is not necessary to thaw frozen meat completely, but when cooking semi-frozen meat the cooking time will have to be increased.

Cured meats such as ham, tongue and salted beef require more water (as well as soaking prior to cooking)—at least 1 pint (generous ½ litre) should be used.

1 Heat a little butter, dripping or oil in the cooker and use to brown the meat on all sides.

2 Using a long-handled spoon remove the meat from the cooker and pour off any surplus fat.

3 Insert the rack in the bottom of the cooker and place the joint on the rack. Add seasoning plus any herbs of your choice and water. (The amount of water depends on the cooker—consult your manufacturer's booklet.)

4 Fix the lid, put the 15-lb. pressure weight on and cook for 10 minutes per 1 lb. (½ kg.) of meat.

5 Reduce the pressure at room temperature. The liquid in the pressure cooker can be served as gravy; if liked thicken with a little flour and add more stock or water if necessary.

Making preserves in a pressure cooker

1 A pressure cooker can be used for softening the fruit (or peel for marmalade) before the sugar is added. *Once the sugar as been added the cooker must be used as an open pan.*

2 When using ordinary preserve recipes reduce the amount of liquid by half—this is because there is no loss of liquid by evaporation when cooking in a pressure pan.

3 Do not fill the cooker more than half full.

4 Use the 10 lb. pressure when softening the fruit for jam or jelly making and 15 lb. pressure when softening the peel for marmalade.

Three-fruit marmalade (Illustrated below and opposite)

Main utensils: juice extractor, pressure cooker	Imperial/Metric	American
Preparation time: 20 minutes	1½ lb./¾ kg. Seville oranges	1½ lb. Seville oranges
Cooking time: 10 minutes at 15 lb. pressure to soften the peel	1 grapefruit	1 grapefruit
Makes: about 5 lb. (2¼ kg.)	1 lemon	1 lemon
	1 pint/generous ½ litre water	2½ cups water
	3 lb./1½ kg. granulated sugar	6 cups granulated sugar

Wash the fruit. Extract the juice from the lemon. Remove the yellow part of the peel (without any pith) and cut it into match-like strips. Tie the pips and pith from the fruit in a muslin bag. Chop the flesh coarsely. Put the strips of peel in the cooker, add the water and muslin bag and leave to soak overnight. Fix the lid, put the pressure weight on and cook for 10 minutes. Reduce the pressure under cold water. Discard the bag of pips and pith. Add the warmed sugar, the fruit pulp (if liked) and lemon juice. Stir until the sugar has dissolved, and then boil in the open cooker until setting point is reached. Cool slightly then ladle into warmed jars; seal and label in the usual way.

A pressure cooker is ideal for softening the peel when making marmalade. The one in the picture has a non-stick lining which makes it easy to clean, even after making marmalade or jam. If you have a juice extractor attachment to your mixer use this for squeezing out the lemon juice.

Place the match-like strips of orange peel in the cooker together with the water and pips and pith tied in a muslin bag—these contain the pectin which helps the preserve to set. After overnight soaking, the lid is fixed and the pressure weight put on. The peel will only need to be cooked for 10 minutes at 15 lb. pressure.

When the peel has been softened and the sugar has been added, the final boiling of the preserve is carried out using the cooker as an open pan. When a set has been reached, allow the marmalade to cool slightly then ladle or pour into warmed jars. Seal and label in the usual way.

A selection of preserves (see pages 142, 144, 145)

Lemon or lime marmalade (Illustrated on page 143)

Main utensils: pressure cooker, small saucepan
Preparation time: 20 minutes
Cooking time: 12 minutes at 10 lb. pressure to soften the fruit
Makes: about 5 lb. (2¼ kg.)

Imperial/Metric
1½ lb./¾ kg. lemons or limes
1½ pints/scant 1 litre water
3 lb./1½ kg. granulated sugar

American
1½ lb. lemons or limes
3¾ cups water
6 cups granulated sugar

Wash the fruit, put into the cooker with 1 pint (generous ½ litre) of the water. Fix the lid, put the pressure weight on and cook for 12 minutes. Cool under cold water. Remove the lemons and halve them. Scoop out the pips and pith and simmer with the remaining water for 10–15 minutes. Cut the lemon peel into fine shreds and put into the cooker with the water in which the lemons were cooked. Strain in the liquid from the pips and pith and add the sugar. Allow the sugar to dissolve over a low heat then boil until a set is reached. Cool slightly, then pot and label in the usual way.

Peach jam (Illustrated on page 143)

Main utensil: pressure cooker
Preparation time: few minutes
Cooking time: 3 minutes at 10 lb. pressure to soften the fruit
Makes: about 3 lb. (1½ kg.)

Imperial/Metric
1 lb./½ kg. peaches
2 tablespoons water
1 lb./½ kg. sugar
juice of 1 lemon

American
1 lb. peaches
3 tablespoons water
2 cups sugar
juice of 1 lemon

Halve and stone the fruit. Place in the cooker with the water, fix the lid, put the pressure weight on and cook for 3 minutes. Cool the cooker under cold water, then add the sugar and lemon juice. Allow the sugar to dissolve, then boil rapidly until a set is reached. Pot and label in the usual way.

Damson jam (Illustrated on page 143)

Main utensil: pressure cooker
Preparation time: few minutes
Cooking time: 10 minutes at 10 lb. pressure to soften the fruit
Makes: about 6 lb. (2¾ kg.)

Imperial/Metric
3 lb./1½ kg. ripe damsons
¼ pint/1½ dl. water
3 lb./1½ kg. sugar
small knob butter

American
3 lb. ripe damsons
⅔ cup water
6 cups sugar
small knob butter

Remove any stalks from the damsons and wash the fruit thoroughly. Put into the cooker with the water. Fix the lid, put the pressure weight on and cook for 10 minutes. Cool the cooker under cold water. Remove as many stones as possible. Add the sugar and butter. Heat to dissolve the sugar, then boil rapidly in the open pan until a set is reached. Pot and label in the usual way.

Variation
Cranberry preserve Use cranberries in place of damsons and pressure cook for 4 minutes only.

Lemon curd (Illustrated on page 143)

Main utensils: juice extractor, pressure cooker
Preparation time: few minutes
Cooking time: 15 minutes at 15 lb. pressure
Makes: about 1 lb. (½ kg.)

Imperial/Metric
2 lemons
2 eggs
8 oz./225 g. granulated sugar
4 oz./100 g. butter
1 pint/generous ½ litre water

American
2 lemons
2 eggs
1 cup granulated sugar
½ cup butter
2½ cups water

Wash the lemons and grate the rind finely. Squeeze the juice (using a juice extractor if available). Lightly beat the eggs in a basin and stir in the sugar, lemon rind and juice. Add the butter cut in small cubes. Cover the basin with two thicknesses of greaseproof paper and tie securely. Pour the water into the cooker, put in the basin, fix the lid, put the pressure weight on and cook for 15 minutes. Cool at room temperature. Stir the lemon curd well, then pot and label in the usual way.

Fruit into jelly

Many fruits can be made into jelly and the method is the same for whatever fruit (or combination of fruits) is used.

1 The fruit is cooked with water to cover until softened.

2 The juice is then strained off overnight, and measured. Sugar is added to the measured juice in the proportion of 1 lb. (450 g.) sugar to each 1 pint (6 dl.) juice.

3 The sugar is then dissolved in the juice and the mixture cooked in the open pan until a set is reached.

4 The yield for jelly is not given as it varies depending on how much strained juice is collected. As a guide, 5 lb. (2½ kg.) jelly can be expected for each 3 lb. (1½ kg.) sugar used.

Note: To make the orange slice preserve shown in the picture on page 143, place softened orange slices in a warmed jar and carefully ladle in orange jelly. Cover and label.

Redcurrant jelly (Illustrated on page 143)

Main utensil: pressure cooker
Preparation time: 10 minutes
Cooking time: 3 minutes at 10 lb.
    pressure to cook the fruit

Imperial/Metric
2 lb./½ kg. redcurrants
¼ pint/1½ dl. water
granulated sugar

American
2 lb. red currants
⅔ cup water
granulated sugar

Wash the currants (there is no need to strip them from their stalks) and place in the cooker with the water. Fix the lid, put the pressure weight on and cook for 3 minutes. Allow the pressure to drop at room temperature then strain the purée through a jelly bag, overnight. Measure the juice and put into the pan with 1 lb. (450 g.) sugar for each 1 pint (6 dl.) juice. Heat slowly to dissolve the sugar, then boil rapidly in the open pan until a set is reached. Pot and label in the usual way.

Stock

Main utensil: pressure cooker
Preparation time: few minutes
Cooking time: 40 minutes at 15 lb.
  pressure
Makes: 2 pints (generous 1 litre)

Imperial/Metric	**American**
4 large marrow bones	4 large marrow bones
2 pints/generous 1 litre water	5 cups water
1 carrot, peeled	1 carrot, peeled
1 onion, peeled	1 onion, peeled
1 stick celery, halved	1 stalk celery, halved
few peppercorns	few peppercorns
1 teaspoon salt	1 teaspoon salt

Put all the ingredients in the cooker. Bring slowly to the boil and remove the scum that rises to the top. Fix the lid, put the pressure weight on and cook for 40 minutes. Reduce the pressure at room temperature. When the stock is cold, skim the fat off the top, strain and use as required.
Note: Stock must be stored in the refrigerator and for no longer than 4 days.

Celery soup (Illustrated on page 25)

Main utensils: pressure cooker,
  liquidiser, saucepan
Preparation time: 5 minutes
Cooking time: 10 minutes at
  15 lb. pressure
Serves: 4–6

Imperial/Metric	**American**
1 head celery	1 bunch celery
1 oz./25 g. butter	2 tablespoons butter
salt and pepper	salt and pepper
bouquet garni	bouquet garni
2 pints/generous 1 litre stock or water	5 cups stock or water
½ pint/3 dl. milk	1¼ cups milk

Wash and roughly chop the celery sticks. Heat the fat in the cooker and sauté the celery for 3–4 minutes. Add the seasoning, bouquet garni and stock or water. Fix the lid, put the pressure weight on and cook for 10 minutes. Reduce the pressure at room temperature. Ladle the slightly cooled soup into the liquidiser, a little at a time, and switch the machine to low speed until the ingredients are puréed. Return to a clean saucepan, stir in the milk, check the seasoning and reheat. Serve with croûtons (see page 24). If liked, sprinkle with a little grated cheese.
This soup freezes well. If liked, cream can be added at the reheating stage.

Veal and tomato ragoût

Main utensil: pressure cooker
Preparation time: 10 minutes
Cooking time: 25 minutes at 15 lb.
  pressure
Serves: 4

Imperial/Metric	**American**
2 lb./1 kg. veal shoulder	2 lb. boneless veal shoulder
1 tablespoon oil	1 tablespoon oil
2 onions, chopped	2 onions, chopped
3 tomatoes, peeled and chopped	3 tomatoes, peeled and chopped
2 sticks celery, chopped	2 stalks celery, chopped
1 pint/generous ½ litre stock	2½ cups stock
bouquet garni	bouquet garni
salt	salt
ground black pepper	ground black pepper
1 oz./25 g. flour	¼ cup all-purpose flour
1 oz./25 g. butter	2 tablespoons butter

Trim the veal and cut the meat into cubes. Heat the fat in the open pan and seal the meat on all sides. Add the prepared vegetables and sauté for 3–4 minutes. Add the stock, bouquet garni and seasoning. Fix the lid, put the pressure weight on and cook for 25 minutes. Reduce the pressure under cold water. Knead the flour and butter together to form a paste. Return the open pan to the heat and whisk in small pieces of the flour and butter paste to thicken the ragoût. Discard the bouquet garni, check the seasoning and serve with rice or noodles.

A guide to entertaining

Entertaining in our own homes is on the increase and as few of us have any help, except husbands and children in the home and as no doubt many of you would not always class the family as a great help, it is useful to have some guide lines when catering for special occasions.

First a word of advice to the new cook/hostess on the food to be served. However tempting a recipe may seem, do try it out on your husband or family first before including it in your dinner party menu. This means that you will know the flavour, colour and texture and you will be able to choose vegetables and the remainder of the meal to complement the main dish. If you are not experienced it may worry you to serve a dish you have not tasted and it helps to build up your repertoire to experiment once a week; it also adds variety to everyday meals. Always remember that a well cooked simple meal will be much more appreciated than one which robs the guests of the hostess because she is slaving away in the kitchen. As one becomes older and perhaps a little more experienced, as well as lazier, you will find that you want to enjoy your own parties; therefore the idea is to choose menus to suit . . .

a The budget; you don't want to live on cornflakes for the rest of the week. Do choose food which is within your budget, but that does not necessarily mean dull food.
b The numbers for which you are catering; this includes remembering the size of your kitchen and serving space. This brings to mind a friend who had prepared a marvellous meal but had forgotten that she did not have enough dishes to serve all the courses. A quick telephone call brought help, but do plan details like this ahead.
c The seating arrangements and the amount of space you have to keep food hot or cold as the case may be.
d The season of the year and the weather; it is sensible to serve food and vegetables in season as then they are very often much nicer and less expensive than frozen out of season food. It is easy now to buy most things all the year round but it can give a lift to a meal to serve for example an apple dessert when they are at their best, or to make a feature of a vegetable in season.

Menu planning

The secret of all successful entertaining lies in the menu. If it is for a special occasion or you are trying to impress the boss or your new mother-in-law then it really is worth a little planning.

When planning your menu it is a good idea to plan around a main course dish. Do not choose all dishes on the menu which require last minute attention—choose for example a starter and a sweet which can be prepared in advance leaving you free to concentrate your energies on the main course. Always bear in mind taste, texture, colour and the season of the year when planning a menu. It would be a mistake to choose three dishes which all contained cream; partner sharp and bland flavours, smooth and crunchy textures and get as much colour into your dishes as possible by attractive garnishing and presentation.

If you are not sure of the order of work it is helpful to make a list beforehand and work your way through it, crossing off the jobs as they are completed. Always start your preparation well in advance to avoid a panic at the last moment. Wash up and keep the kitchen tidy as you go along. If you have a freezer use it to its fullest possible advantage when entertaining. Many dishes freeze well and if frozen in advance of the big day can save you a lot of strain and effort.

A bowl of crisp green salad is always a welcome addition to any meal. Do not dress it until just before the meal and make sure that none of your guests are adverse to French dressing.

Even if you do not have a coffee percolator it is still possible to serve ground coffee to your guests and so much nicer than the instant variety. Pour boiling water onto ground coffee in a heatproof jug, leave it to stand for 5 minutes, then strain through a filter paper or a fine cloth. Many people like black coffee at the end of a meal, but always make sure you put a jug of single cream on the table.

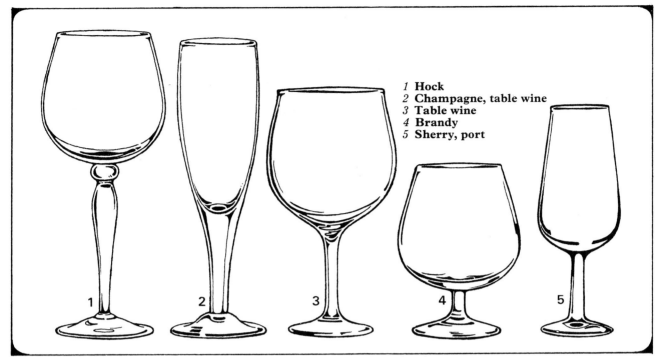

1 Hock
2 Champagne, table wine
3 Table wine
4 Brandy
5 Sherry, port

Glasses

Glasses should be of a clear type to appreciate the colour of the wine and they should be slightly tapered at the top so that the bouquet of the wine may be concentrated and enjoyed.

Storage of wine

Store in a cellar or cool dark place which is free from damp; the ideal temperature of the room should be around 55°F (13°C). Bottles of wine should be stored on their sides if possible.

Simple guide lines on wine

Do not be overcome by the rules and regulations about serving white wine with white meat and red wine with red meats. Most of us are not wine connoisseurs and therefore it is a good idea to serve wines which you enjoy. It is not *wrong* to serve a chilled white wine with cold beef or a red wine with chicken. Wine should really depend on the weather and on a warm day there is nothing better than a slightly chilled white wine or even a slightly chilled Beaujolais; on cooler days a red wine, opened about 1 hour before serving, is ideal. It would be a mistake to serve a sweet white wine with lamb or mutton as the succulent flavour of the meat would kill the flavour of the wine.

It is interesting to note that in the past a formal dinner party would have a different kind of wine with each course; now, even at very grand dinners you are unlikely to be served more than two wines, plus brandy or liqueurs. Imagine drinking and eating your way through the following:

Soup—Sherry
Fish—White wine
Game or roast—Champagne
Entrées—Claret or Burgundy
Desserts—Port or Madeira
Liqueurs with ices and after coffee

For a grand dinner party all you need is your main choice of wine and a bottle of pleasant sweet white wine for the dessert. Offer brandy, port or a liqueur with the coffee.

Opening a bottle

1 Cut the capsule just below the lip with a knife.
2 Clean the top of the cork.
3 Use a good corkscrew which will give maximum grip on the cork; make sure the screw protrudes slightly through the cork otherwise the cork may break in half.

In general all dry and semi-dry wines are suitable to serve with fish—Graves, Muscadet, Chablis, Meursault, Montrachet, white Beaune, Pouilly-Fuissé, Pouilly-Blanc-Fumé, Sancerre, Riesling, Traminer to name but a few popular and easily obtainable wines. Shellfish should be accompanied by a fragrant full-bodied wine such as Meursault, Pouilly-Fuissé, Traminer, Gewurztraminer, Montrachet, or a really good Graves. A good full-bodied rosé could also be served.

White meat, chicken and rabbit are better served with a good red wine which is not too full-bodied such as Médoc, Graves, Beaujolais, Mâcon, Beaune, Volnay.

Darker meat such as duck and guinea fowl are better with a full-bodied red wine such as Moulin-à-Vent, Beaune, Pommard, Châteauneuf-du-Pape, St. Emilion.

Game, pheasant and venison are excellent with really full-bodied wines such as Clos-Vougeot, St. Emilion, Nuits St. Georges. Small feathered game are best served with a good red wine with plenty of bouquet—Beaune, Volnay, Chambertin, Médoc.

The meat course (entrées) can be served with a good quality rosé or a red wine which is light or moderately full-bodied wines such as Clos-Vougeot, St. Emilion, Beaune, Médoc, red Graves.

With sweets and desserts serve a semi-dry or semi-sweet Champagne, or any very good sparkling wine. One is also safe with good sweet wines such as Sauternes, Barsac, Muscat, Alsace.

Final reminders

1 Whether you are serving your meal buffet style or more formally make sure that the table is set correctly and attractively. Have a small flower arrangement or a bowl of fruit as a centrepiece and ensure that all your cutlery and glassware is shining and sparkling.

2 Some white wine chilled, but not iced, and red wine at room temperature. Also have fruit juices on hand for teetotal guests.

3 Offer cheese and biscuits instead of, or as well as the sweet. Allow the cheeses to stand at room temperature for at least 1 hour before serving; serve at least three varieties and have a good selection of biscuits. A few grapes or a bunch of watercress or a sprig of parsley help to make the cheeseboard look more appealing. Strictly speaking the cheese should be served *before* the sweet. This enables you to finish the wine you were drinking with the main course.

4 If you have time, make butter curls, or balls or pats; alternatively cut a block of butter into small cubes.

5 You do not have to use damask napkins—there are paper napkins available in very smart colours and often these can look better if your cutlery and tableware has sleek lines.

To fold napkins

To make a waterlily

1 Take a square and stiffened napkin and find the centre by doubling selvedge to selvedge and then hem to hem, marking the folds well.

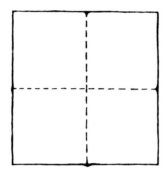

2 Fold the four corners to the centre, turning them in and pressing them down. Repeat this twice more so that the corners have been three times folded to the centre on one side.

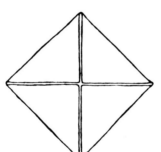

3 Turn the napkin over, holding the points in position and fold the four points once to the centre on the other side. Take a tumbler and place it in the centre to keep the last four points firmly down and pull up the points carefully from underneath.

4 When all twelve points have been pulled up the napkin will look like a waterlily; pull the last four points up rather tightly to help to keep the others in position. A bread roll can be placed in each waterlily if liked.

To make a cockscomb

1 Fold a square napkin in four to make a smaller square and lay it on the table with the four loose points towards you.

2 Fold the loose points up to form a triangle with four single points and one double point at the top. Take the points A and B and fold them over and downwards by the dotted lines.

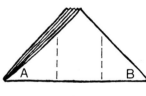

3 Turn in the ends C and D underneath, and turn them to each other slightly to give the napkin an arched appearance on the table.

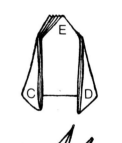

4 Hold the ends in position with your left hand and with the thumb and finger of your right hand pull up the four single points E to form the cockscomb.

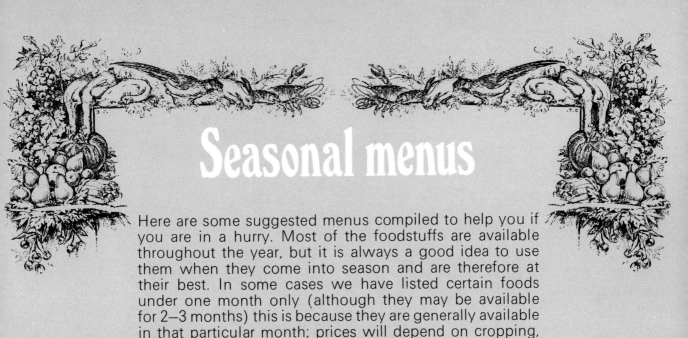

Seasonal menus

Here are some suggested menus compiled to help you if you are in a hurry. Most of the foodstuffs are available throughout the year, but it is always a good idea to use them when they come into season and are therefore at their best. In some cases we have listed certain foods under one month only (although they may be available for 2–3 months) this is because they are generally available in that particular month; prices will depend on cropping, weather and availability.

January
Luncheon and snack menus

Celery soup (page 146)
Omelettes (page 136)
Carrot and raisin salad (page 87)

Minestrone soup and garlic bread (pages 22, 24)

Leek soup (page 19)
Egg cheese cakes (page 136)

Dinner menus

Three-minute liver pâté (page 32)
Roast chicken (page 51)
Roast potatoes
Buttered carrots
Apple delight meringue (page 94)

Scallops au gratin (page 29)
Roast pheasant (page 51)
Game chips
Brussels sprouts
Cheese, fruit and nuts

New Year's Eve family menu

Seasonal notes
Seville oranges (for marmalade making)
Broccoli, celery, seakale, baby onions
Partridge (September to January)
Pheasant (October to January)
Snipe, hare, venison

Salted almonds (page 27)
Canapés (pages 26–7)
Roast pork and accompaniments (page 51)
Roast parsnips
Diced mixed root vegetables
Roast potatoes
Mincemeat flan and cream
Tangerines
Mixed nuts

February
Luncheon and snack menus

Lentil soup (page 21)
Bread rolls (page 120) or French bread

Cheese and fruit

Bacon and tomato flan (page 140)
Baked jacket potatoes (page 84)
Apple and nut salad (page 88)

Dinner menus

Bortsch (page 22)
Scottish hare pie (page 79)
Quartered cabbage
Creamed potatoes
Cheese and biscuits
Fresh fruit

Seasonal notes
Beetroot
Jerusalem artichokes
Spring greens
Mackerel
Goose, wild duck

Scotch broth (page 23)
Gammon steaks with cherry sauce (page 65)
Jerusalem artichokes
Milanaise soufflé (page 99)

March
Luncheon and snack menus

Pasta and tuna salad (page 88)
Cheese and biscuits

Spring lamb casserole (page 67)
Fruit and cheese

Dinner menus

Potted shrimps (page 30)
Leg of lamb roasted with garlic and rosemary
Cream-baked potatoes (page 84)
Peas
Chocolate cheesecake (page 97)

Seasonal notes
Scallops
Pigeon
Turkey

Grilled grapefruit
Chicken tandoori (page 78)
Rice
Green salad (page 89)
Apple cream almond flan (page 93)

April
Luncheon and snack menus

Gougère (page 118)
Raw vegetable salad

Devilled sheep's kidneys (page 70)
Creamed spinach (page 87)

Spinach flan (page 140)
Rice and corn salad (page 87)

Dinner menu

Lettuce soup (page 20)
Mackerel with gooseberry sauce (page 42)
Sauté potatoes
Grilled tomatoes
Syllabub (page 101)

Easter dinner menu

Seasonal notes

Rhubarb
Aubergines
Spinach
Lobster, halibut

Crème de menthe melon cocktail (page 33)
Roast capon with American stuffing (page 54)
New potatoes with parsley
Macedoine of fresh peas, carrots and cauliflower
Raisin and cider tart (page 112)

May
Luncheon and snack menus

Prawn and egg vol-au-vent (page 116)
Tomato salad (page 88)

Cauliflower with cheese sauce (page 92)
Rhubarb flan or pie

Tomato and corn soup (page 21)
Sausage rolls (page 114)

Dinner menu

Asparagus with melted butter
Marinated plaice (page 38)
Courgettes
New potatoes with parsley
Cheese and biscuits
Fresh pineapple in Kirsch

Christening tea menu

Seasonal notes

Apricots
Green peppers
Haddock, prawns, shrimps

Salmon and cucumber sandwiches
Brown bread asparagus rolls
Cream puffs (page 117)
Cut-and-come-again cake iced with ten-minute frosting
   (pages 128, 134)
Florentines (page 132)
Iced fancies (page 130)

June
Luncheon and snack menus

Crab au gratin (page 43)
Green salad (page 89)

Curry puffs (page 118)
Fresh peaches

Stuffed aubergines (page 86)
Cheese and fruit

Dinner menu

Asparagus with hollandaise sauce (page 44)
Normandy trout (page 40)
New potatoes
Creamed spinach (page 87)
Raspberries and cream

Summer buffet menu

Seasonal notes

Strawberries, peaches
Fresh herbs
Crab, crayfish

Gazpacho (page 24)
Cold poached salmon with hollandaise sauce (page 44)
Various salads
Meringue swans with strawberries (page 101)
Fresh fruit salad

July
Luncheon and snack menus

Slimmers' soup (page 24)
Sweet-sour beans (page 82)

Prawns with savoury rice (page 46)
Salad Niçoise (page 89)

Dinner party menus
Seasonal notes
Globe artichokes
Garden peas
Broad beans
French beans
Gooseberries, limes
Raspberries, nectarines
Trout

Avocado with French dressing (page 90) or avocado filled
   with crab meat
Veal birds (page 75)
Broad beans with parsley sauce (page 92)
Lettuce-braised peas (page 86)
Summer pudding and cream (page 102)

Fennel au gratin (page 82)
Roast duck (page 51) garnished with seedless grapes
New potatoes
Broccoli
Cassata (page 97)

August
Picnic menus
Special packs are available which can be frozen in the ice box and packed with the picnic food to keep it cool. Inexpensive insulated bags are also available which enable you to arrive at the picnic with cold drinks and food and crisp salads.

Veal and ham pie (page 72)
Salads packed in polythene boxes
Fruit, French bread and cheese

Marinated chicken (page 76)
Potato and onion salad
Mayonnaise (page 90)
Banana and walnut loaf (page 128)
Seedless grapes

Potted shrimps (page 30) with brown bread and butter
Onion flan (page 140)
Salads
Fresh peaches or cherries

Dinner party menus
Seasonal notes
Blackberries, greengages
Plums, loganberries
Blackcurrants, redcurrants
Marrow, red cabbage
Tomatoes
Grouse (August to December)

Smoked haddock cream (page 30)
Lamb chops with ham (page 67)
Spiced red cabbage (page 85)
Fresh fruit and cream

Eggs in artichokes (page 32)
Moussaka (page 68)
Mixed salads
Blackberry and apple crumble (page 94) with cream

September
Packed luncheon menus for school or college
To keep packed lunches fresh, wrap them in foil or pack in a polythene box. Remember to pack sweet and savoury items separately.

Minestrone soup (page 22)
Marmite, egg, cheese or meat sandwiches
Apple

Pork pie (page 72), tomatoes
Wholemeal scones (page 132)
Pear or banana

Sausage rolls (page 114)
Carrot and raisin salad (page 87)
Chocolate brownies (page 129)

Dinner party menus
Seasonal notes
Apples
Bilberries
Damsons
Figs
Melon
Pears
Leeks
Baby onions
Hare, venison

Lettuce soup (page 20)
Boeuf en croûte (page 116)
Baby onions in béchamel sauce (page 92)
Runner beans
Fresh peaches grilled with brown sugar, served with cream

Anchovy squares (page 27)
Goulash (page 60)
Rice
Braised leeks
Grapefruit cheesecake (page 98)

October
Luncheon and snack menus

Game pie (page 72)
Salads
Baked apples

Cheese and apple pie (page 113)
Rice and corn salad (page 87)

Carbonade à la flamande (page 64)
Stewed damsons

Teenagers' buffet party menu

Pizza (page 122)
Baked jacket potatoes (page 84)
Salads
Meringue shells (page 100)
Fruit gâteau (page 126)

Hallowe'en party menu

Vol-au-vents (page 116)
Sausages on sticks and fried chicken drumsticks with spicy barbecue sauce (page 58)
Veal and bacon pie (page 112)
Various salads
Chocolate mousse (page 101)
Fresh fruit salad
Toffee apples
Fruit punch

Dinner party menus
Seasonal notes
Melon
Quinces
Pumpkin
Turnips
Celery
Beetroot
Brussels sprouts
Chestnuts
Good selection of game

Avocado and grapefruit starter (page 33)
Spaghetti with bolognese sauce (page 63)
Profiteroles (page 117)

French onion soup (page 22)
Stuffed chops (page 68)
Braised celery
Brussels sprouts
Apple delight meringue (page 94)

Melon
Grilled steak with béarnaise sauce (page 59)
Sauté potatoes
Grilled tomatoes
Grilled mushrooms
Green salad (page 89)
Syllabub (page 101)

November
Luncheon and snack menus

Bacon and onion roll (page 117)
Mandarin oranges or tangerines

Ratatouille (page 82) with bread croûtes (page 24)

Sunday luncheon menu

Roast beef, Yorkshire pudding, fresh horseradish sauce
  (pages 51, 55, 56)
Broccoli, roast and creamed potatoes
Apple and cranberry pie

Guy Fawkes party menu

Tomato and corn soup (page 21)
Minced beef hamburgers in bread rolls; sausages with
  mustard, tomato ketchup, relishes
Barbecued spareribs (page 66)
Baked jacket potatoes, cream and chive dressing (pages 84,
  92)
Orange gingerbread (page 129)
Guy Fawkes cake (Victoria sandwich (page 126)
  decorated with butter cream and topped chocolate flakes)

Dinner party menus
Pears
Mandarins
Tangerines
Swedes
Game
Poultry

Taramasalata (page 46)
Roast pheasant (page 51)
Game chips
Watercress and walnut salad, braised celery
Hazelnut meringue gâteau (page 100)
Melon

Scottish hare pie (page 79)
Buttered cabbage, piped creamed potatoes
Golden apricot pudding (page 96)

December
Christmas drinks party menu

Dips (page 28)
Surprise hors d'oeuvre (page 28)
Smoked haddock cream (page 30)
Mince pies
Brandy butter

Christmas menu

Melon or
Crème de menthe melon cocktail (page 33)
Roast stuffed turkey and accompaniments (page 51)
Roast potatoes
Brussels sprouts with chestnuts
Christmas pudding (page 96)

Dinner party menu

Shrimp soup or moules marinière (pages 23, 43)
Steak and kidney pie (page 62)
Broccoli, creamed potatoes
Fruit in jelly and cream, mince pies

Fondue party menu
Seasonal notes
Cranberries, grapes
Halibut
Game

Cheese fondue (page 137)
French bread cubes
Fresh fruit salad

Index